Tourism, Poverty and Development

Poverty alleviation is high on the global policy agenda, its importance being emphasised by its place as the first of the United Nations Millennium Development Goals. As a potentially significant source of economic growth in developing countries, tourism may also play a major role in poverty reduction and alleviation under the right circumstances. The incorporation of tourism into development policy and Poverty Reduction Strategies has special poignancy for those Least Developed Countries where natural resources exist to support a tourism industry and there are limited development alternatives.

This book offers a holistic, explicit and detailed introduction to the relationship of poverty and tourism within the context of developing countries. It is divided into distinct sections, progressing from an evaluation of the key concepts of poverty, tourism and development; to the causal factors of poverty; to the mechanisms of how tourism is being implemented in policy and practice to reduce poverty; and finally to an analysis of the relationship between tourism and poverty alleviation in the future. The adopted analytical approach of the key themes is multi-disciplinary, incorporating tourism studies, human geography, political economy, economics, development and environmental studies. It integrates examples and original case studies from varying geographical developing regions including Africa, South Asia and East Asia and the Pacific, to lend practical insights into tourism's role in poverty alleviation.

The text will be of particular interest to higher education students from tourism studies, geography, political economy, environmental and development studies, and sociology backgrounds. It will also be of relevance to government and policy makers, alongside those who have a more general interest in poverty alleviation.

Andrew Holden is Professor in Environment and Tourism at Bedfordshire University, UK.

Tourism, Poverty and Development

Andrew Holden

Routledge
Taylor & Francis Group

LONDON AND NEW YORK

First published 2013
by Routledge
2 Park Square, Milton Park, Abingdon, Oxon OX14 4RN

Simultaneously published in the USA and Canada
by Routledge
711 Third Avenue, New York, NY 10017

Routledge is an imprint of the Taylor & Francis Group, an informa business

© 2013 Andrew Holden

British Library Cataloguing in Publication Data
A catalogue record for this book is available from the British Library

Library of Congress Cataloging in Publication Data
   Holden, Andrew, 1960–
   Tourism, poverty and development / Andrew Holden.
      p. cm.
   Includes bibliographical references and index.
   1.Tourism–Developing countries.   2. Poverty–Developing countries.
   3. Economic development–Developing countries.   4. Developing
   countries–Economic conditions.   I. Title.
   G155.D44H66 2013
   338.4'791091724—dc23
                                                      2012035581

ISBN: 978-0-415-56626-1 (hbk)
ISBN: 978-0-415-56627-8 (pbk)
ISBN: 978-0-203-86154-7 (ebk)

Typeset in Times New Roman
by RefineCatch Limited, Bungay, Suffolk

Printed and bound in Great Britain by
CPI Group (UK) Ltd, Croydon, CR0 4YY

Contents

Illustrations

FIGURES

TABLES

BOXES

 # Acknowledgements

I would like to begin by acknowledging the lives of the poor people of the world, who are essentially the focus of this book. If in any way it makes a contribution to improving their well-being, it will have been worth writing it. I also gratefully acknowledge the opportunities I have had in my life that have lent me the freedom for a great degree of self-imposed direction – I realise that I am extremely fortunate in that. The list of people I would like to credit would run into pages and therefore I have purposively avoided an extensive list of names but I owe an obvious gratitude to my parents who set me on the path. I would also like to thank my wife, Dr Kiranjit Kalsi, for her support in writing this book, and my brother and sister, who have been very influential to my own 'development'.

In addition, I would like to give special thanks to all of those who have made working in the field of tourism, development and environment so stimulating and great fun over the years. I have met many interesting and knowledgeable people, academics and students from many different cultures, and I can only say that you have greatly enriched my life, so thank you. I would also like to thank Routledge for their continued support with my books, including their patience with a busy author. I hope you enjoy reading this book and by the end feel that you have indeed 'developed' your knowledge of the interaction of tourism, development and poverty.

Introduction

The image on the front cover of this book illustrates a contrast of lifestyles between those living in an up-market area of apartment blocks and those inhabiting a shanty town on their fringes. The image also emphasises that whilst juxtaposed to each other these places have differing characteristics reflective of different paths and levels of development. The unfinished road in the picture could be interpreted as a pathway of development, moving from where we are to where we want to be. Referring to Radcliffe's description of different global lifestyles (1999: 84): 'Cosmopolitan jet setters in São Paulo live one kind of development while women in sub-Saharan Africa walking for hours to collect water experience a completely different kind of development', it is not difficult to transpose this observation to the much smaller spatial area of the front cover. It is this diversity of wealth and development between people and places that this book critically evaluates and analyses, with a central focus resting on how tourism can be adapted to be used for goals of poverty reduction and human development.

As is emphasised in the title, the book has a specific geographical orientation to developing countries, particularly the Least Developed Countries (LDCs), as it is in these countries that people face the most challenging economic and social conditions. The concept of global or world poverty is an interesting one, as a geographical analysis of those people living on less than the World Bank income measure of US$1.25 per day and therefore labelled as being in absolute poverty is limited to sub-Saharan Africa, South and East Asia, and Latin America. However, if poverty is defined as being relative, that is, not having enough to meet the expected norms of living standards of the country one lives in, then poverty can be understood as applying to all countries in the world. Discouragingly, whilst the percentage of the world's population living in absolute poverty has fallen during the last 30 years, the poverty of inequality is simultaneously growing between countries and within countries. As Collier (2008) poignantly puts it in his thesis

'The Bottom Billion', whilst 80 per cent of the world's population now live in countries that are developing, the remaining 20 per cent live in countries that are falling behind and often apart. At the same time, in the context of relative poverty in many developed countries, there is growing disparity between the wealth of the people at the 'top' and those at the 'bottom'.

Nevertheless, when Yunus (2007) writes of 'Creating a World Without Poverty', Landes (1998) evaluates 'The Wealth and Poverty of Nations', and Reinert (2007) explains 'How Rich Countries Got Rich . . . and Why Poor Countries Stay Poor', the inter-connectedness of a global poverty has a resonance beyond purely a geographical limitation. As is discussed in Chapter 1, poverty has moral and ethical associations with it that stretch beyond national boundaries, both in the sense of people who are experiencing it but also in the solutions to 'reducing' it or 'alleviating' it. Sachs (2005) suggests that the solutions for alleviating poverty rest not just with global agencies such as the United Nations or World Bank, but with everyone who is in a position to contribute. This approach emphasises the inter-connectedness of places, a feature of our contemporary society that is explored in Chapter 3, and the trend towards 'time–space' compression that are inherent to the idea of the 'global village' and globalisation that are discussed in Chapter 4.

World poverty also has significance in the implications for peace and security on a global level, as the consequences of poverty inevitably lead to conflict over resources, migration and in some cases aid the recruitment of 'terrorists' or 'freedom fighters'. World poverty also has significance in the sense that when the causes of poverty are analysed, it is apparent that these are not limited to the feature of the place where the 'poor' inhabit but are outcomes of a complicated interaction of historical and contemporary political and economic processes, which have progressively linked countries together into a situation of unequal power relationships of global dependencies and market systems. Whilst this system has brought benefits to the majority of the world's populations, defined by a growth in absolute income and increased material living standards, access to education and health care and life expectancy, it has also left a sizeable minority excluded and falling further behind.

Questions also abound as to who has the authority to define poverty and decide the necessary interactions to alleviate it. Is the poverty reduction project simply one of humanitarianism, with an ethical imperative to do the 'right' thing as a consequence of an empathy of universal suffering, or is it more representative of ideological, political and economic interests? As Hayter (1981: 27) claims, 'The past is not irrelevant' in the context of understanding poverty and development, and the need to expand markets and fields of investments were driving forces of the European imperial and colonial projects, which were to have a significant impact on how countries developed. Similarly, the political and economic rivalry between the capitalist ideology of the United States and the communist Soviet

Union has had a major impact on the then newly independent countries of Africa and Asia in the post-Second World War era.

During the last four decades, a range of interlocking factors emerged that have influenced the relationship between development and poverty. Politically and economically, the end of the Cold War and the collapse of the communist Soviet Union have temporarily led to a lack of a credible alternative economic ideology to capitalism. More countries have been integrated into the global market as the market mechanism has enjoyed an unrivalled supremacy as the most efficient means for resource allocation. One country to have economically benefited from this is China, whose political and economic influence extends worldwide, with an omnipresence of investment in the continent of Africa, ironically whilst it still lays claim to being communist. Other countries have also become economic players on the world stage, referred to in the acronym of 'BRIC', that is, Brazil, Russia and India alongside China. A further change is the influence of environmental constraints on development as the concerns of the United Nations 'Earth Summit' in 1992 in Rio de Janeiro have become reality. Twenty years later, with Rio + 20 having taken place, issues of climate change and the require-ment for sustainable development are key players in shaping approaches to development policy. They also have significant implications for development policy and poverty reduction, as new approaches need to be found as to how coun-tries can combine economic growth with poverty reduction in a sustainable frame-work that will not exceed the ecological capacities of the planet, as exemplified in the United Nations Development Programme's (UNDP) call for a 'Green Economy'.

An evident trend since the 1980s has been the increased mobility of people between and within countries, sometimes referred to as the era of 'hyper-mobility'. A key component of this movement is tourism, the recreational component of which involves people moving between countries out of choice, usually as an outcome of a desire to experience contrasting natural and cultural environments to the ones at home. Although comparatively small in terms of its share of the global tourism market, the fastest growing trend for international travel has been for travel to LDCs. It is the 'comparative advantage' of many LDCs' natural and cultural resources that have appeal to tourists from developed countries and provide the rationale for the use of tourism for economic development and poverty reduction. The emergence of a growing middle class in many developing coun-tries also offers the potential for domestic tourism to play a key role in the battle against poverty reduction, not least because there is a higher propensity for domestic tourists to make use of the tourist services provided by the poor in the informal sector of the economy. Tourism has the potential of taking the consumer, that is, the tourist, to the point of production with the potential to benefit poor people directly, and LDCs do not face the same level of trade restrictions and competitive challenges in the world market for tourism as they do for agriculture or manufactured goods. The key challenge is how to integrate the poor into the tourism industry and system so that they may benefit from its growth in LDCs.

Questions are also being asked within the context of the development project, its purpose and the terminologies that are inscribed within it. The questioning of the purpose of development has become more common, particularly in Western-centric thinking, as questions are asked about where are we 'developing' to, and the extent of the relevance of the term in societies that have reached the stage of mass consumption. The use of labels and terminologies is also sometimes reflecting different economic and political orientations. A range of terms and classifications exist to describe the relativity of countries in terms of their development. These include: developed, developing and underdeveloped; First, Second and Third, and sometimes Fourth, Worlds; Least Developed Countries; high-, middle-, and low-income countries. Then there is the term of the 'poor' and deciding who is in poverty, which, as is explained in Chapter 1, relates to political, economic and cultural constructs as much as it does to deprivation.

The terms the 'First' and the 'Third Worlds' resonate with the geography of post-Second World War politics. The world was divided into 'modern' (the First World) and the 'traditional and underdeveloped' (the Third World). The First World was then subdivided into the 'free', that is, capitalist 'First World', whilst the communist system of the Soviet Union and allies formed the 'Second World'. The term of the 'Fourth World' represents a more recent addition to the lexicon, reflecting the economic and political conditions of some of the world's poorest indigenous peoples. However, since the collapse of the Soviet Union and the end of the Cold War, these terms have considerably less relevance outside their historical context.

A broad distinction is made in the literature between 'developed' and 'developing' countries but there exists no established convention for their designation within the United Nations system. In common practice, Japan in Asia, Canada and the United States in northern America, Australia and New Zealand in Oceania and Europe are considered 'developed' regions or areas (OECD, 2012). The commonality of developed countries is their highly developed economy and advanced technological infrastructure relative to other developing nations. Typically the criteria for evaluating the degree of economic development relates to the level of gross domestic product (GDP), per capita income, levels of industralisation, the level of infrastructure development and general standard of living, but the criteria to be used and which countries are or are not classified as being developed is a contentious issue.

Defining the category of Least Developed Countries (LDCs), the UN General Assembly identified a group of LDCs in 1971 to be afforded special attention in the context of implementing the second United Nations Development Decade of the 1970s. Four United Nations Conferences on the LDCs have been held since, each charting a decade programme for them. The first two were held in Paris in

1981 and in 1990, the third in Brussels in 2001 and the fourth in Istanbul in 2011. However, the General Assembly has never established the development taxonomy for its full membership (Nielsen, 2011). The United Nations identify a total of 48 LDCs of which 33 are in Africa, 14 in Asia and the Pacific, and one in Latin America and the Caribbean. In terms of their geographical characteristics, 16 are totally landlocked, that is, have no coastline or access to the sea, and 11 are small islands (United Nations, 2012). The LDCs also share common characteristics: their exports are heavily dependent on natural resources and low-skilled manufactured goods; almost 60 per cent of the population is under the age of 25; and more than half of the population lives on less than $1.25 purchasing power parity (PPP) per day.

A significant country classification system that recognises the multidimensional character of development is the UNDP's Human Development Index (HDI) which was launched in 1990 and is discussed in Chapter 1. The HDI is a composite index of three indices based upon countries' achievements in longevity, education and income. Other aspects of development, including political freedoms and personal security were also recognised as being important, but the lack of available data prevented their inclusion. In contrast to the UNDP, the World Bank categorises countries by their income levels into categories of low, middle and high incomes per capita per annum. Based upon the Gross National Income (GNI) figures for 2011, the groups are: low income, US$1,025 or less; lower middle income, US$1,026 – $4,035; upper middle income, US$4,036 – $12,475; and high income, US$12,476 or more (World Bank, 2012).

Whilst, it may initially seem odd to suggest some kind of symbiotic relationship exists between tourism and poverty, given the former is generally associated with pleasure and the latter with hardship and misery, it is the collision of two extremes from which a positive outcome can be achieved for the 'poor'. This book seeks to illustrate that this relationship is not as strange as it may first seem, through exploring the characteristics and structure of tourism that makes it a viable development option to reduce poverty in developing countries. It subsequently extends beyond the boundaries of traditional books on tourism development to examine the interaction of tourism development with the poor. It is a book that tries to incorporate a strong message of social justice, to examine tourism as a system rather than purely as an industry, and to embed its relationship with poverty into an ethical framework.

1 Explaining and understanding poverty

This chapter:

- Critically evaluates the concept of poverty
- Identifies its relevance to individuals and global society
- Analyses its characteristics, definitions and multidimensionality
- Explores its spatial distribution

POVERTY AS A SOCIAL CONCERN

The term 'poverty' is embedded into the global vernacular and has relevance to people's lives to varying intensities, from the removed luxury of a subject of dinner table debate to the actual suffering of those experiencing it. Poverty represents a political and moral challenge for society (MacPherson and Silburn, 1998) as is captured in the following statement from the Commission for Africa (2005: 13) with reference to Africa: 'African poverty and stagnation is the greatest tragedy of our time. Poverty on such a scale demands a forceful response . . . The developed world has a moral duty – as well as a powerful motive of self-interest – to assist Africa.' Similarly the Chronic Poverty Research Centre (CPRC, 2009: vii) suggests that: 'tackling chronic poverty is the global priority of our generation'. One of the most cited poverty specialists, Professor Jeremy Sachs, estimates that 8 million people per annum die because they are too poor to stay alive (Sachs, 2005). Poverty is typically conceived as a negative state of being that threatens life and denies livelihood opportunities, a condition that people seek to evade and one for which there exists a moral imperative for the wealthier to help the 'poor' to escape from. It is likely that the majority of us would sympathise with Seabrook's (2007: 35) description of someone as having a 'distended stomach and discoloured hair of malnourishment, the skeletal figures lying listlessly while the flies encrust their eyes' as being in chronic poverty.

This desire to alleviate poverty has been demonstrated through initiatives such as the Make Poverty History campaign run by several British charities and at a global level is embedded in the United Nations Millennium Development Goals (MDGs) as shown in Box 1.1. These represent internationally agreed goals for a civil society amongst 150 Heads of States of the United Nations Millennium Summit in 2000, building on the outcomes of international confer- ences on development and poverty through the 1990s. Whilst there are eight goals, the eradication of extreme poverty and hunger is placed as the first goal as a statement of ambition. More specifically the actual target relating to this goal is to halve by 2015 the proportion of people whose income is less than US$1 per day compared to the figure for 1990. As will become apparent in the following chapters, the other seven goals can also be understood as having a direct relevance to poverty reduction, through providing security and opportunities to break free from the poverty trap in which hundreds of millions of people are currently caught.

BOX 1.1 THE MILLENNIUM DEVELOPMENT GOALS

Goal	Target
1) Eradicate extreme poverty and hunger	Halve, between 1990 and 2015, the proportion of people whose income is less than $1 per day
2) Achieve universal primary education	Ensure that, by 2015, children everywhere, boys and girls alike, will be able to complete a full course of primary schooling
3) Promote gender inequality and empower women	Eliminate gender disparity in primary and secondary education, preferably by 2005, and in all levels of education no later than 2015
4) Reduce child mortality	Reduce by two-thirds, between 1990 and 2015, the under-five mortality rate
5) Improve maternal health	Reduce by three-quarters, between 1990 and 2015, the maternal mortality rate

6) Combat HIV/AIDS, malaria and other diseases	Have halted by 2015 and begun to reverse the spread of HIV/Aids
7) Ensure environmental sustainability	Integrate the principles of sustainable development into country policies and programmes and reverse the loss of environmental resources
	Halve by 2015, the proportion of people with sustainable access to safe drinking water and basic sanitation
	By 2020, to have achieved a significant improvement in the lives of at least 100 million slum-dwellers
8) Develop a global partnership for development	Address the special needs of the least developed countries, landlocked countries and small island developing states
	Develop further an open, rule-based, predictable, non-discriminatory trading and financial system
	Deal comprehensively with developing countries' debt
	In cooperation with developing countries, develop and implement strategies for decent and productive work for youth
	In cooperation with pharmaceutical companies, provide access to affordable essential drugs in developing countries
	In cooperation with the private sector, make available the benefits of new technologies, especially information and communications

Source: UNDP, 2003

The geographical distribution of poverty is typically associated with developing countries or the loosely applied term of the 'South', meaning the continents of Africa, Asia and Latin America. Yet, according to Lister (2004: 1), poverty is not just a problem of the 'South' but also of the 'North', a problem in developed countries as well as the developing, a perspective that is endorsed by the International Monetary Fund (IMF, 2000). Subsequently, to begin to be able to analyse and evaluate how tourism could be utilised for poverty reduction, it is essential to have a clearer understanding of how poverty has been interpreted and categorised. As Lines (2008) points out, before poverty can be confined to history it is necessary to understand the forces that create it and why poor people are indeed poor.

Whilst most people would profess sympathy with those in poverty, it is a highly complex concept and there is divided opinion about whether poverty is primarily concerned with a lack of monetary income or involves other factors such as social exclusion, marginalisation, vulnerability, political repression and victimisation. As will become evident in this chapter, poverty has been interpreted in various ways through the lens of political, economic, cultural, historic and cultural changes. The extent of recognising poverty as a 'problem' is influenced by moral judgement, religious conviction and political beliefs and the effects of its impacts on society. Several questions can be asked about poverty: Why should we be concerned about tackling poverty? What do we visualise and mean by poverty? Why do people end up in poverty? Who has responsibility for dealing with poverty? How can it be mitigated, reduced and alleviated? Is poverty geographically limited to developing countries? None of these questions have easy or straightforward answers, nor are there necessarily definitive ones.

The ethical and social concerns that poverty can raise are evident in the following two commentaries delivered over one hundred years apart. The first was written by Friedrich Engels in the middle of the nineteenth century, describing the living conditions of the proletariat in a rapidly urbanising Manchester in England, the first city in the world to develop as a consequence of the Industrial Revolution. Engels (1845: 100) comments:

> If we briefly formulate the results of our wanderings, we must admit that 35000 working people of Manchester and its environs live, almost all of them, in wretched, damp, filthy cottages, that the streets which surround them are usually in the most miserable and filthy condition, laid out without the slightest reference to ventilation, with reference solely to the profit secured by the contractor. In a word, we must confess that in the working men's dwellings of Manchester, no cleanliness, no convenience, and consequently no comfortable family life is possible, that in such dwellings only a physically degenerate race, robbed of all humanity, degraded, reduced morally and physically to bestiality, could feel comfortable at home.

The social concern is evident in Engels' description, as is a condition of poverty in which alongside physiological hardship rests a psychological denial of one's rights as a human being and citizen. Whilst the conditions of the 'working men's dwellings' have substantially improved in Manchester during the intervening period, over 130 years later Robert McNamara, the then president of the World Bank, made a speech in Nairobi in Kenya which launched the concept of 'absolute poverty', describing it as:

> a condition of life so degraded by disease, illiteracy, malnutrition and squalor as to deny its victims basic human necessities . . . a condition of life so limited as to prevent realisation of the potential of the genes with which one is born; a condition of life so degrading as to insult human dignity – and yet a condition of life so common as to be the lot of some 40% of the peoples of the developing countries.
>
> (McNamara, 1973, cited in George and Sabelli, 1994)

Ironically the absolute poverty that McNamara was describing has itself become a tourist attraction in Nairobi as is described in Box 1.2, lending a direct interaction to tourism with poverty in a controversial way that raises ethical and social issues over the appropriateness of this type of activity.

BOX 1.2 'SLUMMING IT: POVERTY TOURS COME TO NAIROBI'

Whilst Robert McNamara defined absolute poverty during his address in Nairobi in 1973, four decades later absolute poverty has itself become a tourist attraction in the city, raising issues of morality and ethics about the interaction between tourism and poverty. The title of this box is taken from an article by Rice (2009) in a newspaper about tour operators who have started selling guided tours through Kibera, one of the most deprived urban areas in Nairobi, located only a short drive from the luxury hotels where most foreign tourists stay. The tourists pay approximately US$35 for a tour that promises 'a glimpse into the lives of the hundreds of thousands of people crammed into tiny rooms along dirt paths littered with excrement-filled plastic bags known as "flying toilets"'.

The described pattern of interaction offers potential benefits to the local community; for example, through philanthropic tourists giving donations to a local orphanage and buying handicrafts from a women's craft shop, and at least one of the tour operators promises that the profits from tourism will stay in the local community. However, this kind of 'philanthropic tourism', whilst it may bring some benefits to the local residents, raises challenging questions about the ethical aspects of placing the poor in the shop window of wealthy tourists. One tourist from Egypt commented, 'This made more of an impression on me than the pyramids of Giza' – a statement that without further research to provide a richer understanding is open to varying interpretations. Key issues relate to whether this type of experience represents an ultimate form of voyeurism of the 'tourist gaze'; can it be 'right' for poverty to be an attraction for tourists; the extent of the participation of the poor in the planning and development of this tourism; the degree of control by the poor in the operation of this tourism in their own 'backyard'; and the contribution tourism is making to poverty reduction and opportunities for the poor in Kibera. Alongside the possibility of offering direct benefits to the poor, such as employment through tourism and improvement in the infrastructure of Kibera, secondary benefits may also be offered to the poor through the tourism supply chain. To this debate can be added the impact upon the tourist – if this type of tourism provides an educational and moving experience that encourages individuals to take further action when they return home to become active in poverty reduction, is that not a good thing? These questions do not have ready answers but demonstrate the complexity of the interaction between tourism and poverty when they come into direct contact with each other. They also illustrate the necessity for the poor to be involved in participatory mechanisms in tourism, to retain power, have their voice heard and influence its operation and development.

The two commentaries of Engels and McNamara on the conditions of poverty were based upon observations made over 100 years apart and in geographically distinct areas of the world. Yet they describe the characteristics of poverty that would be recognisable to most people. The two commentaries also illustrate that the conditions that create poverty can transcend time, geographies, cultures and economies. Inherent in both descriptions is the indignity that accompanies poverty, the physical discomforts that characterise it, and the denial of opportunities to realise one's potential. The poverty of opportunity to realise one's potential and improve livelihoods is illustrated through the personal circumstances of the life of Simon, a young man living in Uganda, in Box 1.3.

BOX 1.3 POVERTY OF OPPORTUNITY IN UGANDA

Simon is the eldest of eight children living in the village of Kumi situated in the north-east of Uganda. His father deserted the family in 2002 and his mother contracted HIV, stopping her working in the fields which resulted in reduced income and Simon having to take on the duties of running the household. Flooding in 2008 and severe drought a year later has left the family short of food and more urgently focused on procuring it by spending their very limited savings, resulting in an inability to save money to send the children to school. The area also experiences violent insurgencies which have compounded the poverty of this family, now lacking the capital to buy cattle to plough the land. Simon believes that the opportunity for education is the only way to help his family out of poverty. The local primary school was restored with money from Irish Aid but some of the children are hungry and their concentration is low. Headteacher Charles Akol comments: 'You know a child is hungry because his mind is always on the mango tree in the yard. The moment the teacher is distracted, he will go out to the tree to pick a mango. Even if it is unripe, it is something to chew.' The size of the largest classes is 202 students to one teacher, the children are often sharing one pen between two, and the school lacks electricity. Part of the problem is that teachers are paid very poorly, necessitating that they take jobs elsewhere, regularly taking time away from school to cultivate their crops, with sometimes there being just three teachers for a school of 867. Wanting the opportunity for her children to attend the school and gain an education, Simon's mother says her anxieties about education overpower her concerns about food as her children can survive by eating only a small amount, but nothing can replace education.

The situation of Simon's family illustrates the vulnerability of the poor to 'shocks' such as ill health, drought and insurgency. It also demonstrates how a family may fall into a poverty trap, where the harsh circumstances they experience mean their children cannot attend school, so condemning the next generation to limited opportunities and a probable life of poverty.

Source: after Gentleman, 2009

Real-life situations of poverty as portrayed in Uganda and Kenya illustrate the vulnerability of the poor to risks that are often beyond their control but that have significant negative impacts on their lives. Typical risks that have adverse effects upon the lives of the poor include natural disasters such as drought and floods; illness, epidemics and other health hazards; price falls in the world commodity markets for raw materials and agricultural produce; and war and civil unrest. It is also evident that poverty has different guises; for example, as an absolute poverty of not having sufficient to eat but also a poverty of opportunity for education and self-development. The somewhat amorphous boundaries of poverty raise further questions about it, including: How do we quantify the number of people living in poverty if it can take different forms? Is poverty a permanent condition for some societies, transcending the generations? If so, how can this poverty cycle be broken? What is the ethical duty of the economically 'better-off' to help the poor or should the poor help themselves? The ramifications of this question relate not only to the micro-level of individual responsibility but also to the macro-level of collective responsibilities; for example, where should the weight of responsibility for poverty alleviation lie: with individuals; the family; government charities and or non-governmental organisations (NGOs)?

Providing responses to these questions necessitates the consideration of poverty in broader political, economic and cultural contexts. Although now prioritised as a concern of society, poverty as a social issue is a relatively recent occurrence, as until the onset of the Industrial Revolution virtually everyone was poor bar a very small minority of sovereign rulers and large land-owners. As much as poverty was referred to, it was in the context of a spiritual shortage rather than a nutritional one. Food shortages, episodic famine and low life expectancy have been features of most societies for much of human history and even in the wealthier economically developed countries, as recently as the nineteenth century most members of the working class were likely to experience poverty at some time in their lives (Rose, 1972).

In nineteenth-century Victorian England, a state of poverty was viewed as being 'normal', embracing a fatalistic attitude towards destitution, a condition that was often held as being determined by consequences of individual weakness or character rather than processes of economics and politics. More contemporarily in Mozambique, one of the poorest countries in the world, local people's classification of the poor include those of the *Ovelavela* and *Wihacha* who are undeserving of help because they are perceived to have brought poverty upon themselves. The *Ovelavela* are single young people, mostly men, who have not taken family advice and failed to maintain good relationships with their family and community. The *Wihacha* are also mostly young men, who are lazy, divorced and have drug- and alcohol-related problems, deemed to have brought hardship upon themselves through their actions (CPRC, 2009).

It is particularly the economic growth and rapid development in trade since the onset of the Industrial Revolution in the late eighteenth century that has permitted a progression to a situation where food scarcity is no longer a threat to survival for the majority of the world's population. However, whilst the security of regular food supply has become a norm of life for the majority, there still remain hundreds of millions of people in the world for whom this is not the case, and they continue to be vulnerable to changes in their surrounding environment. In many regions of the world where the LDCs are situated a situation of what Gordon (2002) refers to as 'mass poverty' is prevalent, where conversely poverty remains the norm and not to be poor is the exception. The effects of malnutrition extend to other aspects of life which may compound poverty both now and in the future. The prospects for children may be very badly affected by a lack of nutrition, affecting not only their physical growth but also opportunities for education, the consequential effects being not only highly detrimental to the individual but also to a nation's future economic growth, as explained in Box 1.4.

BOX 1.4 CHILDREN AND POVERTY

Globally, 25 per cent or 170 million children aged under five-years-old do not receive sufficient nutrients to grow properly and their development has been stunted by malnutrition. Besides a lack of physical development having consequences for their future livelihoods, malnutrition also affects the educational achievements of children with subsequent negative effects on the economies of nations in the medium to long term, with the World Bank estimating that malnutrition reduces the GDP of developing countries by between 2 and 3 per cent. Increases in the price of food also have an adverse effect on children. In Pakistan, Bangladesh, India, Peru and Nigeria, countries which are home to half of the world's malnourished children, rises in global food prices are forcing parents to buy less food and take children out of school to work. In Afghanistan, six out of ten children are not getting enough nutrients to avoid stunted growth and mothers may be so poor as to not have enough food to eat to produce breast milk.

Between 2006 and 2011, the price of food rose sharply across the globe, an increase explained by a combination of physical and economic factors, including: extreme weather conditions; the removal of land from agricultural production to grow biofuels; the speculative trading of food commodities; and the global financial crisis. The poor who spend the bulk of their income on food have been hit hardest by these events. Neate (2011) comments that Angel Gurria, the secretary-general of the Organisation for Economic Co-operation and Development (OECD), predicts political unrest and that the poor will be forced to eat less and find other sources of income if food prices continue to rise. The increase in extreme weather conditions illustrates the vulnerability of the poor to events such as climate change and how they may suffer disproportionately compared to the rest of the population. The conversion of agricultural land to bio-fuel production also suggests that solutions to climate change will not have equal benefits for all society and may have negative impacts on the poor.

Source: based on Valley, 2012; Neate, 2011

It is evident from this brief introduction to the topic of poverty as a social concern that it is a complex phenomenon, incorporating various dimensions and links to wider society. It is a condition that extends beyond being unable to fulfil our most basic physiological requirements for nutrition and shelter to encompass a lack of opportunities for personal development, marginalisation and an inability to claim one's part as a member of society. It embraces spatial and time dimensions, the highest percentage levels of absolute poverty occurring in LDCs, whilst without successfully alleviating the causes of poverty, a poverty trap will be created that will transcend the generations. For most of human existence, poverty defined as episodic periods of famine and a high degree of risk of exposure to environmental factors, including natural disasters, illness and other health hazards has been a normal condition of the majority. A change in this situation during the last two centuries to where absolute poverty remains experienced by a sizeable minority, but not the majority of the world's population, is indicative of how economic and political processes may 'lift' people out of poverty. However, for political and economic policies to have a positive effect on poverty reduction and alleviation it is necessary to have a comprehensive understanding of poverty. The next section subsequently considers the major typologies of poverty that have been recognised through social science research.

TYPES OF POVERTY

The relevance of being aware that poverty may take various guises and be expressed in different ways is necessary for the identification of strategies to tackle it. As was illustrated in the previous section, poverty is about more than purely being able to meet one's most basic needs for subsistence and survival. It also encompasses a denial of opportunities, freedom and subsequent capabilities to function in life and realise one's potential. Thus whilst income may be an indicator of poverty, so are people's access to resources including health and education, their freedoms of expression and subsequent opportunities for personal development and creativity. Whilst poverty everywhere encompasses material deprivation, it may also involve a denial of opportunities which will cross cultures, subcultures and gender. Subsequently, aspects of human rights, dignity, security and participation in political processes have been integrated into the concept of poverty. This emergent view of poverty is reflected in a growing emphasis upon its multidimensional character, passing beyond physiological concerns to incorporate issues of vulnerability, inequality and human rights. In this paradigm, the concept of poverty is subsequently broadened beyond a measure of income to incorporate aspects of social, political, cultural and environmental capital and a deepening of the understanding of the causal factors of poverty. Utilising these different criteria to understand poverty it is possible to categorise poverty into two main types: 'absolute' and 'relative'.

Absolute poverty

A range of similar terms of emphasis shelter beneath the aegis of 'absolute' poverty, including 'physiological', 'ultra', 'chronic' and 'extreme'. These terms convey the type of images that are frequently broadcast into millions of homes at a time of humanitarian crisis, people who have barely enough for survival and for whom a change in circumstances – for example, drought or war – can cause mass starvation and death. It is an acute condition of poverty that offers people little opportunity to control the destiny of their own lives and makes them vulnerable to death in the most extreme cases. The utter depravation of this situation is conveyed in an agreed definition by the governments of 117 countries at the UN World Summit on Social Development in Copenhagen in 1995 as: 'a condition characterised by severe deprivation of basic human needs, including food, safe drinking water, sanitation facilities, health, shelter, education and information. It depends not only on income but also on access to services' (UNDP, 1995). Similarly Sachs (2005: 20) describes the conditions of people experiencing absolute poverty as those who are: 'chronically hungry, unable to access health care, lack the amenities of safe drinking water and sanitation, cannot afford education for some or all of their children, and perhaps lack rudimentary shelter'. This is the poverty of people who have virtually nothing and live in continued danger from a lack of basic necessities for survival.

These two definitions are recognition that a shortage of income is not the sole determinant of poverty but of equal importance is a lack of access to nutrition and basic services. As Sen (1992) points out, a lack of income is not critical in its own right but it is instrumental to opening choices and opportunities for a person to lead a life they aspire to. Thus, whilst money does not have an intrinsic worth, it has an effect on the lifestyles of the poor, especially in market-based economies where it lends access to the resources needed for survival. For example, being able to access opportunities for health care and utilities such as clean water and sanitation are instrumental to reducing rates of infant mortality and increasing life expectancy. Similarly, having income to access education offers opportunities not only for individuals but also for future generations to break free of the kind of poverty trap experienced by Simon in Box 1.3.

The relationship between a lack of income and a condition of poverty has been understood since the processes of Industrial Revolution became embedded in Western societies during the nineteenth century, causing a rural to urban population drift and a rapid growth in the sizes of towns and cities. Instrumental to comprehending poverty as a condition related to a lack of income were the pioneering works of Charles Booth and Seebohm Rowntree in the late nineteenth century in the United Kingdom. In a positivist stance towards understanding poverty, both men attempted to describe it through measurement. Booth was a wealthy Liverpool ship owner, who attempted to apply a scientific approach to improve the economic and social conditions of the mass of society, emphasising the use of statistical and scientific observations and measurements. Consequently, he attempted to empirically provide an objective measure of poverty that was independent of any moral or emotional assumptions (Rose, 1972), in essence attempting to establish an income line as a determining measure of poverty. His pioneering social maps of areas of London to illustrate the social classes of people inhabiting them are still referred to today.

Booth's work was advanced by Rowntree, a Quaker who was the son of a wealthy cocoa manufacturer. He collected detailed data on families in York in England in 1899 in an attempt to establish the minimum earnings that were essential for establishing a state of nutritional and physical efficiency. The basis of his calculation rested on medical evidence to determine the average nutritional needs of adults and children, to establish the quantities of food necessary to fulfil them, and hence determine the necessary level of income to acquire them (Townsend, 1979). Rowntree's work was fundamental to establishing the concept of a 'poverty line', a measure of income below which it is not possible to meet nutritional requirements and maintain 'physical efficiency'. Rowntree also included a behavioural aspect to the understanding of poverty, making a distinction between 'primary poverty' that resulted from an insufficient income to provide the necessities for physiological well-being and 'secondary poverty' that resulted from the unwise spending of income. This latter category carries implications of poverty as being self-determined, and being caused by unwise decision-making and behaviour, rather than the force of circumstances.

Rowntree also sought to identify the immediate causes of poverty, which he determined as being: the death of the chief wage earner; the incapacity of the chief wage earner as a consequence of accident, illness or old age; the unemployment of the chief wage earner; chronic irregularity of work; largeness of the family; and a low wage (Townsend, 1979: 64). Whilst Rowntree's empirical work was conducted in Britain at the end of the nineteenth century and early twentieth century, it is not difficult to comprehend the parallels to the poor of the LDCs in the world, not least the significance of a chief wage earner for family prosperity and the need for regular and adequately remunerated employment.

As was illustrated in Box 1.3, the loss of the chief wage earner, in this case Simon's mother, can have a detrimental effect on the lives of other members of the family. Whilst for most families any of the causal factors of poverty identified by Rowntree would have a negative impact on their fortunes, in situations where there is no 'safety net' – for example, a state social security system or other wage earners in the family – the effects will be more marked. This is often the situation faced in many LDCs, where the welfare of a household may be solely dependent on the income of one family member, and the state has insufficient resources to be able to provide a social security support system. A characteristic of absolute poverty is a lack of opportunity to control one's own destiny and being highly vulnerable to external 'shocks' that are detrimental to one's well-being in the absence of coping strategies and mechanisms.

In the contemporary era, the use of a minimum income level to identify those in poverty has subsequently been adopted by the World Bank and United Nations. The World Bank is the major player in setting an income level to define poverty and thus categorise the world's poor. Since 2008, a minimum income level of US$1.25 per capita per day has been used to identify those in poverty, a revision upwards from the previous figure of US$1 per capita per day. Whilst minimum income measures may be helpful in identifying the poor, as Townsend and Gordon (2002) point out, amongst those living on less than the World Bank minimum income level, a diversity of situations exist, as income is not the sole determinant of the quality of life. Whilst income remains critical for meeting the most basic needs of food and shelter, absolute poverty may also encompass other dimensions, including social discrimination, physical insecurity and political exclusion that cannot be purchased. In a more polemic stance, Seabrook (2007) is highly critical of the equation of poverty with a lack of income, regarding it as little more than a way of integrating peoples into the capitalist and global market systems. He observes that when Western institutions and governments refer to 'poverty alleviation', this does not entail a return of control of resources to local people or reference to a more equitable distribution of resources. The discussion is rather one of increasing income-generating capacities, typically through loans or micro-credit, so incorporating people into the global financial and market systems.

Whilst absolute or chronic poverty may describe a condition in which physiological, educational and democratic needs and rights fail to be met, the University of Manchester's Chronic Poverty Research Centre (CPRC) adds a time dimension to the condition. They define it as: 'The distinguishing feature of chronic poverty is its extended duration. We use chronic poverty to describe extreme poverty that persists for "a long time" – many years, an entire life, or even across generations' (CPRC, 2009: 15). Once an individual or geographical area becomes poorer, other disadvantages may occur; for example, a lack of opportunity to send one's children to school because it is not possible to pay the fees or the children are needed to work for the family or act as carers, as is the case in Box 1.3. The children are thus denied an education, giving them little chance of realising employment opportunities in the future and improving their well-being. The conditions of a 'poverty cycle' have thus been created, the causes of poverty being so deep-rooted that they pose not only a threat to the well-being of present generations but future ones as well.

A longitudinal dimension to poverty emphasises that the causes of poverty may not lie purely in the fate of natural providence but have underlying structural causes rooted in political and economic processes. The CPRC recognise five poverty traps as the underlying causes of chronic poverty as are displayed in Figure 1.1.

It is not necessary for all traps to be operating simultaneously in one place to cause chronic poverty, one trap may be enough. They represent a mix of political,

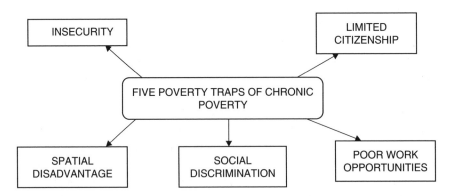

Figure 1.1 *The five poverty traps that cause chronic poverty*
Source: after CPRC (2009)

economic and geographic factors that combine to marginalise the poor and make them vulnerable to long-term poverty by restricting their opportunities for betterment. The traps include 'limited citizenship', which embraces a lack of political voice and representation of the poor in the decision-making process of society. 'Social discrimination' is typically embedded into power relationships in social structures – for example, class and caste systems – whilst gender-defined roles can also deny women a voice and choice in decision-making, severely limiting their opportunities to escape poverty. Geographic remoteness, a lack of natural resource endowment, a long distance to markets and a poor infrastructure are indicative of a 'spatial disadvantage' of places which can contribute to intergenerational poverty traps. The poor may also experience 'poor work opportunities' for reasons of a lack of economic growth; a lack of technical or skills capacity; and social discrimination. Any employment that is generated may be highly exploitative with unhealthy working conditions. Other barriers that the poor may face in attempting to create work opportunities include corruption, excessive bureaucracy, and a lack of access to capital, as is described in the case of Elmina in Ghana in Box 6.5. The combination of these poverty traps is accentuated by the 'insecurity' that can be created by economic crises, natural hazards and political conflicts, the effects of which can be catastrophic for the poor. Given their very limited asset base, the capability of the poor to adjust to these events is low.

Whilst poverty traps may cause long-term poverty and there would be likely common agreement that people living with nutritional deficiencies, a lack of shelter and access to basic resources are poor, other definitions and categories of poverty are more politically contentious, suggesting that poverty is in part a constructed state as much as an absolute measure, a political interpretation as much as a definitive economic condition. As Kane and Kirby (2003) suggest, poverty has been a highly contested issue since the first studies were conducted in the United Kingdom in the late nineteenth century.

Relative poverty

Whilst absolute poverty is understood as occurring when people lack the resources to support a minimum of physical health and efficiency, the second major typology of poverty is termed 'relative poverty'. As the name suggests this type of poverty is determined by what is culturally defined as being poor, usually determined against the normal living standard of societies. This is a common approach taken by researchers to identify those in comparative poverty, typically defined as possessing insufficient resources to meet socially recognised needs and to participate in wider society (Lister, 2004). Subsequently, the basis of the measurement of poverty shifts from an emphasis on 'minimums' to a comparison of averages (Beaudoin, 2007). Using an income line as a measure of poverty, those in relative poverty would be determined by the measurement of a household income level below a given proportion of average national income; for example, 50 per cent of equivalent median disposable income. In terms of how comparative poverty may express itself in developed or high-income countries, Sachs (2005) suggests that it is manifested in a denial of access to cultural goods, entertainment, recreation, and quality health care and education.

The changing characteristics of relative poverty can also be linked to a nation's economic development, as poverty becomes relative to time as well as place, as explained by MacPherson and Silburn (1998: 2):

> As the threat of starvation recedes, questions concerning the appropriate distribution of income and opportunity assume greater importance. In this situation the definition of poverty moves away from a minimal, physical survival notion in the direction of a relative, varying definition which puts increasing emphasis on social survival and starts to attach value to the *quality of life* that even the poorest in a community should be able to enjoy.

The emphasis of poverty subsequently shifts from an inability to meet the most basic needs of the individual to incorporate the ability to play a role in society which include: 'notions of social participation, of inclusion and exclusion, of citizenship, of empowerment' (ibid.: 2). The ability to fit into society and the concept of relative poverty is exemplified in the case of the United Kingdom in Box 1.5.

BOX 1.5 COMPARATIVE POVERTY IN THE UNITED KINGDOM

The concept of relative poverty is exemplified through research conducted by the Joseph Rowntree Foundation in the United Kingdom during 2012. Based upon extensive interviews with families, the aim of the research was to establish the level of 'minimum income' required to create a basket of goods, to permit a family to be able to 'fit into society'. To be able to achieve this 'fit', families should be able to source clothing in cheaper retailers; buy food in Tesco [a multinational supermarket chain]; have a computer and access to the internet at home; take a minimum of a one week holiday in Britain; and own a car. The minimum total household income needed to meet this criteria is UK £37,000 per annum, equivalent to approximately US$55,000. This example illustrates another type of poverty which is not based upon minimum requirements for survival but the minimum requirements relative to the norms of society. This type of poverty is subsequently highly interpretative and open to debate about what are the requirements for individuals to feel a part of society, to what extent 'social exclusion' has become synonymous with 'market exclusion', and indeed what the term poverty really signifies.

Source: after Asthama, 2012

Associated with the inability to play a role in society is the concept of 'social exclusion', which emphasises that as the poor are excluded from mainstream society they subsequently lose the benefits and privileges of citizenship, having a reduced stake in society compared to the norm. They fail to join in activities and enjoy the living standards which are customary and the norm in the societies to which they belong (Townsend, 1979). This inability for individuals to realise their self-potential and play a functioning part in civil society is a theme that has been developed by the influential and Nobel Prize winning economist Amartya Sen (1992, 1999). He suggests that the indicators of poverty should extend to factors that relate to a higher level of human needs than purely the most basic ones. These would include playing an active part in community activities, leading a happy and stimulating life, and having respect for oneself and for others. Thus poverty becomes something not determined solely by an income level or commodities but upon people's quality of life and well-being relative to the rest of society.

Similarly for Kakwani and Pernia (2000), poverty reduction is about improving human well-being, the lives people live and what we can or cannot do. As the United Nations Development Programme (UNDP) emphasises, poverty is more than purely restrictions imposed by a lack of income. It comments: 'It also entails lack of basic capabilities to lead full, creative lives – as when people suffer from poor health, are excluded from participating in decisions that affect their communities or have no right to guide the course of their lives. Such deprivations distinguish human poverty from income poverty' (UNDP, 2006: 271). Consequently, a condition of poverty can exist when people feel that they are excluded from the mainstream of society, denied opportunities to fulfil their own potential and are subsequently marginalised. Thus as Lister (2004) suggests, poverty is not purely a condition of economic disadvantage and insecurity, but can incorporate non-material aspects, including: disrespect; humiliation and low self-esteem; shame and stigma; lack of voice and powerlessness; and diminished citizenship – all factors which limit opportunities to realise one's potential. In this sense, poverty can be understood as an interpretative condition of those who are experiencing it, as much as a state that can be measured.

For Sen (1992, 1999) the ability for individuals to realise the potential of their capabilities is determined by 'freedoms', including the political, educational and personal. In the absence of these freedoms, there is a likelihood of people being socially excluded from mainstream society, including employment and a subsequent lack of income. To work in tourism it is necessary to have skills and knowledge but without having the freedom to access the educational system to achieve these, there is a subsequent denial of opportunity to work in the industry. Tourism development may also take place that totally lacks the poor's political participation in the process, thus socially excluding them from decision-making and the consequent livelihood opportunities created from the development of tourism. Relative poverty can therefore be understood to be about equity in society, the extent to which people are materially wealthier compared to each other and also the relativity of freedoms and opportunities they have to improve their lives. Alongside the importance for individuals to be able to fulfil their abilities to the maximum, it is also important for society and social harmony. Societies in which citizens enjoy political, educational and personal freedoms, have equal access to opportunities, and within which income differentiation is not extreme, are likely to have fewer social tensions and strife than discriminating and unequal societies.

UNDERSTANDING AND INTERPRETING POVERTY

From the previous discussion of the concepts of absolute and relative poverty it is apparent that poverty may be understood as being multicomposite and a complex phenomenon that cannot be easily defined through measurement but also relates to people's experiences, freedoms in society, cultural constructs and social norms. To have a clearer understanding of poverty it is subsequently argued there is a need to engage with people who are marginalised from the mainstream and possess few resources. A failure to enter into participatory processes that attempt to provide rich understandings of poverty may result in the imposition of solutions to alleviate poverty based upon a Western hegemonic construct that fails to respond to the poor's needs. Cultural constructs and interpretation are critical to identifying who is poor and at risk. For example, the rural peoples of many countries define their experience of poverty as the number of months without enough food, to have three months of sufficiency is to be very poor, to have nine months is far less so (Seabrook, 2007). Attaining cultural understandings of poverty is also emphasised by Power (2004: 24), who comments that poverty is increasingly seen as a 'phenomenon of many layers', determined by culture and power relations that range from the micro-level of the household to the macro-level of the nation. This culture and power relationship would embrace minority and oppressed groups who may be marginalised by the structures of the society they live in; for example, women, ethnic minorities, lower classes and the disabled.

Whilst income measures, such as those employed by the World Bank are indicative of poverty, they do not tell the whole story of whether needs are being fulfilled. Nor can it be understood from statistical measurement, which are the key issues of poverty that are relative to a particular place. For people who are heavily reliant on the natural resources of their surrounding environments, grow their own foods, make their own clothes and construct their own shelters, income may have relatively little significance to their well-being. An example of how cultural constructions of poverty may differ is exemplified in the case of the Adivasi peoples, the indigenous people of the Nilgiri mountains of Tamil Nadu in India. Although defined by international measures as experiencing material poverty, they were shocked by their first encounter with Western civilisation as recounted by Marcel Thekaekarka who had spent ten years working with the Adivasi on rural development programmes. Visiting Germany with six of the Adivasi, they expressed sympathy for the Western lifestyle which appeared urbane and isolated, as captured in the following comment: "'It's very nice to be here", Chathi, one of the six told me. "But I couldn't live here. It's not my place. A man needs his family, his community, his own people around him. Just money can't give you a life. You'd shrivel up and die.'"

Similarly, the tribal peoples of Northern Maharastra in India, the 'Warlis' cannot read or write but have a vast store of environmental knowledge, which they utilise to meet many of their needs. They know how to use herbs, shrubs and trees to supplement their diets of cereals and pulses, to make fibre, for fuel and lighting and for medicinal purposes. However, based on the poverty measure of the World Bank, the Warlis are classified as being in poverty and according to the HDI have one of the lowest levels of human development. The cultural influences of poverty are also illustrated in Box 1.6 based upon a folk tale common to many African and Asian societies. The tale exemplifies how statistics and measurements may not reveal the whole story of how people choose to live and emphasises the need for cultural understandings of poverty and interpretations of what it means to be poor.

BOX 1.6 THE FISHERFOLK TALE

As a component of the oral tradition of some regions of Africa and Asia, a tale is told about the encounter between a fisherman and a stranger. The fisherman is sleeping under a palm tree in the shade of the midday sun next to the beach when he is roused by a stranger, who asks him why he is not out fishing. The fisherman replies: 'I have already caught enough fish to feed my family for the day, to which the stranger replies: 'If you worked longer hours and went fishing again in the afternoon, you could catch more fish to sell at the market.' The fisherman asks the stranger why he would want to do that. To which the stranger says: 'If you did this day after day eventually you would save enough money to buy a good boat, employ people, catch more fish and become rich.' When the fisherman asks what he would do with the money, the stranger replies: 'You could have fun and relax, enjoy yourself and sleep in the shade.' The fisherman asks the stranger: 'What do you think I am doing now?'

Just as understanding and identifying what constitutes poverty is more complex than it may first appear, it is also evident that the geography of poverty is more complicated than a simple differentiation between those who live in the developed world and those who are living in the developing world. Since the early 1990s there has been a trend towards an increased divergence of wealth in societies, including those in developed countries. Power (2004: 11) refers to the process of 'Thirdworldisation' in the 'First World' and a vice versa 'Firstworldisation' in the 'Third World', a process of rising inequality within societies as a consequence of unbridled market capitalism. The dominance of neo-liberalism ideology, the dynamics of which are explained in the next chapter, has resulted in a political creed of free market fundamentalism that until the onset of the global financial crisis of 2008 had become seemingly untouchable by political criticism. Its key principle is that the less capitalism and markets are governed, managed or 'interfered' with by the state, the more efficiently they work for wealth creation and the benefit of society.

It is now evident that one of the outcomes of neo-liberalism is an accelerating disparity of wealth between and within countries. The causes of inter-nation inequality can be accredited to various guises of hegemony during recent centuries, which are analysed in Chapter 4, with the wealth gaps between regions of the world having progressively enlarged. At the beginning of the nineteenth century, the marked inequalities in wealth and poverty witnessed today did not exist, with Europe, China, India and Japan all having similar income levels (Sachs, 2005). For example, in 1820 the United Kingdom was the richest country in the world and had an average income per person approximately three times greater than that of sub-Saharan Africa, the poorest region. In 2005, the per capita income differential between the richest country, now the United States of America and sub-Saharan African had grown to approximately 20 times (Sachs, 2008).

Disconcertingly, the wealth gap between the richest and the poorest is also accelerating; for example, in 1990 the average American was 38 times richer than the average Tanzanian, but by the first decade of the twenty-first century the gap had grown to 61 times (UNDP, 2006). Countries in the developed world are also experiencing growing inequality; for example, wealth inequality in London now makes it the most unequal city in the developed world with the richest tenth of the population possessing 273 times the wealth of the poorest tenth (Ramesh, 2010). The scale of this wealth disparity has not been witnessed since the days of the slave-owning elites, one consequence being a rising health gap and a geographic polarisation of city according to class.

In an attempt to move beyond purely a simple income measure of poverty and lend more recognition to its multidimensional character, a widely referred to broader multidimensional analysis of poverty is the United Nations Human Development Index (HDI). The HDI is a summary composite index that prioritises measurements of levels of health and education provision alongside income, permitting a comparative measure of development between countries that stretches beyond income (UNDP, 2011). The HDI was developed by the late Pakistani economist Mahbub ul Haq in collaboration with Amartya Sen for the first Human Development Report produced by the United Nations Development Programme (UNDP) in 1990. Traditionally included in the HDI are indicators that reflect three basic dimensions of human development: a long and healthy life measured by life expectancy at birth; being educated, measured by mean and expected years of schooling; and a decent standard of living, measured by Gross National Income (GNI) per capita (UNDP, 2006).

Besides permitting an inter-country comparison of levels of human development, the HDI also allows a monitoring of the progress countries are making against these different criteria. Countries are ranked by order according to the key criteria and the UNDP recognises four main categories of development into which countries are placed: Very High Human Development; High Human Development; Medium Human Development; and Low Human Development. Examples of ranking scores for the top ten and bottom ten nations from the 2011 Human Development Index are given in Tables 1.1 and 1.2. The top ranks of the index are dominated by the economically developed countries of North America and Europe, emphasising a link between economic development and improvements in human welfare, determined by educational opportunities and access to health care. In contrast the list of the bottom countries is dominated by those of the region of sub-Saharan Africa.

The indicators in the tables demonstrate that the vast difference in the quality of life an individual will experience is dependent upon which country they are a citizen of. In the top ranked country, Norway, life expectancy is approximately 37 years longer than in the lowest rated country, the Democratic Republic of

Table 1.1 *Human Development Index and Country Scores (2011) – the 'Top 10'*

HDI Rank	Country	HDI Value	Life expectancy at birth	Mean years of schooling	Expected years of schooling	Gross National Income US$ per capita
1	Norway	0.943	81.1	12.6	17.3	47,557
2	Australia	0.929	81.9	12.0	18.0	34,431
3	The Netherlands	0.910	80.7	11.6	16.8	36,402
4	USA	0.910	78.5	12.4	16.0	43.017
5	New Zealand	0.908	80.7	12.5	18.0	23,737
6	Canada	0.908	81.0	12.1	16.0	35,166
7	Ireland	0.908	80.6	11.6	18.0	29,322
8	Liechtenstein	0.905	79.6	10.3	14.7	83,717
9	Germany	0.905	80.4	12.2	15.9	34,854
10	Sweden	0.904	81.4	11.7	15.7	35,837

Source: UNDP (2011) http://hdr.undp.org/en/media/HDR_2011_EN_Table1.pdf

Table 1.2 *Human Development Index and Country Scores (2011) – the 'Bottom 10'*

HDI Rank	Country	HDI Value	Life expectancy at birth	Mean years of schooling	Expected years of schooling	Gross National Income US$ per capita
178	Guinea	0.344	54.1	1.6	8.6	863
179	Central African Republic	0.343	48.4	3.5	6.6	707
180	Sierra Leone	0.336	47.8	2.9	7.2	737
181	Burkina Faso	0.331	55.4	1.3	6.3	1,141
182	Liberia	0.329	56.8	3.9	11.0	265
183	Chad	0.328	49.6	1.5	7.2	1,105
184	Mozambique	0.322	50.2	1.2	9.2	898
185	Burundi	0.316	50.4	2.7	10.5	368
186	Niger	0.295	54.7	1.4	4.9	641
187	Congo, Democratic Republic of the	0.286	48.4	3.5	8.2	280

Source: UNDP (2011) http://hdr.undp.org/en/media/HDR_2011_EN_Table1.pdf

Congo; the average time spent in school by an individual in Norway is nearly four times greater; and the Gross National Income per capita approximately 170 times higher.

Whilst the HDI represents an advancement in the recognition of the multidimensional character of poverty and permits a 'broad brush' comparison of levels of human development, it also has a number of limitations. A central criticism is that the three core components of life expectancy, education and income fail to embrace the rich variety of human developmental capabilities and deprivations. An evident limitation is that whilst the HDI presents an accurate snapshot of a comparison of health, knowledge and income levels between countries, it reveals little about the quality of the experiences of individuals, being reliant on measurement. Criticisms also exist that the three measures are not independent variables but that they are multicollinear; for example, good health improves educational attainment which improves opportunities for employment and income earning, which in turn increases the propensity for higher standards of education and health. Further criticisms are that regional, cultural and ethnic differences are not reflected in the statistics; and that measurement errors may exist (NSAC, 1999; Power, 2004). Additionally, the HDI does not incorporate a measure of wealth disparity between the richest and the poorest within countries.

THE SPATIAL DISTRIBUTION OF THE POOR

Identifying the numbers of poor people and the places they inhabit would probably seem evident building blocks of policies and strategies for poverty alleviation and reduction. Yet as Power (2004) points out, after six decades of development strategies, few if any of the international agencies know the exact number of poor people in the world. Reflecting on the complexities of defining poverty, the resources necessary to employ even a simple income measure of poverty in every country in the world, a rapidly expanding and migratory world population, and the political insecure situations in many countries that dictate against census collection, trying to attain an accurate picture across a large geographical scale is difficult. For example much of the poverty data for sub-Saharan countries is either out of date or does not exist, with the most current data for Malawi of people living on incomes of less that US$1 per day being from 1998 and for Niger from 1993 (Ibrahim, 2009). Power makes the point that this makes it extremely difficult to assess with any degree of scientific accuracy the extent to which efforts to raise people out of poverty are successful or not.

According to the UN International Fund for Agricultural Development (IFAD), who undertook the most comprehensive survey there has been of rural poverty, approximately 75 per cent of the world's poorest people live in rural areas. Many of the poorest of the rural poor live in geographically remote regions and on marginal lands; for example, at high altitude or areas with low levels of rainfall, areas with the lowest agricultural potential and furthest from the main national markets. Typically they live at subsistence or near subsistence level, growing all the food that their households eat or buying a very limited amount of food using the income from the small amount of their own produce they can sell, a situation of little earned monetary income and limited interaction with the market mechanism.

Using the latest available data to give a projection of the spatial distribution of the world's absolute poor, defined by having an income of less than US$1.25 a day in 2005, poverty is most prevalent in East Asia, South Asia and sub-Saharan Africa, as shown in Figure 1.2. However, the trends of prevalence of poverty within these three regions have different trajectories, with the numbers of extreme poor having risen in sub-Saharan Africa but fallen in East Asia and risen only slightly in South Asia. In real numbers this means 596 million people are living in extreme poverty in South Asia, 391 million in sub-Saharan Africa and 316 million in East Asia and the Pacific in 2005, the latest year for which completed data sets are available. The decline in the actual numbers of people in extreme poverty in the East Asia and Pacific region has been particularly dramatic, falling from 873 million in 1990 to 316 million in 2005. The principal reason for this decline has been the rapid pace of economic growth and development in China during this period. The increase in South Asia in real numbers is relatively small, rising from 579 million in 1990 to 596 million in 2005. However, the increase in sub-Saharan Africa is much more substantial, rising from 299 million in 1990 to 391 million in 2005 (IBRD, 2009).

In terms of the percentages of population living in poverty, all three regions display a decrease in the percentages of their populations living in extreme poverty. Between 1981 and 2005 the poverty rate in South Asia fell from 59 per cent to 40 per cent, in East Asia and the Pacific from 78 per cent to 17 per cent over the same period; and in sub-Saharan Africa from 54 per cent in 1981 to 51 per cent (ibid.). The characteristic of falling percentages of people living in extreme poverty at the same time as actual numbers are rising is reflective of increasing population numbers in sub-Saharan Africa and South Asia, in a situation where the birth rate has been exceeding the death rate.

The issues of population growth, associated demographic changes and resource pressures represent significant challenges to the reduction and alleviation of global poverty. During the twentieth century, the world's population grew exponentially, from approximately 1 billion at its start to 6 billion by its end. In 2011, the world's population surpassed 7 billion and by 2050 it is expected to be 9.3 billion; reaching 10.1 billion by 2100 in a medium growth scenario (United Nations, 2012). The geographical distribution of this population growth was also

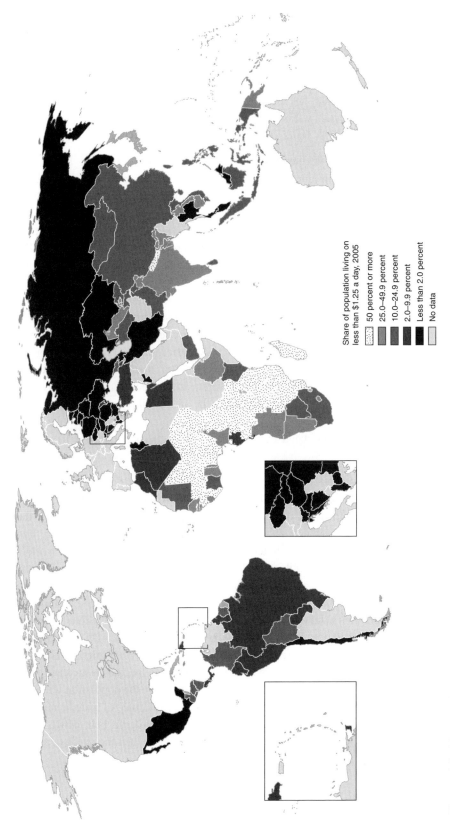

Figure 1.2 Map to show the global distribution of the poor

Share of population living on less than $1.25 a day, 2005

- 50 percent or more
- 25.0–49.9 percent
- 10.0–24.9 percent
- 2.0–9.9 percent
- Less than 2.0 percent
- No data

uneven during the twentieth century, with 80 per cent occurring in developing countries (World Bank, 2008). A key reason for this disparity relates to the availability of modern medicines in developing countries during the second half of the twentieth century that has permitted the control of infectious diseases and increased life expectancy. For developing countries as a whole, life expectancy at birth increased from 41 years in 1950 to 66 years by 2006 (ibid.).

Conversely, in the developed world of high-income countries, birth rates have been decreasing since the 1960s. The decrease in developed countries is attributed to social changes, particularly the role of women, as they have gained increased access to education, employment and career opportunities. Unlike the LDCs, an issue facing many developed countries is that of 'low-fertility', with 42 per cent of the world's population living in low-fertility countries, that is, where women do not have enough children to: 'ensure that, on average, each woman is replaced by a daughter who survives to the age of procreation (i.e. their fertility is below replacement level)' (United Nations, 2012: 6). This presents challenges to the future availability of human resources for the economies of these countries and a probable future reliance on immigrant labour. Expressed in terms of fertility gradings of countries, 42 per cent of the world's women live in low-fertility countries; 40 per cent in intermediate-fertility countries where each woman gives birth on average to between one to one and a half daughters; and the other 18 per cent live in high-fertility countries where on average a woman has more than one and half daughters (ibid.). It is in the high-fertility countries, dominated by the LDCs, where the population is increasing most rapidly.

Whilst falling populations may present a challenge for many developed countries, the extra 3 billion people that will be added to the world's population during this century will be mostly in developing countries, particularly in Africa and the Indian subcontinent, which will create new challenges for global society and policy. It is forecast by the United Nations that the populations of the world's poorest 48 nations will double to 1.7 billion by 2050 with Africa experiencing the most rapid population growth, rising from approximately 1 billion in 2012 to 2 billion by 2050, that is, from 15 per cent of the world's population to approximately 22 per cent (United Nations, 2012). Within the United Nations' medium variant of projected population, by 2100 the population of the LDCs is expected to be twice that of the more developed regions (ibid.). Examples of country-specific growth include Kenya, whose population is expected to increase from 40 million in 2010 to 96 million in 2050 and Niger where the population will over the same time period increase from 15 million to 55 million. An added challenge for Niger is its geographical situation in the Sahel semi-desert belt, which poses its own climatic challenges to agricultural production to meet the needs of such a rapid population increase.

Population growth is a controversial political issue with divided and sometimes extreme viewpoints about whether there are too many people in the world. Whilst it is theoretically possible to produce enough food to feed a growing world population and *technocentrics* place a strong belief in the advancement in science; for example, Genetically Modified (GM) crops and technological improvements to increase food yields, the combination of factors of political economy and distribution mean that 1 billion people remain constantly at risk from malnutrition and famine. Although it can be argued that improved governance and infrastructure development can help to alleviate this situation, the combination of population growth and resource pressures pose significant challenges to poverty reduction.

It is the poor who will be the hardest hit from population growth, as they face increased economic, environmental and natural resource pressures, including access to land and water. Access to resources is important to determining the choices in one's life and corresponding levels of economic and social well-being. As Power (2004) points out, for the poor who have access to few resources, their choice is severely constricted. In a situation where population growth outstrips economic growth, poverty will increase, placing pressures on land and water resources, contributing to deforestation and desertification, and increasing the propensity for conflict over resources. Land pressure for use for agriculture will be an increasing challenge in the future, as the majority of the poor live in rural areas and most of the land available to meet food requirements is already in production, meaning further expansion will be into marginal environments. The intensification of agricultural production in developing countries reliant on increased irrigation and the use of chemicals to meet the growing demand for food will result in soil erosion, salinisation, deteriorating water quality and desertification. Conflicts that may arise from resource competition will also have a detrimental effect on poverty, with 73 per cent of the 1 billion poor having recently been in a civil war or still being in one (Collier, 2008). The devastating effect that war can have on the livelihoods of the poor is illustrated in the case of South Sudan as described in Box 1.7.

BOX 1.7 THE IMPACT OF CIVIL WAR ON POVERTY IN SUDAN

In the recently created state of South Sudan, founded in 2011, local militias are fighting over water, cattle and land resources. The intensity of the fighting has led to 1 million political refugees fleeing northwards to the Nuba mountains in the hope of finding safety.

However, the area offers little real security as it is occupied by the Sudan People's Liberation Army which is regularly bombed by the air force of the Sudanese government. The mountainous region also has a poor infrastructure with roads becoming impassable in the wet season. The harsh conditions faced by the refugees have been high-lighted by the actor George Clooney who is the co-founder of the Enough Project, which aims to raise awareness of the humanitarian situation in Sudan and South Sudan. Of particular concern is that common vaccines against childhood diseases are not reaching chil-dren because of the violence, leading to death and ill-health. Combined with the effects of malnourishment, it is estimated that 20 per cent of the children will die and many of the survivors will be disfigured or left blind without the vaccine.

This case illustrates how conflict, especially civil wars, can displace the poor and have a marked effect on their well-being. This point is highlighted by Collier (2008: 18) who states: 'Seventy-three per cent of people in the societies of the bottom billion have recently been through a civil war or are still in one.' In an empirical study of civil wars and their relationship to economic growth, Collier (ibid.) found that there was a strong positive correlation between civil wars and a lack of income, with civil wars much more likely to break out in low-income countries, to the extent that if the starting income of the country is halved, the likelihood of civil war doubles. In a vicious cycle, one effect of civil war is to reduce economic growth and lower income and if the economy is weak, the government is also likely to be weak, heightening the chances of rebellion. In the context of using tourism as a tool for poverty reduction, the insecurity and chaos that is created through civil war makes tourism development a non-viable option, and any country that already has an established tourism industry will experience a reduction in tourism demand if civil war breaks out.

Source: after McClenaghan and McVeigh, 2012

In a self-perpetuating poverty circle, poverty may be the major cause of popula-tion growth, and population growth a major cause of poverty. In many LDCs, where population growth is outstripping economic growth, there is a subsequent possibility of being caught in a poverty and development trap, where today's poverty results in long-term poverty for future generations as a consequence of a lack of economic development. The ability to be able to meet the needs of billions more people during the course of this century also raises issues about the environmental limits of the planet, an issue which is fully evaluated in Chapter 3 in the context of resource dependency and Chapter 6 in relation to new development trends. A combination of population growth, climate change and a loss of fertile land could lead to famine, migration and conflict.

The challenges of population growth in LDCs related to scarce resources points to the need for a reduction in fertility rates if rates of population growth are to be reduced. However, the most basic human requirement is for security and survival and in the absence of a state 'safety-net' of social welfare, kin and family represent the most important and central resource for the poor. High infant mortality rates and the requirement for children to work to support their parents further encourage high birth rates. Birth rates generally begin to fall as a country's economy grows, with parents typically choosing to have smaller families as health conditions improve, as they no longer have a fear of a high incidence of infant mortality, nor do they have to rely on their children for labour or to take care of them in old age.

Reducing the economic necessity for children to work on the family farm or business also creates opportunities for parents to send their daughters to school. This is important because women with even a basic education tend to produce healthier children and smaller families (United Nations, 2012). A situation of women having children from an early age denies them future opportunities as they have less chance for education and childbirth may also adversely affect their health. An emphasis on education as the way to laying a foundation for poverty alleviation and reduction is reflected in the UN Millennium Development Goals shown in Box 1.1, one of which relates to ensuring that by 2015 all children will be able to complete a full course of primary education. Globally, tens of millions of children never attend school or have opportunities for education – the World Bank (2008) estimating that in 2005, 75 million children remained out of primary school, with 75 per cent of those living in sub-Saharan Africa and South Asia.

Of the children attending school in LDCs, a higher number of boys than girls are enrolled and also complete primary school. Children from poorer families and rural areas are also more likely to drop out of primary school before completing their education or never attend. As was illustrated in the case of Simon, the boy from Uganda in Box 1.3, the reasons for non-attendance are caused by poverty, whilst ill-health of adult family members and a need for children to labour for income are typical causes. It may also be too expensive for parents to send their children to school and schools may be geographically remote and inaccessible, especially in rural areas, and may also be of a poor quality and offer little educational value.

SUMMARY

- Poverty is a complex phenomenon whose definition will vary according to political, economic, historical, cultural and ethical interpretations. Absolute or chronic poverty can be understood as being a lack of ability to meet one's most basic requirements – for example, for nutrition and shelter – and raises ethical issues about the relationship and responsibilities of humankind. Poverty can also be understood as a lack of opportunity to fulfil one's potential as a consequence of being marginalised in society. Poverty is not purely a condition of economic disadvantage and insecurity, but can also incorporate non-material aspects, including: disrespect; humiliation and low self-esteem; shame and stigma; lack of voice and powerlessness; and diminished citizenship. The concept of relative poverty is also used particularly in developed countries to identify marginalised people who cannot have the quality of life, including types of diets, living conditions, access to amenities and participation in the types of activities that are the norm of the societies to which they belong.

- For most of human existence, poverty has been a 'normal' state for the majority of people, making them at risk and vulnerable to any event or 'shock' that may negatively affect the status quo. These include illness, natural disasters (e.g., drought and floods), and events of human activity (e.g., wars). Industrial revolution and the economic development of many countries during the twentieth century means that chronic poverty is now the condition of a sizeable 'minority' rather than the majority. Nevertheless, this sizeable minority includes between 1 and 1.5 billion people living on an income of less than US$1.25 per day. It was towards the end of the nineteenth century that poverty began to become associated with a deficiency of income through the pioneering work of Charles Booth and Seebohm Rowntree in their attempts to improve the economic and social conditions of the mass of society in the United Kingdom. The high number of people living in absolute poverty, often referred to as 'the poor', means that poverty alleviation and reduction is a focus of supranational agencies, including the United Nations and the World Bank. The prioritisation of poverty alleviation is reflected in its inclusion as the first goal of the Millennium Development Goals.

- In an attempt to reflect the multidimensionality of poverty, rather than purely recognising it as a deficiency of income, the United Nations Development Programme (UNDP) uses the Human Development Index (HDI) as an indicative measure of countries' level of development. Four main categories of development are recognised: 'Very High Human Development', 'High Human Development', 'Medium Human Development' and 'Low Human Development'. It is apparent that poverty may be understood as being multi-composite and a complex phenomenon that cannot be easily defined through measurement but also relates to people's experiences, freedoms in society, cultural constructs and social norms. To have a clearer understanding of poverty it is subsequently argued there is a need to engage with people who are marginalised from the mainstream and possess few resources. A failure to enter into participatory processes that attempt to provide rich under-standings of poverty may result in the imposition of solutions to alleviate poverty based upon a Western hegemonic construct that fails to respond to the poor's needs.

- The geographical distribution of the poor is dominated by Least Developed Countries (LDC) which are located in sub-Saharan Africa, South and East Asia and Latin America. The predominant location is in sub-Saharan Africa and the majority of the poor are located in rural areas. Whilst population rates are declining in the developed countries of the world, they are increasing in the LDCs, where the population of the world's poorest 48 countries is expected to double by 2050, raising key economic and social challenges for the future. In a situation where population growth outstrips economic growth, there is a subsequent danger of people and countries being caught in a poverty and development trap.

Tourism development

2 A relationship to poverty?

This chapter:

- Critically evaluates the term 'development'
- Explains development theories and paradigms
- Analyses the relationship between tourism and development
- Explores tourism's relationship with poverty reduction

UNDERSTANDING 'DEVELOPMENT'

The title of this chapter has been formulated as a question to encourage the reader to think about the relationship between tourism development and poverty. Chapter 1 evaluated the concept of poverty, highlighting its multidimensional character and typologies. It was also discussed that the recognition of poverty as a matter for political and social concern has arisen relatively recently. For the majority of human history, poverty has been a condition of familiarity across most societies. However, economic growth and associated development means that absolute poverty is now a condition of a significant minority rather than the majority of the world's population, yet this is a recent transformation. As Collier (2008) observes, as recently as the 1960s the development challenge was one of a rich world of 1 billion people facing a poor world of 5 billion people. However, during the course of the last four decades, the pace of development for 80 per cent of that 5 billion has been so rapid that the real challenge to development is the remaining 1 billion who live in countries that are often dysfunctional and failing.

Since the Second World War the term 'economic development' has become one that is widely used in reference to the nation state, yet, the term 'development' is one that has application in different contexts. For example, a common usage is to talk of an individual's development or perhaps lack of it, referring to changes in their behaviour, intellectual capabilities and skills, and physique. The theory of human evolution and development presented in Darwin's seminal *Origin of the Species* in the nineteenth century was simultaneous with the great economic and social changes of the Industrial Revolution occurring in the same century in Europe and the USA. Philanthropists, liberals and social commentators such as Friedrich Engels, referred to in Chapter 1, shared concerns over the appalling living and working conditions of many working people during this period. The transition of agricultural societies to industrial economies and the effect on living standards for the majority resulted in interest in how societies develop. This led to observations that society may also pass through organic evolutional stages of development similar to the human body, the final stage being that of a created utopia. Subsequently, the process of development may be interpreted as taking on the guise of a remedy attempting to address pressing social problems such as population increase and scarce resources; job losses and unemployment; urban squalor and poverty (Cowen and Sheraton, 1996).

It was in the immediate post-Second World War period in the 1940s that a strong association was established between global economic progress, national development and political ideologies. This epoch was defined by the ideological divide of capitalism and communism and an emergent political independence of the countries of Asia and Africa from European powers. Within this changing global political order, a significant event in establishing the terminology of international development was President Truman's speech on 21 January 1949. He distinguished between the 'developed' and the 'underdeveloped' worlds, and the 'First' and the 'Third' worlds, terms defined by the quantitative measure of national income and political orientation. In other words, he divided the world between those who were modern and those who were not and established modernity as the standards to which other societies would be compared and judged (McMichael, 2004).

The First World encompassed the industrialised and capitalist countries of the world, those of North America, Western Europe and Australasia. The Third World countries were the economically developing countries of the world who were beginning to demand their sovereign independence, geographically situated in the continents of Africa, Asia and Latin America. In between the First World and the Third Worlds, was a Second World that consisted of the industrialised countries of the Soviet Union and other communist allies. The political dimension of Truman's speech can be understood as interpreting the world's poor as a possible threat to the established global political economy unless they could be integrated into the wider capitalist and market system. His speech also emphasised the role of America in using its scientific and industrial knowledge to relieve the suffering of the poor, stating: 'More than half the people of the world are living in conditions approaching misery. Their food is inadequate. They are victims of disease. Their economic life is primitive and stagnant. Their poverty is a handicap and a threat to both them and to more prosperous areas.' Alongside their economic power in the post-war era, the United States also possessed an ideological supremacy, given its superior standard of living with a per capita income three times that of Europe, an anti-colonial heritage and a commitment to liberal domestic and international relations. The significance of this constructed world political geography was the imperative for the use of Western aid to rework the political and economic spaces of several Third World countries, administered through the Bretton Woods establishment, which is explained in Box 2.1.

Beside the conflict in political ideology between capitalism and communism, a major concern amongst the leaders of the 'allied nations', including the United States and Britain, was to establish a system of rules and regulations to govern the post-war global economy. A priority was to avoid the economic hardships of the 1930s 'Great Depression', a significant causal factor of the rise of fascism and political division. To help to achieve this aim, a meeting of international leaders was convened at Bretton Woods, New England, in 1944, which resulted in the establishment of institutions to regulate the world economy, the most significant of which, the World Bank and International Monetary Fund (IMF), remain highly influential in determining the political economy of global policy.

BOX 2.1 THE BRETTON WOODS TRIO'S INFLUENCE ON INTERNATIONAL DEVELOPMENT

There are key global and international institutions and organisations, sometimes referred to as multilateral and supranational agencies that have a decisive influence in setting the paradigms and conditions for global and national economic development. These institutions are particularly influential in setting the terms of continued financial support for LDCs in the form of aid and loans. Their establishment can be traced to the immediate re-building of the European and international economy in the aftermath of the Second World War. In 1944, delegates from 44 nations met at the New England resort of Bretton Woods, to devise a new framework for the global economy. They were concerned to try to stabilise the international economy to avoid a repeat of the Great Depression that had proved economically and politically damaging. The title 'Bretton Woods Trio' refers to the three governing institutions which emerged from the conference to coordinate the global economy. These are:

The International Monetary Fund (IMF)

The role of the IMF was to create economic stability in the world and to oversee a system of fixed exchange rates. The idea of this initiative was to stop countries devaluing their national currencies to gain a competitive trading advantage over other countries, a strategy that was believed to have been a major factor contributing to the global economic downturn in the 1930s. The IMF was to provide limited loan amounts to members when they fell into a trade deficit. The other role of the IMF is to act as a 'lender of the last resort', supplying emergency loans to countries with short-term cash flow problems.

The World Bank (International Bank for Reconstruction and Development (IBRD))

A key goal of the Bretton Woods conference was to rebuild the economies of Europe after the Second World War. The IBRD was established to facilitate this process, being funded from payments from its members and money borrowed on international money markets. Emphasis was placed upon the giving of loans for the development of infrastructure, including dams, roads, airports, ports, power stations, agricultural development and education systems. Although the bank lent lots of money for the redevelopment of Europe, the continent's reconstruction was also facilitated by the USA through the form of grants in what was termed the 'Marshall Plan'.

The statutes of the World Bank also specifically enjoin it to promote the flow of private investment to developing countries, and as Europe's economy began to recover in the 1950s, the attention of the IBRD moved towards the developing world and it became widely known as the World Bank. Linked to the 'stages of growth' economic theory (see Figure 2.1), a strong infrastructure was believed to be essential for economic development. Consequently, the Bank funded hydroelectric projects, bridges and highway systems throughout Latin America, Asia and Africa. However, it was soon clear that the poorest countries would find it difficult to meet loan repayments. In the late 1950s, the Bank established the International Development Association (IDA) to provide 'soft loans' with very low rates or no rate of interest at all.

General Agreement on Tariffs and Trade (GATT)/World Trade Organisation (WTO)

Similar to the creation of the World Bank and the IMF there were plans in 1945 to create an International Trading Organisation under the auspice of the United Nations to regulate world trade in an attempt to ensure that the economic conditions of the 1930s that led to the rise of fascism and the Second World War were not repeated. However, the influence of powerful business interests led to a downgrading of an organisation to an 'agreement', made between 23 of the West's richest countries and that excluded the countries of the Soviet Union. The General Agreement on Tariffs and Trade (GATT) was founded in 1948, the purpose being to establish rules to govern world trade, reduce national barriers to trade, and to resolve trade disputes through negotiating rounds.

Seven rounds of tariff reductions were negotiated under the GATT treaty, the final Uruguay Round being in 1986. In 1994, a new institute the World Trade Organisation (WTO) was established in Morocco, which had the official status of an international organisation rather than a loosely structured treaty. It includes the GATT agreements, and also a new General Agreement on Trade in Services (GATS), which includes banking, insurance, telecommunications and tourism. The effect of GATS on tourism is to open a country's resources to foreign investment as is exemplified in the case of Kenya described in Box 2.2. The effects of GATS is commented upon by Badger *et al.* (1996: 22) as: 'Power is increasingly resting in the hands of these large northern-based companies, who can direct flows of international tourists to particular destinations because of their high-tech globalised reservation systems. An estimated 80 per cent of all tourists travel with a tour operator package, so it is easy to appreciate the power of the tour operator vis-à-vis the host country'. Whilst this figure of 80 per cent has been reduced with the growth in independent travel in the two decades since Badger's work, the power of large tourism companies based in developed countries is emphasised in her statement. In the general context of trade, the WTO also concentrates on 'hard cash', ignoring issues of human rights and the rights of the natural environment. Both GATT and the WTO have been subsequently criticised as a 'rich man's club' dominated by the Western nations on the basis that the global trade rules are biased against developing countries. Similar criticisms have also been made of the World Bank and IMF, including the lack of representation from developing countries, an issue that is explored in Chapter 6.

The contemporary importance of the institutes of Bretton Woods for global and nation state development, particularly the World Bank and the IMF, cannot be understated. Referring to the World Bank, George and Sabelli (1994) observe that although the Bank's charter defines it as an economic institution, it wields immense political power. One reason for this is that since the collapse of the Soviet Union, the World Bank as a supranational agency with its close ties to the United States government can operate and enforce policies on a global scale, imposing its own view as the norm. As George and Sabelli (ibid.) point out, the Bank has more to say about state policy than many governments. However, Pieterse (2010) observes that American hegemony played out through the World Bank is being challenged by the rise of China as an economic superpower which has substantial foreign reserves for investment in other countries, making it an alternative source of funding to the World Bank. The role of China as a major foreign investor in Africa since the beginning of the twenty-first century is especially significant as is discussed in Chapter 6 in the context of a changing global political economy.

The World Bank was instrumental to the linking of development with poverty, notably under the stewardship of Robert McNamara who was its president during the 1970s. Although a controversial figure, not least because of his pro-Vietnam war stance, McNamara's 1973 Nairobi speech cited in Chapter 1, was instrumental in redefining the notion of 'development' as perceived by the World Bank (George and Sabelli, 1994). The previous sole emphasis of development in the World Bank had been to make sure that states had sufficient electrical power, transport and communications, that is, the infrastructure for progression to a state of modernity. The linking of development with poverty and the World Bank as having a role in relieving it, represented a new departure.

During the early decades of the second half of the twentieth century, the conception of development encouraged by the World Bank became synonymous with economic progress. This can be dated to President Truman's speech, which whilst a watershed in politicising the global politics of development, also equated development with economic growth and increasing world trade. The concept of development subsequently became defined by economic progress and quantifiable measurement through indicators of growth, ignoring other types of wealth as Reid (1995: 140) comments: 'The wealth of a range of societies with flourishing cultures was simply ignored . . . for it could not be assessed in economic terms.' Consequently, the dominant measure of development became correlated to increased economic and material wealth, marginalising the range of democratic, gender, political and environmental issues that determine the individual and collective quality of life. The concentration on the economic at the expense of other issues that determine the quality of life has led to subsequent criticism of the World Bank.

Building on Truman's speech, through equating development with economic growth, logic would suggest that if a country is underdeveloped, it requires growth in its economy to raise living standards and benefit the poor. The further association of Third World countries with notions of backwardness, underdevelopment and poverty provided a powerful context for economic and political intervention by developed countries on the pretence of humanitarian grounds. Intervention and the desire to 'develop' countries would similarly offer opportunities for the expansion of the capitalist model into new markets, at a time when the post-colonial world was dividing on ideological lines between the capitalist and communist systems. The origins of national development as a focus of international policy can therefore be understood as having a strong political context, causing neo-Marxists to interpret development as a form of neo-colonialism and a global domination of capitalist ideology in the post-communist era.

CHANGING PARADIGMS OF DEVELOPMENT

The changing political economy of the post-Second World War period, encapsulated in President Truman's inauguration speech, marked the beginnings of the study and theorising of development, and the formalisation of policies for economic development at national and international levels. Different frameworks of main ideas or 'paradigms' on international development have been formulated since the post-war period, predominantly based upon a comparison of economic levels of growth between countries of the 'developed' and 'developing' worlds. Inherent to these paradigms are political doctrines and concerns, reflective of the opposing political ideologies of capitalism and communism, and a relative freedom of the World Bank and IMF since the early 1990s to apply development models rooted in capitalist and market doctrines. Development has subsequently been subject to political and economic analysis which has influenced its aims and policies and routes to achieving it. The most recognised theories of development are modernisation, dependency, neo-liberalism and alternatives, which in turn reflect broader paradigms of classical and neo-Marxist socio-economic theories, as is explained in the following respective subsections.

Modernisation

The association between the concept of organic development and the development of societies manifested itself in the first significant theoretical perspective on international development – that of modernisation theory. Modernisation theory views socio-economic development as an evolutionary and linear path from a traditional society to a modern society, combining economic growth with political modernisation and national benefits (Pieterse, 2010). Its roots lie in a variety of different perspectives applied by non-Marxists to developing countries in the

1950s and 1960s but is epitomised by the work of Walt Rostow who was an economic policy advisor to President Johnson of the USA. The title of his most influential work, *Stages of Economic Growth: A Non-Communist Manifesto*, published in 1960, indicates the political orientation of Rostow's work: an analysis of development that extended beyond the theoretical into a political manifesto to fight off the threat of communism or the 'disease of transition' as he referred to it. In Rostow's view, the rationale for financial aid for development should surpass the purely economic to include the political, that is, supporting non-communist elites, democracy and pluralism.

The work of Rostow was heavily influenced by the organic analogy of functionalism, that is, the idea that societies, like natural beings, mature through different stages of evolution driven by an internal dynamic. Rostow stresses that progressive stages of economic growth are the route to a more developed status, the ultimate state being that of the 'Age of High Mass Consumption'. His theory emphasises development as being synonymous to modernity, following Western models of evolution through defined stages of economic growth as displayed in Figure 2.1. This paradigm of development was framed by an optimistic approach to development, the general assumption being that the development problems of the less developed world would be solved quickly through national economic planning and the transfer of finance, technology and experience from the 'West' to the 'Rest' (Elliott, 1994; Mowforth and Munt, 2009; World Bank, 2000).

Rostow detailed the five main stages of economic growth that he understood societies would evolve through under optimum conditions to a final age of mass consumption. In his modernisation model, Rostow suggested that rapid economic development could only occur if barriers to tradition and superstition could be overcome, and the values and social structures of traditional societies are changed (Harrison, 1992). In direct reference to organic analogy, Slattery (1992: 270) comments: 'Just as we often talk of a child being immature, even retarded, when its mental development doesn't match its physical growth, so we talk of underdeveloped even backward societies, of Third World countries held back by illiteracy, ignorance and superstition.' In Rostow's progression such a change would involve the expansion of investment capital, entrepreneurial skills and technical knowledge. He further suggested that if such features are absent, possibly because of the conservative nature of tradition, they could be diffused from outside. Constant to the theme of modernisation remains one of 'Westernisation' in which the structures of less developed countries become like those of the West, emulating their development patterns (Harrison, 1992). In this sense it can be argued that Rostow appears to justify colonialism (ibid.), on the basis that the European powers transferred elements of investment capital and technical knowledge to their colonies, albeit based upon the pursuit of their own national interest and economic benefits.

STAGE ONE – TRADITIONAL SOCIETY
Pre-industrial, typically agricultural societies that are characterised by low economic output, ancient technology and poor communications. The culture is hierarchical with little social mobility and values orientate towards the fatalistic.

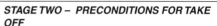

STAGE TWO – PRECONDITIONS FOR TAKE OFF
New ideas favouring economic progress arise, leading to the idea of economic change through increased trade and the establishment of infant industries. A new political elite emerges, such as the entrepreneurial bourgeoisie of the Industrial Revolution to challenge the power of the landed classes. Infrastructure is developed to facilitate economic growth

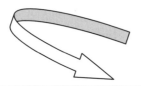

STAGE THREE – THE TAKE OFF
Industrialisation replaces agriculture as the driving force of the economy. This happens through new technology or the influence of the entrepreneurial class who prioritise modernisation of the economy. Agriculture also becomes commercialised with a growth in productivity. The influence of the market leads to new political, social and economic structures. Rural to urban population drift takes place.

STAGE FOUR – THE DRIVE TO MATURITY
Over a period of approximately 40 years, the country builds on its progress. Investment grows, 10–20 per cent of the national income is invested in industry, technology spreads to all parts of the economy, and the economy becomes a part of the international system. There is a move away from heavy industry, as what is produced now becomes a matter of choice rather than necessity.

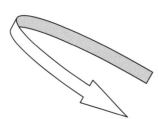

STAGE FIVE – THE AGE OF MASS CONSUMPTION
The economy matures, the population can enjoy the benefits of mass consumption, a high standard of material living and, if it wants, a welfare state. According to Rostow, in the United States this stage was symbolised by the mass production of the motor car. The balance in the economy progressively shifts to a service economy vis-à-vis an industrial one.

Figure 2.1 *Rostow's five main stages of economic growth*

Given its capitalist emphasis and Western ethnocentrism, unsurprisingly modernisation theory has received substantial political and economic criticisms. These include that the unidirectional path of development suggested in Rostow's model is incorrect, as later developing countries can learn from the West and through borrowing Western skills, technology and expertise subsequently leap a stage or two. For example, a LDC may plan to use tourism as primary economic driver for development as a replacement or accompaniment to heavy industry. Modernisation theory has also been criticised for its cultural superiority and the assumption that traditional values are not compatible with modernity. A significant further criticism came later upon environmental grounds, that if the developing countries industrialise using natural resources as the same way in the West, the strain on the world's natural resources would be insupportable.

A significant change in the world economy since Rostow constructed his five main stages of growth has been the growth in the global service industries in which tourism plays a significant part. Tourism is embedded into the contemporary age of mass consumption of developed countries, which presents opportunities for LDCs with the natural and cultural resources to develop an international tourism industry. A consideration of tourism for development is also symbolic of how economic opportunities shift with time, as in the period when Rostow was writing the idea of considering tourism as a form of international trade and being used as a means to modernise economies was improbable.

Dependency theories

The criticisms of modernisation theory were encapsulated in an alternative school of thought originating in Latin America known loosely as 'dependency theory'. In a radically alternative view to modernisation theory, dependency theorists or *dependinistas* argue that developing countries have external and internal political, institutional and economic structures that keep them in a dependent position relative to developed countries (Bianchi, 1999). Subsequently, development theorists attempted to formulate an explanation of the causes of underdevelopment in a holistic framework, based upon the interaction of economic and social structures within an international system.

Through analysing the comparative underdevelopment of Latin America to the West, *dependinistas* agreed that this occurred because of the operation of the capitalist system, within which a 'core' of industrialised countries developed their economies through the exploitation of the non-industrialised peripheral countries (Willis, 2005). As one of the most recognised dependency theorists, Andre Gunder Frank commented in the 1960s: 'I believe, with Paul Baran, that it is capitalism, both world and national, which produced underdevelopment in the past and which still generates underdevelopment in the present' (Frank, 1967: vii). Subsequently, emphasis is placed upon analysing the exploitative nature of the exchange relations between historically powerful metropolitan states, that is, the United States and Western European countries and their dependent satellites; for example, countries of Latin America, Africa and parts of Asia. Andre Gunder Frank, a major influence on dependency theory, viewed the 'development of underdevelopment' as being deliberate and a part of the same world capitalist system. Frank argued that the lack of development in Third World countries was because the Western nations deliberately aimed at underdevelopment and not because of its own inadequacies or a failure to develop a 'culture of enterprise'. He subsequently argued that industrial development in the periphery would only begin when it severed its ties with the capitalist First World.

Frank emphasised that this relationship of exploitation and dependency can be traced back to the seventeenth century and colonialism, when European powers conquered and colonised the continents of Africa, Asia and Latin America, making them a part of their imperial system. Subsequently, with the Industrial Revolution of the nineteenth century and the emergence of a world capitalist system, an international division of labour was created that forced colonies to specialise in the production of one or two primary products. The colonies supplied the mother country with cheap raw materials and food and in turn provided markets for manufactured goods. For example, an essential component of the beginnings of the Industrial Revolution in Britain was the importation of cotton from its 'Jewel in the Crown' colony of India, which was then manufactured in England into clothes for return for sale in the Indian market. The scale of this enterprise made a significant contribution to making Britain into the richest country in the world during the nineteenth century.

Frank argued that through this model emerged a 'world system' of dependency and underdevelopment, in which core nations such as Britain exploited 'peripheral ones' such as India. A key element within this relationship was the city, as colonial powers built cities or used existing ones as a means of governing areas and forging points of connection with ruling local elites. The ruling upper class generally collaborated with colonial powers, using their control of local markets to exploit the peasantry in the countryside, progressively becoming more linked to a Western way of life and removed from that of the majority of their own people. Frank (1967) also drew attention to how ruling elites may use military means to suppress local people at times of political unrest with arms supplied from the West to preserve their wealth and power. There subsequently existed a system of 'metropolises and satellites', in which development in one part of the world system occurred at the economic and political expense of another part. Through this mechanism of unequal exchange, economic value was transferred from the relatively underdeveloped to the relatively developed regions (Harrison, 1992). Subsequently, *dependinistas* argue that instead of aiding their development, the world system actually hinders the development of LDCs, as it is to the advantage of the wealthier countries to ensure that the poorer ones remain undeveloped.

Since the end of colonialism in the post-Second World War period, it is arguably multinational organisations that maintain this unequal relationship through co-operation with elite counterparts in the LDCs and the ownership of resources. As to how this system of development and underdevelopment should be corrected, dependency theorists have different approaches (Willis, 2005). A major distinction exists between the 'reformists' who advocate a reform of the existing capitalist trade system and revolutionary neo-Marxists who hold that the overthrow of capitalism is the only solution. Frank was one of the most vociferous advocates of the latter solution, believing that within the capitalist system the peripheral countries would always be exploited (ibid.).

The influence of dependency theory on policy has been limited and it has been criticised that its theoretical concepts are vague and its ideas are too radical and too Marxist. Modernisation theorists argue that multinationals and Western aid bring considerable benefits, and the premise that the economically advanced countries keep other countries underdeveloped is wrong, as developed countries need other countries to economically develop as a source of new investment and new markets. Frank's work is also criticised as being too generalised and failing to recognise the differences between countries and levels of economic development. Marxists have also maligned Frank's failure to provide a revolutionary programme for how countries can break free of the world capitalist system. A further reproach originated from the ability of the 'newly industrialising countries' (NICs) or 'newly industrialising economies' (NIEs) of East Asia, including Hong Kong, Singapore, Taiwan and South Korea to generate rapid economic growth based on labour-intensive manufacturing industries in the post-Second World War epoch. The economic success of these countries challenged the notion that it was in the interests of the developed core to purposefully under develop the periphery.

Economic neo-liberalism

An incumbent part of modernisation theory was to make available international aid through the World Bank and IMF as a catalyst for the economic development of poorer countries. The general principle of aid involves the transfer of resources, including loans, grants and technical advice on terms that are more generous than is available in the world's capital markets. During the 1950s and 1960s, aid was typically channelled into industrial development, the technological advancement of agriculture to improve crop yields, and large-scale infrastructure projects such as dam construction, road and bridge building (Willis, 2005). Despite aid programmes, economic growth in developing countries was lower than expected, leading some economic analysts during the 1970s to begin to dispute the Keynesian theories that were driving international policies for economic growth in developing countries and that had dominated post-war development thinking.

The Keynesian model followed the philosophy of the economist John Maynard Keynes, whose theories were highly influential for international development policy in the post-Second World War era. He rejected the ideas of free markets and classical economics as the best route for economic growth. Instead he stressed that governments had a key role for promoting economic growth, through government expenditure as a stimulus and effective control of monetary policies; for example, interest rates. In the 1970s doubts were raised over the ability of government planning to solve the problems of under development and poverty. The consensus of neo-liberal economists was that the control and interference of the state in economic development was causing inefficiency and resulting in growth at a slower rate than if resource allocation was left primarily to the market mechanism. It was also argued that foreign aid was contributing to inefficiencies and that this type of market intervention should be reduced.

This re-evaluation of development took place in the context of a debt crisis as many developing countries failed to meet their debt repayment requirements on loans taken to finance large-scale infrastructure projects. These loans had been taken from various sources including private banks, foreign governments and the World Bank. The failure of developing countries to meet debt repayments was a consequence of a fall in the late 1970s of commodity prices in world markets that led to a decline in import earnings. Developing countries' reliance on primary industries, especially agricultural and mining products as their chief exports and earners of recognised foreign currencies, meant a decline in world commodity prices was catastrophic for them.

The advocacy of markets was supported by a re-vitalised form of classical economic thinking, 'neo-liberalism', which became favoured in influential policy decision-making circles. Developed in the USA by influential philosopher–economists such as Milton Friedman (Power, 2004), it purports an ultimate belief in the economic rationalism and efficiency in the free market as a path to development. Integral to neo-liberalism is market liberalisation, the privatisation of state assets and a minimum role for state intervention in the market. Key components of these themes included recognition of the private sector as the engine of economic growth vis-à-vis the state, whilst simultaneously shrinking state bureaucracy and public expenditure; removing barriers to foreign investment and resource ownership; privatising state-owned industries through open international competition; and increasing exports of services including health care and education.

Essentially the implementation of this set of measures could theoretically integrate a country's resources, including human and natural capital into an open and free global market. In terms of the relationship between the developed and the developing worlds, this agenda was forced onto developing countries as a precondition for the continuation of loans from the IMF and World Bank, in part a response to the vicious cycle of indebtedness that had been created between the rich and the poor worlds (Maathai, 2009). The dominance of the market system and neo-liberalism was given further credence as the pathway for development following the collapse of the socialist statist systems of the Soviet Union. A mix of political coercion and bureaucratic inefficiency had led to their collapse, an event that was seized upon by the West (Seabrook, 2007), as being indicative proof that it is only via the operation of free markets and the integration of the global economy through trade and information sharing that poor countries can be lifted out of the economic doldrums (Maathai, 2009).

Key drivers of neo-liberal policy were the World Bank, the USA and Britain, through the personas of President Ronald Reagan and Prime Minister Margaret Thatcher respectively, the new direction being captured in Regan's 'magic of the market' speech at the 1981 North–South Conference in Mexico. The package of neo-liberal measures recommended by USA, Europe and the World Financial Institutions including the World Bank, IMF and World Trade Organisation are referred to as the 'Washington Consensus'.

Integral to the implementation of neo-liberal measures has been the use of structural adjustment programmes (SAPs), which have been adopted by national governments in return for continued financial support from the World Bank and IMF (Willis, 2005). SAPs were based upon free market economic principles, the aim being to improve a developing country's propensity for attracting foreign inward investment through stabilising its economy, typically being implemented in stages. The first step involved a structural change in the economy by diminishing the role of the state in the running of the national economy and reducing government deficits through spending cuts, including ones on health, education and welfare. Once stabilised, adjustment measures are then introduced into the economy to lay the foundations for long-term changes that should contribute to a more prosperous future (ibid.). These adjustment measures typically include the privatisation of government-owned enterprises, business deregulation, wage suppression and, if appropriate, currency devaluation to boost exports. According to neo-liberal theory, through removing restrictions on the ownership of resources and introducing wage suppression in the public sector, a country should become more attractive for foreign inward investment. This in turn should lead to economic development and a comparative advantage in specialised economic sectors which should boost exports.

The imposition of SAPs on developing countries during the 1980s and 1990s raised substantial controversy over their impacts and demonstrates how economic policies contrived in the North can be imposed in countries in the South in the absence of the acknowledgement of cultural differences (Burns, 2004; Power, 2004), forcing governments to pursue 'specific policies not of their own design' (Mowforth and Munt, 2009: 303). Commenting specifically on the effects of the range of measures enforced on African countries under the aegis of SAPs, Maathai (2009) views them as having had a range of highly negative impacts on the poor, including a cutting of essential services in infrastructure development, health and education. The sum effect has been that the quality of the lives of the majority of Africans has declined and the governance of many states failed to improve. The effects of SAPs are also evident in the tourism industry as described in Box 2.2.

BOX 2.2 THE INFLUENCE OF SAPS ON KENYA'S TOURISM INDUSTRY

The influence of SAPs on the tourism industry is illustrated through Dieke's (1994, 2000) analysis of changes to the Kenyan tourism industry during the 1980s. Since political independence in the 1950s, the resources for tourism, including national parks, transport and accommodation suppliers, were all under state control. The subsequent privatisation of these tourism assets beginning in the 1980s meant that a cadre of elites who were able to purchase them within the terms of the SAP. Acquisitions included hotels and transport companies, which were then either sold or the new owners went into partnerships with foreign-owned chains. There was a subsequent switch from an industry that was too controlled by government to one that was largely unregulated and lacked local ownership. This transfer of Kenya's tourism resources to foreign control, combined with increased levels of foreign inward investment, effectively shifted hegemonic control of the industry and the bulk of revenue earnings to outside the country.

Alongside increased economic leakages, the environmental effects on Kenya's tourism resources of the desire to maximise foreign exchange earnings as part of Kenya's Structural Adjustment Programme are reported by Hawkins and Mann (2007), citing a World Bank (1990) report entitled the 'Wildlife and Tourism Project'. Whilst the report acknowledges the role of the development of wildlife tourism in improving foreign exchange earnings, it emphasised that little attention had been given to environmental planning and management, leading to natural resource degradation and threatening the sustainability of both the environment and the tourism. Within ten years of the report, the Kenyan government had to request World Bank support for a 'Protected Areas and Wildlife Services Project' to mitigate the environmental problems caused by tourism.

SAPs have encouraged LDCs to develop their natural and cultural resources for tourism as a component of the neo-liberalism emphasis on market-orientated growth and increased levels of exports, specifically in industries in which countries have a comparative advantage in world markets. This emphasis on export-led production has led to a shift in development strategy away from an inward perspective towards an outward orientation (Brohman, 1996). This includes the expansion of previously ignored economic sectors such as international tourism, which can be grouped with other new 'growth' sectors; for example, non-traditional agricultural exports to Western countries. It is these sectors which are believed by the World Bank and IMF to show much promise for stimulating rapid growth using the comparative advantages of developing countries. The emphasis on tourism as an export industry and foreign exchange earner, combined with a simultaneous reduction in state protection to fledgling industries such as tourism, has led to increased interest from multinationals as they continue to attempt to secure new markets for their products. They also wish to have unimpeded access to resources (Scheyvens, 2002), including the natural, cultural and human. Some developing countries have also wanted to increase tourism arrivals as a consequence of falling world commodity prices during the 1980s and 1990s, and the requirement to fulfil debt repayments to the IMF and World Bank.

The 'Post-Washington Consensus': alternative and sustainable development

The implementation of SAPs has in the majority of cases led to serious negative consequences for society, increasing poverty levels rather than decreasing them (Willis, 2005). By the late 1990s, the growing concern over this detrimental effect and a call for a global agenda for poverty reduction challenged the Washington Consensus. It became evident that the economic inequalities between the developed and the developing worlds were growing rather than shrinking and that the 'miracle growth' witnessed in the NIC economies of East Asia had been encouraged by strategic state intervention of infant industries (Scheyvens, 2007).

There has been a subsequent re-evaluation of the usefulness and direction of SAPs, causing a stated refocusing of economic growth on reducing poverty and levels of inequality by supranational agencies, as evidenced in the MDGs shown in Box 1.1. This shift since the beginning of the millennium to focus on the poor has sometimes been labelled the 'Post-Washington Consensus' (PWC) that incorporates a 'New Poverty Agenda'. Subsequently, in 1999 the IMF and World Bank replaced SAPs with Poverty Reduction Strategy Papers (PRSPs), as the preconditions for countries to obtain further loans and debt relief. A stated intended shift of PRSP is that the importance of country ownership of economic reform programmes is recognised by the IMF and World Bank. There are five core principles that underlie the PRSP approach, they are:

> country-driven, promoting national ownership of strategies through broad-based participation of civil society; result-oriented and focussed on outcomes that will benefit the poor; comprehensive in recognising the multidimensional nature of poverty; partnership-oriented, involving coordinated participation of development partners (government, domestic stakeholders and external donors); and based on a long-term perspective for poverty reduction.
>
> (IMF, 2012: 1)

Whilst these core principles would appear to represent a change in focus to poverty reduction from prioritising purely economic growth, and offer a framework for achieving the MDG targets, the extent that PRSPs represent a real break with the characteristics of neo-liberalism is very uncertain and highly disputed. For Scheyvens (2007) the solutions to poverty remain embedded in neo-liberalism, whilst Storey *et al.* (2005: 34) emphasise that from the perspective of the World Bank and IMF the main determinants of whether a PRS is pro-poor or not is determined by the 'soundness' of its macro-economic policy. This is in turn is determined by the extent of liberalisation and privatisation of the national economy, and development of the private sector, which leads Storey *et al.* (ibid.) to refer to PSRPs as being 'remarkably similar to their predecessor structural adjustment programmes'. Similarly, Mowforth and Munt (2009) liken PRSPs to SAPs in that countries remain forced to pursue policies not of their own design, but externally imposed by international agencies, whilst Power (2004: 275) terms the process as: 'neo-liberalism with a human face', leading him to suggest it as premature to refer to a PWC. The use of tourism as a tool for poverty reduction is reinforced through the PRSPs, with 80 per cent of the 56 countries with poverty reduction strategies citing tourism as an option for economic growth, poverty reduction and employment. Several, including Ghana, Cambodia, Honduras and Kenya, give it an equal weighting with agriculture and manufacturing (Hawkins and Mann, 2007).

Whilst the World Bank replacement of SAPs with PRSPs may represent a less radical shift than the name would infer, the recognition that decision-making on development should be made at the national rather than international level infers a degree of devolvement of power. It is also representative of an emphasis towards more localised decision-making which is inherent to the alternative paradigm of development, a challenging of externally imposed policies for development, a key tenet being 'agency' or the capacity of people to influence and direct local change, consequently stressing local participation and being social-centred. There exists a subsequent prioritising of objectives of development that are reflective of locally defined needs, and methodologies of development decision-making that are participatory and endogenous. However, beyond this basic principle, alternative development is more problematic to define as Pieterse (2010: 85) observes: 'Over the years alternative development has been reinforced by and associated with virtually any form of criticism of mainstream developmentalism, such as anti-capitalism, Green thinking, feminism, eco-feminism, democratisation, new social movements, Buddhist economics, cultural critiques, and poststructuralist analysis of development discourse.'

Whilst the alternative development paradigm may be difficult to define and represents a broadly based and eclectic consensus, the criticisms of modernisation and neo-liberal theories has resulted in new methods for assessing development that extend beyond simple economic measurement; for example, the Human Development Index (HDI) as explained in Chapter 1. As Mowforth and Munt (2003) emphasise, these new systems of social, environmental and economic quantification, represent a move towards people-focused and participatory approaches to development. Indicative of this change is the increasing use of the term 'social capital', which refers to the ability of people to work collectively to fulfil common goals, a theme now advocated by the World Bank (Power, 2004). An emphasis on community and local participation is also a decisive break from a dominant reliance on development through either state directives or supranational directives. The emphasis of development subsequently becomes one of fulfilling human needs with direct attacks on problems such as infant mortality, malnutrition, disease, literacy and sanitation. It can be argued that the influence of the alternative paradigm on mainstream supranational agencies is evidenced through the creation of the MDGs. In the planning process, emphasis is placed upon inclusive and participatory processes that recognise indigenous theories of development as they incorporate local conditions and knowledge systems, rather than purely Western models of development. This is in marked contrast to the earlier modernisation theory that held local customs and traditions as barriers to economic development and to neo-liberalism that seeks a universal blueprint of nation state comparative advantages and free markets.

Alongside participatory approaches and the development of civil society, inherent to the alternative paradigm is a strong environmental discourse that necessitates the conservation of natural resources and ecosystems. The linking of human development with the conservation of natural resources is epitomised in the concept of 'sustainable development' which has subsequently been adopted and adapted into the paradigm of sustainable tourism development. The term 'sustainable development' is typically associated with the Brundtland Report, officially the report of the World Commission on Environment and Development (WCED, 1987). Arising from concerns over the effects of economic growth on the natural environment and commissioned in 1984 by the United Nations, the Brundtland Report is the outcome of an investigation carried out by an independent group of 22 people from various member states representing both the developing and the developed world who constituted the World Commission on Environment and Development. Led by Gro Harlem Brundtland, the then prime minister of Norway, the aim of the commission was to identify viable long-term strategies for development that could be established on a sustainable use of natural resources and the environment. Accompanying a heightened awareness of environmental problems was a realisation that the environment and development are inexorably linked. Development cannot take place upon a deteriorating natural resource base; neither can the environment be protected, when development excludes the costs of its destruction. The way industrial development has been pursued, characterised by a general lack of concern for nature, has led to the use of natural resources in a way that is unsustainable, that is, many finite resources are being exhausted whist the capacity of the natural environment to assimilate waste is being exceeded.

Significant to the Brundtland Report is the premise that poverty alleviation based upon sustainable development is critical for the long-term environmental well-being of the planet and for human development. Poverty is a major cause of environmental destruction, a relationship that is particularly exacerbated in regions of the world where the population is growing rapidly, and forced into more marginal environments. Alongside poverty and destruction, the report also emphasises the need for consideration of both intra- and inter-generational equity as an important part of a more harmonious society and environmental conservation. Not only is there a necessity for a fairer distribution of wealth in society in the present but there also needs to be provision in planning and policy for development to ensure that future generations have the availability of a quality of natural resources and eco-system services to ensure their well-being.

The term 'sustainable development' gained greater recognition in international policy through Agenda 21 following the United Nations Conference on Environment and Development (UNCED), held in Rio de Janeiro in June 1992, popularly referred to as the 'Earth Summit'. The action plan was subsequently reaffirmed at the World Summit on Sustainable Development (WSSD) held in Johannesburg in South Africa in 2002, of which one outcome was the delinking of economic growth and environmental degradation, promoting sustainable development that does not exceed the carrying capacity of ecosystems (La Viña et al., 2003). It was recognised in 'The Plan of Implementation' that was the outcome of the summit that ethics had to be considered in development, the first time that an explicit reference to ethics had been made in an official UN document (ibid.). The plan includes reference to tourism, specifically recognising it as offering sustainable development potential to certain communities.

The term 'sustainable development' has become widely used by governments, international lending agencies, non-governmental organisations, the private sector and academia. The fact that the term can be readily adopted by such a diverse range of organisations, some of whom could be viewed as having divergent and politically opposed objectives, is a reflection of the inherent ambiguity of the concept permitting a variety of perspectives to be taken on sustainability (Holden, 2005; Sharpley, 2009). Much of this ambiguity can be traced to the most commonly quoted definition of sustainable development taken from the Brundtland Report: 'Yet in the end, sustainable development is not a fixed state of harmony, but rather a process of change in which the exploitation of resources, the direction of the investments, the orientation of technological development, and institutional change are made consistent with future as well as present needs' (WCED, 1987: 9). The inherent problem being that whilst most people would agree with this statement, the divergence of opinion of how to achieve it is large, and political tensions underlie much of the debate about its interpretation. At a broad level of generalisation, distinctions can be made between a 'light green' or 'technocentric' approach to achieving sustainable development and a more radical 'dark green' or 'ecocentric' approach. This latter approach is more radical because it challenges excessive patterns of consumption in developed countries, calling for a change in economic and political structures, and a re-organisation of society to smaller-scale types of organisations. This fundamental division is between those for whom sustainability represents little more than improving technology and environmental accounting systems, whilst preserving the status quo of existing hierarchies and power structures in society, and those who have more radical political agendas involving changing the value systems, power structures and political economy of society.

LINKING DEVELOPMENT THEORY AND TOURISM

Given the potential of tourism to contribute to development, it is perhaps surprising that, as several authors (Hall, 1994; Telfer, 2002; Wall, 1997) have commented, the linkage of development theory to tourism remains relatively limited compared to other economic sectors. Referring to tourism, Bianchi (1999) suggests that the origins of this lack of engagement with the paradigmatic debate of development studies is a consequence of an emphasis in tourism studies of an applied and practical nature. Despite an early lack of theoretical interest in tourism, recognition of its potential for development by the supranational agencies has its origins in the late 1950s, when it was enthusiastically prescribed as a top economic policy for Third World governments by the World Bank (Srisang, 1991). Other UN specialist agencies, including the United Nations Development Programme (UNDP), the International Labour Organisation (ILO), alongside Western governments supported the World Bank's plan. Recognition from the UN of the potential for tourism as a way for development was emphasised through the creation of the World Tourism Organisation (WTO) in 1970, later re-designated the United Nations World Tourism Organisation (UNWTO) in 2003. As the major international agency for development, its relationship with tourism is shown in Box 2.3.

BOX 2.3 THE WORLD BANK'S RELATIONSHIP WITH TOURISM

According to Mann (2005, cited in Scheyvens, 2007), the World Bank began funding tourism projects from 1966 with an emphasis on income generation, growth and modernisation at a time when commercial air travel was beginning to generate substantial numbers of international air travellers. However, in the intervening decades its support of tourism projects has been mercurial, reflecting both changing development paradigms and shifting views on the effectiveness of tourism as a tool for development.

In the decade up to 1979, the World Bank operated a special department, the Tourism Projects Department, which was established in 1969 to assist directly in the financing of tourism projects, although only 24 projects were actually supported in 18 out of a possible 120 countries (Badger et al., 1996). The emphasis in the 1970s was on macro development and the use of tourism as a tool for economic growth (Hawkins and Mann, 2007). The department was shut down because of demands on its resources from other sectors and also a shift to neo-liberalism, with the World Bank subsequently placing its faith in the markets and the private sector as the best routes for development, negating a need for focused lending. There was also growing criticism of the social and economic impacts of tourism which would necessitate that the World Bank invested more resources and time in the preparation of their projects. Hawkins and Mann (ibid.) also point to a range of other concerns that the World Bank has had and continues to have about the use of tourism for development, including the volatility of tourism demand to factors such as fashion and changing consumer taste, fluctuating political and economic conditions, natural and human disasters, and internal political instability such as civil wars.

The World Bank became more directly involved in tourism projects again from the 1990s as sustainable development gained credibility with the major international agencies and national governments. As an industry based on climate sensitivity and natural resources, the link between tourism and sustainable development is axiomatic. The establishment of the 'Global Environmental Facility', which was a partnership between the UNDP and the World Bank, created a route for tourism to be used in projects to generate economic benefits to justify the sustainability of investments for environmental and cultural preservation (Hawkins and Mann, 2007). The extension of the sustainable development debate and its interaction with tourism extended to poverty reduction as the connection between poverty and environmental degradation was becoming more evident and emphasised.

The interest in tourism as a tool for tourism development is not just limited to the World Bank and Hawkins and Mann (2007) identify a minimum of 12 supranational agencies supporting tourism projects, including the United Nations Education and Development programmes, the United Nations Conference on Trade and Development (UNCTAD) and the Asian, African and Inter-American Development Banks. They also list 13 bi-lateral institutes that have a commitment to tourism development, including the Netherlands Development Organisation (SNV), Irish Aid and the United States Agency for International Development (USAID). They also suggest that the attitude of the World Bank to tourism development is critical as it will influence the way that governments perceive the role of tourism in their economies. In the context of the relationship between tourism and poverty, Hawkins and Mann (ibid.) recount that 80 per cent of the 56 countries with poverty reduction strategies cite tourism as a tool for poverty reduction and economic growth. Several, including Ethiopia, Tanzania, Uganda, Ghana, Nigeria, Mozambique, Kenya, Cambodia and Honduras, lend tourism equal weighting with agriculture and manufacturing. However, the World Bank's specific country assistance strategies were supporting tourism in only eight of these countries in 2007.

Whilst the linkage of development theory to tourism may be limited compared to other economic sectors, distinct stages of thought on the application of tourism to development are evident, beginning with the modernisation paradigm of the 1960s. Wall (1997) equates this era with the 'trickle down effect', that is, the idea that investment in large-scale development will lead to economic benefits being passed down to the lower social classes of society, in a classic 'top-down' approach to development. Typically, macro-economic benefits were sought from investment in tourism and tourism expenditure, including the earning of foreign exchange, employment creation and the stimulation of different types of economic multiplier effects in national, regional and local economies (Telfer, 2002). Unlike a requirement for the private sector-led development that characterises neo-liberalism, in some cases the large-scale development of tourism was initiated by state investment; for example, the Mexican strategy of building a number of very large resort complexes in such places as Cancun in the hope that economic benefits would accrue to a larger geographical area. Consequently, tourism as a form of modernisation involved the transfer of capital, technology, expertise and 'modern' values from the West to LDCs. Little consideration was given to how the poor could be integrated into the tourism industry and markets; instead, a reliance was placed on economic benefits trickling down to them. Nor was consideration lent to the environmental, cultural and social impacts of tourism and their management, as in the 1960s tourism was predominantly viewed by policy makers as a 'smokeless' and clean industry.

During the 1970s as part of the wider re-evaluation of development captured in dependency theory, there was a similar re-evaluation of the economic and social effects of tourism by political economists, anthropologists and sociologists. Whilst international tourism demand increased during the decade from approximately 166 million arrivals in 1970 to 277 million by 1980 (WTO, 2003), the benefits were questioned as economic studies pointed to lower multiplier effects and higher levels of economic leakage than were expected. The application of the social sciences to tourism also emphasised the negative social and cultural impacts that could be caused by exploitative situations arising from marked economic inequalities when wealthier tourists from developed countries and poorer communities in developing countries came into contact with each other, including the sexual exploitation of women and children. Emphasising dependency theory, a central criticism was that tourism perpetuates exploitative economic relationships between metropolitan-generating countries and peripheral-destinations societies, epitomised in the work of Turner and Ash (1975), who referred to the tourist-receiving destinations of the developing world being the 'pleasure-periphery' of the developed world.

The corollary of tourism to a new type of plantation economy also emerged as the exploitative relationship between the developed and developing world with colonial overtones became more of a focus of the academic study of tourism. The political and geographical analysis of tourism into core areas of the developed world where tourists come from and peripheral ones of developing countries where they were increasingly travelling to, led to tourism being labelled as a form of 'neo-colonialism' and 'imperialism'. The analogy to cultural imperialism is aptly summed up in the words of Turner and Ash (1975: 129) who view tourism as: 'a form of cultural imperialism, an unending pursuit of fun, sun and sex by the golden hordes of pleasure seekers who are damaging local cultures and polluting the world in their quest'. Hall (1994) suggests that the terms 'neo-colonialism' and 'imperialism' are powerful metaphors to describe the relationship between core and periphery areas, illustrating the potential loss of control that the host community may experience in the face of foreign tourism interests and the actions of local elites. Similarly, Nash (1989: 39) comments that: 'metropolitan centres have varying degrees of control over the nature of tourism and its development . . . It is this power over touristic and related developments abroad that makes a metropolitan centre imperialistic and tourism a form of imperialism'. The power that Nash (ibid.) refers to is typically one that is built upon the possession of superior entrepreneurial skills, resources and commercial power that exists in core areas. This sentiment of imperialism is also expressed in Britton's (1982) seminal work, which through the case study of Fiji described in Box 2.4, exemplified the probability that when a developing country, in this case a small island developing state (SIDS), uses tourism as a development strategy, it will enter a global system over which it has little control.

BOX 2.4 TOURISM IN THE PERIPHERY: THE CASE OF FIJI

In a seminal and detailed study of tourism development in Fiji, Britton (1982) highlighted the dependency that peripheral areas have upon core areas. As an island of the Polynesian archipelago, Fiji has used international tourism to develop its economy. However, it is heavily dependent upon foreign airlines to bring tourists to the island. In 1978, Quantas and Air New Zealand were responsible for 80 per cent of the airline seats to Fiji, illustrating the control of core and metropolitan organisations on tourist flows. The ability of regional carriers, such as Air Pacific or Polynesian Airways to compete with these airlines, was negated by high operational costs, limited equipment capacity, and interference by foreign management and share-holding interests. Direct pressure by metropolitan governments also ensured protection for their national airlines and carriers.

The case of Fiji also illustrates the problems faced by a country or region that has a limited manufacturing base. Although Fiji is in fact one of the largest Pacific island economies, it relies upon 53 per cent of hotel food purchases; 68 per cent of standard hotel construction; and 95 per cent of tourist shop wares to be supplied by imports. The granting of management contracts for hotels to foreign companies further extends the influence of foreign control. This gives effective corporate control to foreign companies without them having to commit large sums of money in capital investment thereby negating any risk factor in their investment. The consequence of this heavy dependence upon foreign interests is that over 70 per cent of tourist expenditure is lost to pay for imports, profit expropriation and expatriate salaries.

Source: Britton, 1982

Dependency theorists also point out that the social and structural frameworks existing within a society determine the way in which the international economy integrates with it. Applied to international tourism, a model of multinational companies working with elites thus replaces the model of colonial governments working with local elites. Only the privileged commercial and political groups in the periphery, along with foreign interests, are in a position to coordinate, construct, operate and profit from the development of a new industry such as tourism. It is consequently argued that the economic outcome of such a model is the removal of part of the economic surplus by foreigners, and the non-productive use of much of the remaining surplus by ruling elites (Britton, 1982). However, the reality of developing countries successfully entering the global tourism market without a reliance on international partnerships is small. Small island developing states such as Fiji are especially dependent on multinational and foreign investment and support in their airline and hotel operations. As Britton (1982: 336) suggests: 'the establishment of an international tourist industry in a peripheral economy will not occur from evolutionary, organic processes within that economy, but from demand from overseas tourists and new foreign company investment, or from the extension of foreign interests already present in that country'. Recognition of this reality partly explains why the focus of Pro-Poor Tourism (PPT), which is described in Chapter 5, emphasises the 'tilting' of the existing mainstream tourism industry to the needs of the poor rather than a reliance on the evolutionary and organic development of small-scale community-based schemes.

Whilst the application of dependency theory to the international tourism system highlights aspects of the unequal economic and political relationships between countries of the developed and developing worlds and the negative social and environmental impacts of tourism, it falls to other solutions to remedy these problems. To attempt to find solutions to these issues, it is necessary to consider the alternative development paradigm in the context of tourism, the most popular manifestation of this being sustainable tourism development. Given the Brundtland Report (WCED, 1987) was concerned with issues of environmental degradation, poverty, gender equality, democracy, human rights, and intra- and inter-generational equity, it could be expected that sustainable tourism would emphasise these different components. However, the concept of sustainable tourism has a similar ambiguity inherent to the concept of sustainable development, with no agreed common definition, which has meant its emergence in different ways in tourism.

In a review of how sustainable tourism development has manifested itself, Saarinen (2006) identified three main traditions. The 'resource-based' tradition is primarily focused on the conservation of natural resources and mitigation of negative environmental impacts arising from tourism. The 'community based tradition' embeds small-scale and participatory approaches that epitomise a more radical interpretation of the alternative development paradigm. The third tradition of 'tourism first' emphasises the sustainability of the tourism industry. The three traditions illustrate the ambiguity of the paradigm in its application to tourism with varying degrees of emphasis placed upon nature conservation, community development and business goals. They also support Butler's (1998) observation that it is not possible to separate sustainable tourism from the value systems of those involved and the societies in which they exist. As Mowforth and Munt (1998: 122) remark: 'If it [sustainable tourism] remains a "buzzword" which can be so widely interpreted that people of very different outlooks on a given issue can use it to support their cause, then it will suffer the same distortions to which older-established words such as "freedom" and "democracy" are subjected'. Writing 11 years later in reference to sustainable tourism, Mowforth and Munt (2009: 100) comment that there remains: 'no unarguable, comprehensive and all-encompassing definition that is accepted by all'.

The debate about the meaning and interpretation of sustainable tourism development also applies to other types of 'new tourism' that have emerged under the aegis of appearing to offer an alternative form of development. Ecotourism is often juxtaposed to sustainability yet similar confusions exist as to its real meaning because of its ambiguity. Similar to sustainable tourism, there are different interpretations ranging from it representing an alternative philosophy of tourism development to it being little more than a business or marketing tool. Other concerns also arise over the economic and political relationship of ecotourism to developing countries. In an early treatise on ecotourism, Wheeller (1994) referred to the concept of 'ego-tourism', in reference to ecotourism's high cost and possible elitist perception. Mowforth and Munt (2009) similarly emphasise the duality of discourse between its perception of being elitist by protagonists in developing countries and its perception by proponents in developed countries as a means of protecting ecologically endangered habitats in the developing world. Despite the contestation over the term, there exists a recognised UNEP/WTO declaration on ecotourism: the 'Quebec Declaration', resulting from an international meeting during the United Nations' International Year of Ecotourism in 2002. Embedded in this are five key principles to define ecotourism: a nature based product; management to minimise the negative environmental impacts of tourism; environmental education; contribution to conservation; and a contribution to the community.

The debate about sustainable tourism and ecotourism raises issues about the extent that they truly represent a break in political ideology with mainstream neo-liberal discourses and paradigms or are a more ethical representation of it. The same question can be asked of Pro-Poor Tourism (PPT), which is critically evaluated in Chapter 5. At the very least, to achieve a more radical alternative tourism agenda that will target poverty reduction, there is a need to politicise the tourism industry – a requirement that Mowforth and Munt (1998) highlighted in the late 1990s in the context of sustainability. The issue of how tourism is developed and how it is used to provide livelihood opportunities for the poor and enhance their social well-being is subsequently a political one as much as it is economic. Can real change be achieved with what House (1997) refers to as 'reformist' school of thought of the existing political economic structures or is a much more radical agenda that challenges existing structures and development paradigms necessary?

THE ECONOMIC BENEFITS OF TOURISM: LINKAGES TO POVERTY

The advocating of the use of tourism for poverty reduction is a consequence of a convergence of trends in international tourism and shifts in global development policy. Tourism's growth in global economic importance, a trend for increasing international arrivals to developing countries especially LDCs, the need to develop export-driven industries in which LDCs could demonstrate a comparative advantage under the terms of SAPs, and a recent shift in development policy to PRSs, are significant factors to explain why tourism has become linked to poverty reduction and alleviation. Tourism also offers an opportunity for economic diversification in LDCs, as the 49 least developed countries of the world depend upon agriculture and fishing for more than 36 per cent of their GDP and 80 per cent of export revenues (Seabrook, 2007).

It is the reported growth in the economic size of the tourism industry that is the most likely rationale of why it should attract policy makers' intervention as a means for poverty reduction. Accepting an allowance for slight statistical error in the compilation of visitor arrival numbers from countries of the world, the UNWTO figures provide an indicative account of the rapid growth in international tourism during the last few decades. In 1950 there were approximately 25 million recorded international arrivals, in 1980 there were 270 million, 435 million in 1990, by 2011 this number has risen to 940 million and is expected to surpass 1,600 million by 2020 (UNWTO, 2012). This growth in international tourism demand has presented opportunities for an ever-increasing number of places to become tourist destinations, making tourism a key driver of socio-economic progress. The growth in its global economic significance is underlined by it contributing approximately 30 per cent to the world's exports of commercial services and 6 per cent of the overall export of goods and services in 2011 (ibid.). In addition to this mobility between countries, there exists substantial movements and flows of residents between places within countries, referred to as domestic tourism. The significance of domestic tourism for poverty reduction is that domestic tourists are more likely to display a higher propensity of utilising tourism enterprises initiated by the poor than the majority of international tourists, as they are familiar with local quality standards of service and produce.

Whilst international tourism flows are unevenly distributed between various regions of the world, with Europe, North and South-East Asia, and North America accounting for an overwhelming proportion of both supply and demand, it is the growth in international tourism arrivals to LDCs that is significant in the context of utilising tourism for poverty reduction. Particularly since the first decade of the twenty-first century, there has been a marked increase in tourist arrivals to LDCs. During the period 2000–2005, arrivals in LDCs grew by 48 per cent, compared to 34 per cent for all developing countries and 17 per cent worldwide (UNWTO, 2006b). For sub-Saharan Africa, the poorest region in the world, the total number of international arrivals grew from 6.4 million in 1990 to 30.7 million in 2010, with an average annual growth rate for the period 2000 to 2010 of 6.6 per cent (UNWTO, 2012). For the same period, the average annual growth rate in international tourist arrivals to South Asia was 6.2 per cent, with recorded international tourist arrivals having risen from 3.2 million in 1990 to 11.1 million in 2010 (ibid.). These average annual growth rates in international tourist arrivals compare to 2.1 per cent for Europe and 0.7 per cent for North America over the same period. The significance of this growth is that for some LDCs tourism has remained or become the largest export sector during the period 2000–2008, including the Maldives, Samoa, Eritrea, Gambia, Rwanda, Nepal and Senegal (UNDP, 2011).

Whilst the orientation of the tourism industry towards poverty reduction is relatively recent, the potential macro-economic benefits of tourism have been evident since the 1950s. As part of the development process, the creation of export-earning industries is essential and for many developing countries tourism is especially important in this aspect. Neo-liberalism stresses the requirement for countries to develop their economic comparative advantages within a free trade system for countries to boost their export earnings, particularly LDCs and developing countries. Whilst LDCs can expand and increase their range of agricultural and mineral exports, primary products are subject to price fluctuations in the world markets, making economic and development planning difficult. The development of manufactured goods to export is also highly problematic given the domination of the markets by existing manufacturing countries. Subsequently, the combination of the natural and cultural resources belonging to many LDCs and an increased tourist demand to see and experience them offers opportunities to national governments to gain economic benefits from tourism development.

It is particularly the macro-economic benefits that may be realised through tourism which are attractive to governments. These include the earnings of foreign exchange and contributions to the balance of payments. The importance of governments to have a positive balance of payments figure is that it enables them to service foreign loans and build up capital reserves, whilst a negative balance of payments is likely to necessitate increased levels of borrowing and a running down of capital reserves. The requirement to increase levels of borrowing through foreign loans from supranational agencies such as the IMF may also lead to a loss of government autonomy of national economic development plans, including imposed expenditure reductions on education, health and welfare for the poor, as was explained in the case of many developing countries under SAPs.

The use of tourism to stimulate extra economic demand is a further macro-economic benefit that has a potential direct relationship to poverty reduction when the created economic opportunities are targeted at poor people. One measure of this demand is tourism's contribution to the Gross Domestic Product (GDP) of a country, which is indicative of the level of tourism's importance to the economy. In small island developing states (SIDS), the contribution of tourism to GDP can be highly significant. For example, in Antigua and Barbuda, tourism made a direct contribution to the GDP in 2011 of 17.7 per cent and an estimated total contribution, including both direct and indirect contributions of 74.9 per cent. In the Maldives, the figures were 31.3 per cent and 70.6 per cent respectively (WTTC, 2012). Whilst the importance of tourism to the economies of many SIDS is widely recognised, there is a danger of creating economic over-dependency upon tourism, making the economy and associated livelihoods vulnerable to downturns in tourism demand.

Essential for comprehending how tourism investment and expenditure can create economic opportunities for the poor that extend beyond direct engagement in the tourism industry are economic multiplier effects. The basic rationale of the multiplier effect is that investment and expenditure raises not only the level of demand directly in the tourism industry but also generates extra indirect demand in the economic sectors that supply it, which in turn induces demand in other sectors of the economy. For example, in the case of an investment project in a new hotel, the financial capital used for the goods and services needed to construct it, such as building materials and construction workers' wages, will circulate in the economy. The recipients of this first round of investment spending will in turn enter into additional spending of their own, as the suppliers of building materials purchase extra products to replace the ones they have used and the construction workers spend their remuneration on goods and services they require, in turn generating another round of spending.

From the investment in the hotel, money could theoretically circulate many times in the economy, generating extra demand at each stage and, importantly, opportunities for the poor in the tourism supply chain if they are integrated into it and in other sectors of the economy in which they work. However, the extent to which employment and income opportunities are created for the poor in the supply chain will depend upon several factors. If tourism enterprises choose foreign suppliers over local ones, then money will 'leak' out of the economy to pay external providers. Issues of the ability of local producers to supply goods, such as agricultural products that are of the right quality and can be supplied with the necessary regularity to meet demand, are often cited by the tourism industry as the reason for their choice of foreign suppliers. Another reason cited by the industry is that the mass tourism market prefers Western food with which they are familiar. Other factors that dictate against the inclusion of the poor in the local supply chain, either as employees or as small enterprises, include a lack of capacity relating to education, training and skills.

As a part of a programme for the use of tourism to reduce poverty, the creation of employment opportunities in the industry and supply chain for the poor will be essential. The pressure of a population demographics in LDCs, with a high percentage of young people constituting their populations, makes the creation of employment opportunities a priority concern for governments. Tourism has advantages for employment creation compared to other industries, including that the investment costs to create jobs are less than for manufacturing industry. The economic importance of tourism is reflected in figures for global employment, with 8.7 per cent of the global workforce being employed directly or indirectly through tourism, an actual figure of approximately 255 million people (WTTC, 2012).

Similar to income, the multiplier effect also works for employment, generating extra jobs not only in the tourism sector but also indirectly through the supply chain in other sectors of the economy. The total percentage of the workforce employed directly and indirectly through tourism is indicative of its importance to the economy. In several SIDS there is a heavy reliance on tourism employment as emphasised in the case of Antigua and Barbuda, which has approximately 18 per cent of employment directly generated by tourism and a combined total of 70 per cent directly and indirectly generated by tourism (WTTC, 2012). Similar to GDP, there is the danger of creating an over dependence upon tourism as a source of employment, making the workforce vulnerable to a decrease in tourism demand.

Issues also arise over the quality of employment opportunities created through tourism with criticisms having been made that the majority are low skilled, part time and seasonal, whilst also lacking trade union recognition. It is therefore important that in any strategy for tourism's use in poverty reduction, structures are put in place to increase the poor's technical capacity to work at a higher level in the industry and to ensure they have employee rights. However, the part-time character of tourism employment may be advantageous in terms of adding tourism as an additional income source to work in agriculture, which is likely to remain the most significant economic activity for the rural poor. Part-time employment may also provide opportunities for women to gain paid employment in patriarchal societies where there remains an expectancy that their primary role is one of taking care of the family household and children.

Other factors that contribute to a rationale for the use of tourism for poverty reduction as shown in Figure 2.2, include that tourism brings comparatively wealthy consumers from developed countries to the point of production, which offers a market for local entrepreneurs and the poor. Besides making a difference to the livelihoods of individuals, the poor can also make a contribution to the national economy because as the consumer travels to the destination it offers the opportunities for the sale of extra goods and services, and the poor can become 'exporters'. From a neo-liberal perspective this fits well in the context of increasing exports but critically from the perspective of poverty reduction incorporates the poor into the equation of export orientated economic growth.

Tourism can also offer a diversification of the local economy when tourists visit peripheral regions of countries, defined by their geographical remoteness from major urban areas, which often contain the natural and cultural 'resources' that often appeal to tourists. It is the release of an economic value from these assets through tourism that offers an opportunity to diversify the local economy to meet the needs and wants of tourists. Other aspects that favour the use of tourism as a tool of poverty reduction is that compared to other economic sectors there are minimum trade barriers to overcome, permitting more opportunities for LDCs to be active in the global and international markets. The character of tourism also favours small-scale entrepreneurship – for example, curio-sellers, drink vendors

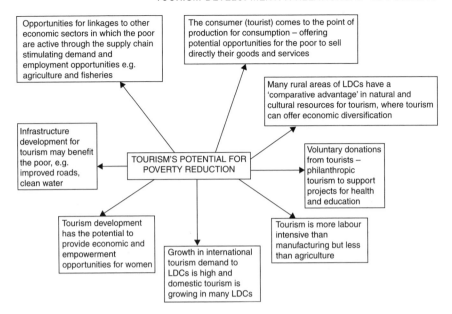

Figure 2.2 *Tourism's potential for poverty reduction*

and renting bicycles – which, providing suitable micro-finance schemes and political support for capacity building exists, will afford opportunities for the poor to be involved in the tourism industry.

Despite evident advantages of the use of tourism for poverty reduction, a significant challenge to persuading government ministries and politicians to utilise tourism for poverty reduction relates to the accuracy and availability of data. There are a number of issues of measurement that make the economic impact of tourism difficult to comprehend and diminish its possibility as an option for development and poverty reduction in the view of government ministers and other politicians. Alongside the ongoing definitional problems of what actually constitutes the 'tourism industry', tourism is not a clearly identifiable sector of the economy in the international standard system of national accounts (SNA), implemented since 1993. Referring to economic activity generally in the tourism sector, Mitchell and Ashley (2010: 8) comment that: 'activity in this sector is usually estimated simply by summing the economic subsectors of hotels, restaurants and transportation'. Alluding to the problems of collecting accurate data on employment, the WTO (1998: 87) observe that:

> the contribution of tourism to employment and tourism's potential to generate new jobs ranks as one of the paramount questions related to the social and economic importance of tourism. However it is difficult to make accurate assessments of its volume and impact on the economy. Unfortunately reliable

and comparable data about tourism employment on the international level is very scarce.

The difficulties of the collection of comparable data are partly a consequence of the disparate character of the tourism sector being composed of defined industries; for example, the airline industry, hotel industry, attractions industry and tour operating industry. The use of various data collection methodologies by separate countries in an attempt to measure the same characteristics compounds this problem. These difficulties are pointed out by the WTTC (2004: 6) which comments: 'Over the last three decades, countries have estimated the economic impact of Travel and Tourism through a range of measures using a variety of different definitions and methodologies.' A further challenge of measurement arises from the large informal tourism sector that characterises many developing countries and within which the poor are most likely to be involved. The numbers of people working in the informal tourism sector – for example, hawkers, handicraft sellers and street vendors – is extremely difficult to estimate.

As a consequence of this lack of coherence, and a commonality in economic definition and methods for data collection, the UNWTO has been working with the WTTC since the early 1990s to improve tourism statistics worldwide (ibid.). The common framework that is being developed is termed the 'Travel and Tourism Satellite Account', which lays out a comprehensive recommended methodological framework for the compilation of tourism statistics and the assessment of its economic importance in all countries, which should permit a more meaningful comparison of tourism's role in different national economies in the future. Despite the problems of the accuracy of statistics and a lack of data about tourism's impacts on poverty reduction, many LDCs have a comparative advantage in natural and cultural resources for tourism. A continuing global net loss of biodiversity and a trend towards urbanisation (in 2011 over 50 per cent of the world's population was living in urban areas for the first time in human history) are indicative that in the future, as Mitchell and Ashley (2010) suggest, the value of these natural resources will increase in conjunction with their scarcity.

SUMMARY

- Whilst specifically targeting poverty alleviation has become a part of global development policy since the 1990s, its relationship to development can be traced to the immediate aftermath of the Second World War. It was in this era that a strong association was made between economic progress, national development and political ideologies in a speech by US president Truman in 1949, who made a distinction between the 'developed' and 'underdeveloped worlds' based upon criteria of national income. From a Western-centric viewpoint there was an imperative to integrate the poor into the capitalist and market system, rather than allowing them to ally themselves with the communist Soviet Union. This was a time when many ex-colonial countries were attaining their independence and both the USA and the Soviet Union were willing to lend large amounts of foreign aid in attempts to secure political allegiances. The association of underdeveloped countries with backwardness and poverty lent a powerful context for economic and political intervention by developed countries on the pretence of humanitarian grounds.

- The separation of countries into categories of 'developed' and 'underdeveloped' sets a standard for countries to develop to, illustrated in modernisation theory. In contrast, dependency theorists held that the rest of the world (i.e., the 'periphery') would not be permitted by dominant powers to develop like the West (i.e., the 'core') because it was in the interests of the core to ensure that these countries remained underdeveloped. The rationale of this thesis was to ensure that they did not develop to be economically competitive with the countries of Europe and America, and to ensure a regular supply of primary and raw materials for their industries. The lack of development in many parts of the world by the 1980s, despite billions of dollars of foreign aid, led to a rethink of the best way for developing countries to economically grow. The dominant paradigm became one of neo-liberalism that encouraged 'free trade', the rule of the market and minimum government interference in the functioning of the national economy. The need to repay foreign debts, especially after the end of the Cold War in 1989, necessitated that many developing countries had to accept Structural Adjustment Programmes (SAPs) from the World Bank and IMF to ensure the continuance of their support. Amongst the conditions of SAPs were that governments boosted export-driven growth in goods and services with which they enjoyed a 'comparative advantage' to the rest of the world and reduced their expenditure, including on health and education programmes. The impact of this on the poor was to reduce the self-sufficiency of agriculture as more land was used for cash crops for agriculture and to restrict opportunities for health care and education.

- By the 1990s, the growing concerns over the detrimental effects of SAPs led to a 'New Poverty Agenda' in what is loosely and contentiously referred to as the 'Post-Washington Consensus'. The World Bank and IMF replaced SAPs with Poverty Reduction Strategy Papers (PRSP) that emphasised more national ownership of development policy and a long-term perspective for poverty reduction. Alternative development strategies also came more to the fore that advocated participatory mechanisms for development at a more local level; for example, community-based tourism and recognition of environmental constraints on development. The concept of sustainable development, although ambiguous in its meaning and interpretation, became widely adopted by different stakeholders following the United Nations Conference on Environment and Development held in Rio de Janeiro in 1992, including international agencies, national governments, the private sector and non-governmental organisations. An emphasis on sustainable development combined with poverty reduction presents a political and economic challenge of how best to achieve this and whether neo-liberalism and free markets will be able to deliver on these goals. Following the global financial crisis that began in 2008, there is a growing challenge to this paradigm, and calls for more government intervention in economic policy.

- The linkage of tourism to poverty reduction has arisen for a variety of associated reasons. The emphasis in neo-liberalism of the utilisation of a country's economic comparative advantage gave a rationale for many developing countries to develop their tourism industries around their natural and cultural resources. If a global net loss on biodiversity continues into the future, then the scarcity value of natural resources and ecosystems is likely to increase their economic worth for tourism. The growth in international tourism to LDCs has been higher over the last decade than for other regions of the world, although the LDCs' share of the world market remains comparatively small. An emergent middle class in many developing countries also offers opportunities for a growth in domestic tourism and the linking of domestic tourists to the informal tourism sector in which very many of the poor are employed. The development of the tourism industry also offers other opportunities to the poor, including links to other parts of the supply chain and economic sectors in which they are economically active, including the agriculture and fishing industries. The tourist also comes to the point of production for consumption of goods and services, offering the poor the opportunities to sell them directly. Compared to other economic sectors, tourism has the potential to directly benefit women, which is important for their empowerment and ability to play a full participatory role in society.

3 | Geography of poverty

This chapter:

- Analyses the geography of poverty
- Evaluates the influence of the characteristics of place on poverty
- Critiques the influence of climate change on poverty and tourism interaction

The preceding two chapters have evaluated the three inter-related key themes of the text: poverty, development and tourism. The next two chapters attempt to explain the causal factors of the geographical distribution of poverty, which, based upon the World Bank income measure of US$1.25 per capita per day, is dominated by the countries of sub-Saharan Africa, East and South Asia, and Latin America as was illustrated in Figure 1.1. However, that poverty is endemic to these regions is not a product of chance, but a range of interlocking geographical, political and economic factors. The foci of Chapters 3 and 4 are subsequently grounded in attempting to explain the spatial geography of poverty, focusing on the interaction of place, environment and political economy. Emphasis is placed upon processes of change in place and space over time and the impacts upon people's livelihoods. The thematic analysis of these two chapters may be subsequently understood in the context of geographical and political economy perspectives, epitomised in a definition of geography as being: 'about the understanding of the people, places and environments of our world, the processes by which they are changing, and the interactions between them – both locally and globally' (RGS, 2011: 21). Inherent to this definition are understandings of people; the concepts and interactions of place and space; and the processes that induce change within them across varying spatial dimensions. It is through such understanding and knowledge that foundations can be laid for creating solutions for poverty reduction and evaluating the role tourism has to play in it.

PLACE AND SPACE: AGENCY AND STRUCTURE

Analysing the geographical distribution of poverty it would seem that the place, location and environment one is born into is determinantory to livelihood opportunities and also the likelihood of experiencing poverty. Whilst the concept of 'place' is a central one to human geography and a part of our common vernacular, similar to the concepts of 'tourism', 'development' and 'poverty', it eludes a simple definition. Often association is made between place and 'location', which Agnew (2005) argues represents a point in space with specific relations to other points in space. The relevance and importance of space in attempting to give a definition to place is also emphasised by Mackinnon and Cumbers (2007: 3) who comment: 'Place refers to a particular area [space], usually occupied, to which a group of people have become attached, endowing it with meaning and significance.' There is in this sense a relationship between what geographers would call place and space – at its most simple, space referring to a location, and place to the occupation of that location (Agnew, 2005). Thus 'place' can be understood as having a strong anthropocentric interpretation, being defined by human occupation and cultural perception.

Whilst historically there has been a strong reliance and attachment to the environment and resources of place for survival, many places in the world are now more inter-connected than at any time before, an outcome of advancements in transport and technology, the development of trade, political and economic sectors, and financial freedoms to move large amounts of capital. Whilst the evolution of mass transport systems can be traced to the railways during the Industrial Revolution in the nineteenth century, it is particularly during the second half of the twentieth century that rapid advancements in transport and information technology, combined with neo-liberalism and the effects of free trade, that there has been a notable acceleration in place inter-connectivity. Despite this heightened inter-connectivity of places, for much of human history the majority of the world's population have relied heavily upon the resources of the place in which they resided, that is, upon their 'surrounding' natural environment, a characteristic which has made them highly vulnerable to natural shocks such as drought and consequent crop failure. Although processes of economic and cultural globalisation have quickened and strengthened, many hundreds of millions of people continue to remain exempt from a profound inter-connectivity with other places, notably the poorest 1 billion. This is a point advocated by De Blij (2009), who stresses the continuing importance of the influences of locality on life experiences and opportunities, emphasising that the 'power of place' on the lives of many of the world's population is something that is frequently overlooked in the era of globalisation. As he observes in his profound thesis on how place continues to shape lives, hundreds of millions of people remain remote from the forces of globalisation, living in a predominantly similar fashion to their ancestors.

Commenting on the position of the countries of sub-Saharan Africa in relation to shifts in nation-state inter-connectivity, Castree (2003: 176) states that they: 'remain partially cut-off from the rest of the world or else subject to very one-sided relationships that exacerbate poverty'. Using the example of Ethiopia, Castree (ibid.) explains how the one-sidedness of this relationship may lead to harmful effects on the local population. During the mid-1980s, when faced with horrific food famines that gained global media coverage and led to a campaign for famine relief headlined by popular music mega-stars in the collective of Band Aid, ironically Ethiopia continued to produce large quantities of food. However, this was being produced by wealthy landowners as export crops for European and North American markets, rather than food crops for their own people. This seemingly strange anomaly was a consequence of one of the conditions attached by the World Bank and IMF to Ethiopia's Structural Adjustment Programme, that is, to increase export production and earnings, which had to be met for continued World Bank and IMF support. The case of Ethiopia is illustrative of how the structure of the global political economy into which places become inter-woven and the power relationships between them may act as an important determinant of the economic and social benefits and costs that accrue to the poor.

Alongside geographical and environmental characteristics of place, cultural factors may also influence the extent of the opportunities that are available to improve well-being. The limitations of place may not be purely restricted to the properties of nature but may also be influenced by characteristics of culture and language and the degree of ease that they permit integration into the global system. De Blij (2009) draws attention to how being born into a family whose language is globally dispersed and regionally dominant potentially offers a lifetime of opportunities, particularly when constructed upon a cultural legacy from imperial times. For example, as a consequence of the legacy of the British Empire, the English language has become the 'lingua franca' of the world economy, a characteristic that gives an advantage to those who are born in places where English is prevalent as the first language.

Cultural factors may also be highly influential in the marginalisation of peoples within the community according to characteristics such as gender, religion, ethnicity and sexual orientation. Women may find that they are exempted from decision-making or other democratic freedoms as is discussed in Box 6.5 in the context of Elmina in Ghana, whilst similarly cultural differentiations on principles of religion and ethnicity may lead to one section of the community being marginalised and disadvantaged in their opportunities. For example, within the tradition of the Indian caste system, the 'untouchables' caste have historically been given few opportunities for self-development to improve their livelihoods, a situation that is now being challenged through government legislation for positive discrimination and equal opportunities for this group. Similarly, ethnic minority groups may find that their opportunities are limited by discrimination, as may the homosexual community. These examples emphasise the necessity for people to have access to freedoms to realise their opportunities as was discussed in Chapter 1.

Whilst cultural factors of place can be highly influential for livelihood opportunities, they are also central for the creation of tourism demand to LDCs. The tourism system is reliant upon the inter-connectivity of a differentiation of places between the home and destination environments, usually centred on natural and cultural characteristics. The growth of mass participation in domestic tourism in the nineteenth century in Europe and the USA was built upon the new inter-connectivity of urban with coastal areas through the construction of railways. More contemporarily, the growth in international tourism to LDCs has been facilitated through the innovation of jet travel. It is the differentiation between the characteristics and features of the home and destination environments that partially explains the pull of places where we choose to recreate and is essential for providing a rationale for tourism.

The importance of differentiation between places is emphasised by Entriken (1994), who notes the 'value' placed on spatial variations. This value is often at its highest in places that are seen to be free from global forces of homogenisation and retain an individuality of culture. Such places are often valued highly in tourism with a pull factor of having retained some degree of authenticity in an increasingly globalised world. The centrality of authenticity attached to a place's natural and cultural resources is important for the use of tourism for poverty reduction in LDCs as was referred to in Chapter 2, whilst the pace of global development means that the quantity and quality of natural ecosystems and biodiversity is constantly being reduced (Mitchell and Ashley, 2010). This will add a scarcity value to resources in those countries and regions that maintain sound environmental management of their natural resources for tourism, lending them a future added value.

Entriken (ibid.) recognises a further differentiation of place based upon its epistemological significance, which embraces scepticism towards general theories that claim applicability everywhere and emphasises sensitivity to where knowledge comes from. This epistemological differentiation between places has a direct relevance to strategies of how development can be used for poverty reduction, and similarly how tourism is used. Although not specifically defined as such, the epistemological differences between places can be interpreted as being recognised in the World Bank's Poverty Reduction Strategies which, as was discussed in Chapter 2, acknowledge the need for the diffusing of policy to at least a national level. To this can be added the need to recognise the inherited knowledge of place, especially indigenous knowledge which has been deliberately or inadvertently overlooked in development decision-making. Applied to tourism development, there is a subsequent emphasis on participatory opportunities and the use of indigenous and local knowledge, typified in community-based tourism (CBT) programmes.

Whilst the recognition of indigenous factors of place are important for its 'value', differences between places are not just a product of their internal characteristics but are also a product of systems of global relations between them. Thus networks between places become important in shaping the character of places, rather than the global being portrayed as a collection of local places and peoples with clearly delineated geographical boundaries, collectively forming a global mosaic. Tourism is such a force that shapes the character of places through integrating them into networks, ironically sometimes acting as a catalyst towards the cultural and economic homogenisation that some tourists may be attempting to escape. The demonstration effect of wealthier tourists can lead to a copying of behaviour and acculturation of local people, whilst when a destination becomes more popular there is a propensity for inward investment from global multinational players and the likelihood of a transfer of power over development away from local stakeholders.

An increased inter-connectivity of places and the political and economic hegemony that accompanies this process raises questions over the extent that the poor have influence in directing development and livelihood opportunities in the face of external forces. The ability of people to have control and direct their lives in the face of powerful global political economic forces, a balance between 'social agency' and 'social structure', is an issue that has consequences for development and poverty. Marxist geographers emphasise that the global political economy constrains people's agency in their home places to improve their lives, stressing that local inequalities are caused and accentuated by global inter-linkages (Castree, 2003). Subsequently, processes of local control and democracy within a place, and the ability to shape community and individual destiny are challenged by forces of globalisation, including external political structures and decision-making, and flows of capital, goods, services, information and people. It is therefore argued by Marxist geographers that poverty in a particular place is caused or at least exacerbated by global forces that limit people's capacity and agency to develop coping strategies and alleviate poverty in the medium to long term. Within this paradigm, the likelihood of the success of a community-driven tourism development to alleviate poverty and provide livelihood opportunities would be typically challenged by determinants of the global political economy that may counteract local agency.

The social agency vis-à-vis social structure debate has direct relevance to the last chapter of this book, which explores the ways forward for how tourism may be used for poverty reduction. If one accepts the diktat of globalisation and the imposition of social structure on local initiatives, there would appear to be very limited opportunities for the poor to improve their livelihoods through independent initiatives in the face of the supranational-directed global political economy and associated corporate powers. Conversely, the argument for social agency would advocate that individuals are capable of building direction and innovation in their own lives; for example, individuals can take action to make and sell handicrafts to tourists or form partnerships with larger corporations for mutual benefit through tourism. These concepts and tensions of social agency and social structure are also evident in Chapter 5, which explains the initiatives that are being taken to use tourism to combat poverty; for example, through Pro-Poor Tourism (PPT).

The increasing inter-connectivity of many places challenges the notion of place remaining synonymous with local. Massey (1994) refers to a 'global sense of place', a meeting place where wider social relations and connections come together, subsequently calling for a re-visioning of places as not being set areas within locally defined geographical boundaries. There is a subsequent need to rethink the concept of place in terms of geographical connections and relations across space, of cultural and economic integration. The relevance of this concept to tourism is exemplified in the economies of countries and livelihoods of many people in small island developing states (SIDS), which may be heavily dependent on the source markets of tourists in the developed world.

A global essence of place, a relationship of connection between place and space can also be symbolically represented by the contemporary adage of 'think local act global'. This expression lends recognition to the realisation that place is connected to space by political, economic and environmental systems, that the decisions and actions taken in one place influence the livelihoods and environments of other communities in other locations. An evident example of this reciprocity is the impact of individual action on the process of global warming and climate change, and the subsequent influence on our well-being. Similarly, the purchasing of fair trade goods by people in developed countries has beneficial effects for people involved in their production in developing countries. The purchasing of fair trade commodities such as tea and coffee may have significant positive impacts on the producers in developing countries, permitting families to have the income to send their children to school or provide access to health care. Although the fair trade system is more embryonic in tourism than in the agricultural commodity market, the concept has been employed in South Africa as is discussed in Box 5.5.

CHARACTERISTICS OF PLACE AND DEVELOPMENT

Whilst there is an increasing inter-connectivity of places defined by spatial range and depth of relationships, the geographical characteristics of place have and continue to exert influence on development. Whilst it is important to stress that as Sachs (2008: 11) refers to it 'geography is not destiny' and refute any notion of the discredited and politically manipulated theory of 'environmental determinism' and the accompanying racist overtones, geographical characteristics of place can influence opportunities for development. Whilst not pre-determined barriers or insurmountable obstacles to development, Lines (2008) identifies key character-istics that are common to many of the poorest countries, including a small popula-tion, remoteness from world markets, and a commodity export dependency.

The influence of a small population is that it offers only a limited domestic market for manufactured goods and services, making economies of scale and price competitiveness difficult in comparison to mass-produced imported goods. Although not the sole reason to explain the rapid economic growth and develop-ment in China and India since the 1980s, their populations of approximately 1.3 billion and 1.1 billion respectively offer large internal markets. In comparison, the current total population for all the countries of Africa is approximately 1 billion, although as stated in Chapter 1 this is projected to reach 2 billion by 2050.

The geographical situation of countries may also act as a hindrance to develop-ment. As is explained in the next chapter, the emergence of commercial expansion through ocean trade from the late fifteenth century onwards was critical for wealth creation in many European countries. Several centuries later, a geographical remoteness from access to the oceans continues to limit trade, with nine of the 13 countries with the lowest HDI scores being landlocked. Many of the poorest land-locked countries are in Africa but also include Bolivia and Moldova, the poorest countries in their respective continents, and several Asian countries with very low per capita incomes, including Laos, Mongolia, Tajikistan and Nepal. Sea-based transport costs are lower than those of land and air, and at their cheapest when places are located on the main trading lanes. Of the world's 20 biggest container ports, 13 are in Asia whilst none are in Latin America or Africa. The demographic geography of the world, with 75 per cent of the world's population located on the Eurasian landmass, means that coastal populations in Europe, the Middle East and Asia find themselves located on principal sea-lanes, whilst African and Latin American populations find themselves more geographically isolated (Sachs, 2008).

The effect of location on development may also act at a spatial level within coun-tries as a contributing determinant of development. Within countries, especially ones of large geographical extent, the internal regions often lag behind coastal areas in their level of economic development. For example, in China the economic development in its eastern provinces along the coast has far exceeded that of inland regions, causing a mass migration to and rapid growth of urban areas situated on the coast. The third shared characteristic of poor countries is a dependency on primary goods for exports. This dependency on agricultural and commodity export markets makes countries highly vulnerable to acute price changes in the world markets, a characteristic of trade in commodities.

Geography will also influence levels of agricultural productivity which are linked to the ecology of place, including the quality of the soils, water supply, topography, pests and pathogens, and local crop varieties (Sachs, 1999). It is not a coincidence that the earliest recognised civilisations in Mesopotamia and the Indus valley coalesced in areas where there were ample river plains, rich soils and a good climate for growing crops. Sachs (ibid.) also draws attention to how an endowment with primary energy sources has lent an economic advantage to places. The most obvious example of this is the development of the United Kingdom during the Industrial Revolution, where an abundance of coal combined with the development of technology to exploit its use in the form of the steam engine led to rapid industrial development. Whilst Sachs (ibid.) points to several *caveats* of why mineral energy and mineral resources may not lead to economic development, including poor governance and a lack of technology to exploit the resource, in optimum conditions the combination of energy and mineral resources are an important asset for economic growth.

A further characteristic of place and geography that Sachs (ibid.) identifies as having a significant influence on economic productivity and development is what he terms 'disease ecology'. The term stresses the relationship between human health and productivity, and that a high prevalence of life-threatening diseases, such as malaria, acts as an impediment to development as productivity is impeded by illness. Disease-prone regions are also much less likely to attract tourists and be less desirable for foreign investment and to skilled migrants. A further geographical influence on development is the occurrence of natural disasters. Sachs (2005) emphasises that countries that are repeatedly hit by natural disasters face long-term set-backs to development. Natural disasters include those that are meteorological in character – drought, floods, hurricanes, tornadoes and heat waves – and those that are seismological – earthquakes, tsunamis and volcanoes.

DEPENDENCY ON PLACE

Whilst hundreds of millions of the world's population still remain exempt from the forces of globalisation and are highly dependent on the resources of the surrounding environment, this situation has been a common one for the majority of the world's population for much of human history, as Beaudoin (2007: 15) comments: 'Before the sixteenth century, both the causes of poverty and the reactions it inspired were primarily rooted in the internal dynamics of individual civilisations and their immediate surroundings.' Similarly, Ponting (1991) observes that since the evolvement of settled societies between eight and ten thousand years ago, the majority of the world's population has been living in conditions of vulnerability, their primary concerns resting with obtaining enough food to stay alive. If it is possible to envisage a world stripped of industrial development, information technology and with very limited trade, we can begin to understand the reliance of communities upon the 'resources' of their surrounding environment. Such was the normality of consistently struggling to meet one's basic needs that the application of 'poverty' to the human condition denoted a spiritual dearth rather than one of physical deficiencies. This dependency on local resources is emphasised in the description of the life of a European peasant in the early modern age in Box 3.1.

BOX 3.1 DEPENDENCY ON PLACE: PEASANT LIFE IN EARLY MODERN EUROPE

The life of the peasant masses, *das gemeine Volk* ('the common people') during the fifteenth and sixteenth centuries bears similarities to those who experience absolute poverty today. The life was predominantly one of hard physical work, aiming to produce enough food to subsist with very little technological support and highly vulnerable to vagaries of climate and disease. The economy was 'organic' based largely on the productive capacity of land combined with human and animal power (Beaudoin, 2007). There was a subsequent requirement to attempt to maintain good health to be able to work, resulting in ordinances in many sixteenth-century European villages that forbade fighting or insulting each other at assembly meetings. Injuries sustained in physical fights sometimes resulted in the bringing of civil suits against the inflictor.

The role of women was pre-determined and devoid of opportunity, being responsible for childcare, and female work was centred on the household. Typical duties would involve cooking, cleaning and washing, fetching water, livestock care, the preparation of food and tending the garden. Women would also work in the fields at harvest time and take rural produce to the local market. Once married it was expected that a couple would have children, the teaching of the Church was that the procreation of children was one of the main purposes of marriage. A good marriage partner was deemed to be one who would bring some property to the marriage and be willing to work hard after. Typically a woman would have six to seven children,

of which between two and four could expect to survive, a consequence of the high levels of infant mortality with 40–50 per cent of
children dying before they had reached the age of ten.

Average life expectancy was 30 years with the most common cause
of death being disease, including plague, dysentery, smallpox and
fevers. Other significant causes of mortality included death in childbirth, accidents and for men as a consequence of fights. Resistance
to disease was typically lowered by harvest failures as a consequence of bad weather and resultant food shortages. A sense of
localism was dominant in sixteenth-century Europe, a sense of place
being rooted in the village and environs, which ranged in size from
hamlets of five or six households to larger settlements with 60 or
70 households. Decisions about village life were typically made by
village assemblies comprising all household heads. Whilst the
agrarian economy was geared towards subsistence and self-
sufficiency, few households were self-sufficient and most had limited
economic linkages to other villages and market towns.

Source: Rowlands, 2001

There are parallels that can be made between the life of a peasant household in
middle age Europe and that of many households in rural areas of the Least Developed Countries. A common characteristic is a high dependency on a small
geographical area to meet one's needs and a lack of opportunities for successive
generations to break free from the poverty trap. Whilst the development of
mercantile commerce from the late sixteenth century and the impact of the Industrial Revolution would progressively lead to increased levels of economic productivity, and an improvement in living standards for the majority, for much of
human history no society has been free from the risks of food shortages and
famine. Similiary, in the ancient city states that acted as the forerunners of modern
civilization, food shortages and poverty were not uncommon. For example, in
Ancient Athens, one in every six years had food shortages between 403 and 323
BC, whilst the rate was one in every five years for Rome between 123 and
50 BC and in China agricultural disasters were recorded in 119 years between
AD 22 and 220 (Beaudoin, 2007). As a consequence of restricted trade, these
communities were highly vulnerable to natural disasters including drought or
agricultural pests.

In medieval Europe, the necessity of focus on meeting the basics of life meant that
much of the available if very limited expenditure went on foodstuffs, restricting
opportunities for saving or capital accumulation. It is estimated that 80 per cent of

the expenditure of the mass of the population went on food but the diet remained poor, with similar conditions existing in China and India (Ponting, 1991). The economic livelihoods of peasants were also vulnerable to demographic changes, with population growth posing a real threat to survival. Observations on how population growth could be a causal factor of famine and conflict were proposed in the seminal thesis of Thomas Malthus in 1817. He argued that whilst population will increase geometrically, 2, 4, 8 . . . , agricultural production will continue to grow arithmetically, 1, 2, 3, 4, 5, eventually resulting in a situation within which the combined nutritional requirements of the population will exceed the productive capacity of agriculture, leading to famine. Malthus argued that events such as famine and war were necessary checks to redress the level of population to a supportable level. Although the theory of Malthus has subsequently been proven to be incorrect for the majority of the world's population, as advancements in agricultural sciences and technologies have led to dramatic increases in agricultural productivity to a level where there exists a theoretical food surplus relative to the global population, it illustrates the continuing vulnerability of communities that are unable to access the benefits of these agricultural advancements owing to a lack of technical capacity and capital or are placed in a vulnerable position through the constraints of the global economy, as in the case of Ethiopia and SAPs discussed in Chapter 2. Dramatically, the fine balance between resource usage, vulnerability to external shocks and population growth is illustrated by the decline of the Maya civilisation explained in Box 3.2.

BOX 3.2 POPULATION AND RESOURCE ISSUES OF THE MAYA CIVILISATION

The influence of climate and limited resources upon the well-being and longevity of civilisations is demonstrated through the case of the Maya civilisation of Central America which inhabited a landmass covering approximately 500,000 square kilometres, including Guatemala, Yucatan, western Honduras, Belize and El Salvador. Having its origins in the Yucatan peninsula between 2600 and 2500 BC, their culture reached a peak between AD 600 and 800, having developed sophisticated astronomy and mathematics, hieroglyphic writing and impressive architecture. The society was complex, based upon a hierarchical system of government dominated by the rule of kings and nobles and the development of city states, notably the city of Tectihuacan in the Mexican highlands, which had a population estimated to be as high as 200,000. However, between AD 800 and 900, Mayan civilisation appears to have declined rapidly and dramatically, with the estimates of population decline varying from 66 to over 90 per cent. Disease, overpopulation, warfare between city states, invasions from outside, deforestation and environmental degradation have all been suggested as possible causes. The evidence of environmental causes in the decline of the Maya has recently become more compelling as an increasing number of tests have been performed on sediment cores from lakes in Yucatan, which demonstrate prolonged periods of drought around this period. The responses of the Mayans to environmental problems are uncertain but clearly a scarcity of resources, such as water, leading to food shortages, malnutrition and disease increases the propensity for internal unrest and conflict. It is argued that the situation of the Maya was worsened by the high population densities that required an intensive system of agriculture, which even in the years of higher rainfall may have been pushing the boundaries of what was sustainable in the short term, never mind the long term. The effects of drought were made worse because it occurred at a time when population densities and levels of agricultural exploitation had reached unsustainable levels.

Source: after Whyte, 2008

The historical vulnerability of communities to population growth can be exemplified through the situation of sixteenth-century France, where the population of 7 to 8 million in 1450 increased to approximately 16 million a century later, a demographic expansion resulting from a decline in crisis mortality as a consequence of reduced outbreaks of plague and war and fewer harvest failures (Rowlands, 2001). Population growth outstripped agricultural production causing a rapid inflation in grain prices, which increased by an average of 400 per cent across the countries of Europe during the sixteenth century. Conversely, wages increased by only half that amount as demographic expansion meant the supply of labour exceeded demand, hence suppressing wage levels. Similar situations were reported across the countries of Europe and whilst for the minority of peasants with enough land to generate grain surpluses for sale, including the yeomen in England, *coqs de village* in France and *Volkbauer* in Germany, there were financial benefits, for the majority the changing demographic and economic conditions of the sixteenth century brought hardships.

Population growth and the resultant pressure on land led to an increase in the number of peasants who possessed holdings that were too small for subsistence. They were subsequently forced into a position of having to attempt to buy grain that became increasingly expensive, whilst selling their labour at a cheaper rate as a consequence of oversupply. By the late sixteenth century, many villages in

France and other European countries had a majority of land-poor and landless households, and a state of poverty was normal as subsistence became an increasingly unattainable ideal. The poor's diets began to suffer as an increasing amount of income was designated to attaining grain and a state of almost constant malnutrition was interrupted by times when starvation became a real possibility. During the famine years of 1570–74, many peasants were reduced to eating bread made with bran, acorns, sawdust and even grass, mixed with milk or animal blood as their staple diet as grain became unaffordable (Beaudoin, 2007).

In the contemporary era, the dependency of the world's poor on the resources of place is emphasised by Duralappah (2004) in the exploration of the links between poverty and ecosystems. In a report commissioned by UNEP to further understand the linkages between poverty and the environment, Duralappah (ibid.) identified ten determinants of well-being and poverty reduction that are related to ecosystem services as shown in Box 3.3.

BOX 3.3 THE TEN DETERMINANTS OF WELL-BEING AND POVERTY REDUCTION RELATED TO ECOSYSTEM SERVICES (DURALAPPAH, 2004: 5)

1. Being able to be adequately nourished
2. Being able to be free from avoidable disease
3. Being able to live in an environmentally clean and safe shelter
4. Being able to have adequate and clean drinking water
5. Being able to have clean air
6. Being able to have energy to keep warm and to cook
7. Being able to use traditional medicine
8. Being able to continue using natural elements found in ecosystems for traditional cultural and spiritual practices
9. Being able to cope with extreme natural events including floods, tropical storms and landslides
10. Being able to make sustainable management decisions that respect natural resources and enable the achievement of a sustainable income stream

An important caveat for the reader here is that as Duralappah (ibid.) recognises, there are many other constituents and determinants of well-being not listed – for example, education – but the focus is on constituents and determinants linked to ecosystem services.

Integral in Duralappah's (ibid.) work is the recognition of humans as an essential part of the ecosystem and not as an entity that is separated from it. There exists a subsequent reciprocal relationship where the quality of the ecosystem influences human well-being and human action influences the quality of the ecosystems. The listed determinants respond to human needs related to themes of physical well-being, mental and spiritual nourishment, and having the capacity to be able to formulate economic prosperity on sustainable foundations. There is also an evident link in the last constituent in the list to a model of sustainable tourism development that conserves natural resources whilst meeting long-term livelihood needs.

The report recognises that many of these determinants of well-being are closely linked to three broad services that are provided by ecosystems. They are: *provisioning*, that is, the supply of food, fibre and fuels; *regulating*, that is, purification, detoxification and the mitigation of droughts and floods; and *enriching* through the spiritual, aesthetic and the social values we lend to ecosystems. It is stressed that besides providing 'goods' for humans, ecosystems also provide critical life-supporting systems, alongside the cultural and spiritual values that have historically and continue to support the psychological well-being of human societies. Duralappah (ibid.) emphasises that the cultural services of ecosystems are amongst the most overlooked by official agencies, ignoring the wisdom built upon beliefs and values surrounding natural forces which have provided spiritual guidance to societies for many generations. Subsequently, any breakdown of these cultural and spiritual norms may have a potentially devastating effect on social relationships, and between people and their surroundings. This is poignantly demonstrated in the case study of Easter Island in Box 3.4, where deforestation and a loss of cultural practices led to a questioning of the belief systems and the social foundations upon which a complex society had been established. Related to the cultural services and belief systems, ecosystems also have an important role to play in the provision of traditional medicines, which can be especially important to the poor, who lack the income to purchase manufactured medicines.

BOX 3.4 EASTER ISLAND: UNSUSTAINABLE RESOURCE USAGE, A DESTROYED CIVILISATION AND CULTURAL TOURISM

The case of Easter Island, a Polynesian island located in the Pacific Ocean 3,700 kilometres off the west coast of Chile, illustrates community dependence upon the resources of place and the immediate environment. It also highlights how the unsustainable use of natural resources can cause poverty, especially when places are isolated from wider networks. When the first European, Dutch Admiral Roggevenn, arrived on the island on Easter Sunday in 1722, he was amazed to see the evidence of a previous flourishing and advanced society in the form of massive stone statues over 20 feet high. Yet the population was in a primitive state, living in squalid reed huts or caves and practising cannibalism to survive.

Seeking to explain this decline from an advanced civilisation to squalor, in a period between the fifth century when the island was first visited by Polynesian settlers and the eighteenth century, the issues of the unsustainable use of natural resources and human competition become central ones. Owing to the high temperatures and humidity, poor drainage and a lack of permanent streams on the island, the diet of the inhabitants was largely limited to chickens and sweet potatoes. Whilst boring, the advantage of this system was it left plenty of time for the pursuit of cultural practices, which were actively pursued by clans consisting of closely associated extended families.

A cultural practice for which the island is now renowned was the construction of large stone statues, big headed figures, called *moai* statues. However, in the absence of any draught animals and a reliance purely on human power, a major challenge was how to transport them to chosen sites for display. The chosen method is accepted to be the use of tree trunks as rollers, which, combined with a population growth from an initial 20 or 30 settlers up to a maximum of 15,000, caused deforestation. Alongside their use for moving the statues, the trees would have been felled to make clearings for agriculture, use for fuel and as construction materials. The shortage of trees forced many people to abandon building houses from timber and live in caves, eventually people having to dig stone shelters into the hillsides and construct flimsy reed huts. Fishing was made difficult because nets had been made from the paper mulberry tree which was now no longer available and there was a lack of wood for canoes.

The lack of tree cover also caused soil erosion and the loss of essential nutrients, affecting soil quality for agriculture. Without canoes, the islanders were trapped on the island, unable to escape the consequences of their self-inflicted environmental collapse. The social and cultural impact of deforestation was equally important, as the inability to erect more statues led to a questioning of belief systems and the social foundations on which this complex society had been built. Conflict over diminishing resources became almost permanent, slavery common and cannibalism was practised. When Admiral Roggevenn arrived in the eighteenth century, the remaining islanders no longer had any knowledge of how their ancestors had moved the statues, saying that the huge figures had walked across the island.

The subsequent recent establishment of air routes to Chile, Tahiti and Peru has led to the development of cultural tourism to the island with the opening of its first high-class hotel in 2012. The immediacy of this change from a place of isolation to a tourist destination is emphasised by the commentary of one tourist: 'My tour guide, Hugo tells me his 87-year-old great grandmother used to live in a cave. She and many islanders also remember their confusion the first time they saw a plane circling overhead, causing children to run off screaming with fear.' Now cars and motorbikes are the preferred means of transport around the island and the population has recovered from just 111 in 1877 to approximately 5,000. The development of a tourism industry has brought opportunities for economic diversification as described by one local tour operator: 'I am fishing man, I am farming man, I am artist man (sic) . . . and now I am *tourismo* man' (Baker, 2012: 3).

Source: after Ponting, 1991; Baker, 2012

Duralappah (ibid.) also recognises that whilst all of humankind is dependent to differing degrees upon ecosystem services for their well-being, the poor are much more heavily dependent on these services than the rich, as the rich have the means to access coping strategies. For example, in a situation of inadequate access to clean drinking water, the rich can buy bottled water or purification tablets. Similarly, the poor are much more vulnerable to extreme natural events such as floods and tropical storms as they do not have access to resources to be able to build resistant shelters, or they are forced to inhabit more marginal lands, such as steep slopes that are at high risk from landslides at times of heavy rain.

Enhanced vulnerability may also be an outcome of ecosystem changes that are made in the absence of consultation with local people. Duralappah (2004) gives the example of how the destruction of mangroves for commercial shrimp farming has removed a natural protective barrier against storm activity, enhancing the vulnerability of many poor coastal communities to nature. A major reason for this occurring was a lack of well-defined property rights of the mangrove swamps, permitting a small elite class to capture the rights, even though local people have been using them as a resource for generations. The exclusion of women from the decision-making process about the use of mangrove swamps and the ecosystem, despite them often being the primary users and custodians of the land, also contributed to their destruction. Whilst within modernisation and neo-liberal development paradigms it can be argued that the conversion of ecosystems services for economic development will provide the poor with the financial resources to purchase the nourishment they require, Duralappah (2004: 14) disputes this, commenting: 'empirical evidence over the last five decades shows that the conversion effect has produced mixed results with many instances whereby the poor have not only *not* [author's emphasis] benefited from the conversion of ecosystems, but have also lost an important source of nourishment, especially in times of distress'.

Given the reliance of the majority of the poor upon natural resources, the condition of the environment has important implications for them and future generations (DFID, 2000). If the creation of livelihood opportunities in rural areas is the objective of government policy in developing countries in an attempt to arrest population drifts to urban areas and an increase in the numbers of urban poor, there is a requirement to ensure that economic growth is sustained on a conserved and environmentally well-managed natural resource base. This necessity can be illustrated through the example of coral reefs which are both an important ecosystem and a highly attractive natural resource for tourism upon which to develop an industry and provide livelihood opportunties. After tropical rainforests they are the second most biodiverse ecosystem on the planet, being home to approximately 25 per cent of all marine species despite covering only 0.17 per cent of the ocean floor (Goudie and Viles, 1997). This biodiversity is a great attraction to tourists but the well-being of the reefs can be threatened by tourism development. Examples of threats include the mining of reefs for building materials in Sri Lanka, India, Maldives, east Africa, Tonga and Samoa (Mieczkowski, 1995) and inadequate sewage disposal measures to deal with human waste as a consequence of the increase in numbers of hotels and other types of tourist accommodation (Holden, 2008). The addition of untreated sewage into the water causes nutrient enrichment or eutrophication, stimulating the growth of algae, which can cover coral reefs, in effect suffocating them. For instance, the discharge of partially treated sewage into the sea off the Hawaiian island of Oahu stimulated the growth of the alga *Dictyosphaeria cavernosa*, which overgrew and killed large sections of the reef (Edington and Edington, 1986). Similarly parts of the Great Barrier Reef off the coast of Australia have been destroyed by the proliferation of 'crown-of-thorns' starfish, *Acanthaster planci*, which feed on the reef and have become abundant as a consequence of pollution and over fishing of their predators.

The behaviour of local people, tourists and tour operators may also damage the coral. Local people may break it off to sell as souvenirs, as in the Bahamas and Granada, where rare black coral is made into earrings for sale to tourists. Local operators taking tourists out in boats to visit reefs sometimes drag their anchors through the coral causing localised damage, whilst tourists harm the coral by touching and standing on it. Additionally, shells are sometimes collected by local people to sell to tourists, as in areas of the Red Sea, the Caribbean and off the coast of Kenya. These negative impacts caused by the behaviour of local people, tour operators and tourists, are partly as a consequence of a lack of awareness and poverty. The destruction of a reef not only means a loss of biodiversity but also threatens the tourist industry and the livelihoods of those who depend upon it. It may also have negative consequences for the fishing industry, an activity in which the poor are traditionally employed, as coral offers as abundance of food for fish. To safeguard natural resources there is a subsequent need for coordination of environmental management and environmental education as components of Poverty Reduction Strategies to ensure that livelihood opportunities through tourism are created in a sustainable way.

ENVIRONMENTAL CRISIS, CLIMATE CHANGE AND POVERTY

Our dependency on ecosystem services discussed in the last section means any challenges to their functioning threaten our own well-being. The poor are placed particularly at risk from negative environmental change given their limited resources to adapt to change. Crises in climate and loss of biodiversity particularly threaten the ecosystem services upon which the poor depend, including the provision of water, food, building materials and fuel, meaning they may suffer disproportionately. The reliance of the poor upon their surroundings is underlined by the Commission for Africa (2005: 248) who comment: 'In surveys, poor people consistently highlight the importance of the environment to well-being in terms of health, security, clean water, sanitation, safe energy, safe housing, food security and access to agricultural inputs.' Of major consequence for the poor is the process of global warming and resultant climate change, which may simultaneously diminish the qualities of the natural resource base and reinforce conditions of poverty. Given the reliance of many of the world's poor on natural resources and climate-sensitive industries, especially agriculture, fishing and also increasingly tourism, combined with their inhabiting of marginal land areas, there is significant future uncertainty and threat posed to their livelihoods by climate change.

Whilst a limited amount of contention may still exist over the extent to which global warming is a consequence of human activity or a natural occurrence, the real debate has now shifted to whose responsibility it is to deal with its causes and mitigate its impacts. Global warming models predict that increasing global temperatures are likely to impact upon many atmospheric parameters, including precipitation and wind velocity, leading to more frequent extreme weather events, including storms, heavy rainfall, cyclones and drought (UNEP, 1999). The number of extreme weather events have quadrupled since the 1950s, and the frequency of high level hurricanes and typhoons has doubled since the 1950s (De Costa, 2001). As the effects of Hurricane Katrina on New Orleans in 2005 demonstrated, with flooding causing a mass evacuation of the city and thousands becoming homeless, even the most advanced economy in the world is vulnerable to the power of nature. Combined with rising sea levels and coastal erosion, there is a real threat from 'natural' or climatic disasters to tourism. The poor are also highly vulnerable to a rise in extreme weather events as a consequence of their lack of resources to adapt to natural disasters. They also live in marginal areas that are subject to flooding and landslides and live in less robust shelter than the non-poor. The frequency of hurricanes and typhoons is also at its highest in the tropics, the geographical area between which latitudes the majority of the world's poor are found as shown in Figure 1.1.

The causes of global warming and climate change are now well charted and it is not the intention to re-iterate them in detail in this text, as its focus rests on the interaction of climate change with poverty. However, the causes of climate change are not without considerable political and economic controversy that have context in the wider debate about development. The chief sources of the Greenhouse Gas (GHG) emissions that cause global warming have come from the developed countries, especially North America and Europe. Since 1850, North America and Europe have produced around 70 per cent of all the world's GHG emissions due to energy production (Stern Report, 2006), although this situation is changing with the growth of China and India as global economic powers. Unsurprisingly, this has led to political contention over the rights and hegemony of the developed world to dictate controls over GHG emissions for developing countries as they attempt to develop their own economies to similar levels of those enjoyed in the West.

The practice of unsustainable consumption endemic to developed countries, the undervaluing of the common pool of goods and services provided by the environment leading to a propensity for over consumption and over pollution, and poor and ineffective governance that leads to environmental neglect, all contribute to a deteriorating global environmental quality that also has local consequences (DFID, 1999). The failure of the market system to adequately accommodate negative environmental externalities may push costs onto the most vulnerable. For example, the zero costs for airlines and tourists of depositing emissions from air travel into the atmosphere that contribute to global warming has potential negative consequences for the poor. The emissions contribute to climate change, resulting in rises in ocean levels that threaten communities inhabiting low-lying areas; for example, in the Pacific Isles and flood plains of Bangladesh. The latter is particularly vulnerable to climate change given its low-lying coastline, high population density and economic dependence on agriculture. A one metre rise in sea-level could result in more than a fifth of Bangladesh being under water, a possibility by the end of this century (Stern Report, 2006).

The progressive changes in climatic zones as a consequence of global warming, shifts in precipitation patterns, increases in the magnitude and frequency of extreme weather events including droughts, floods and storms, and accompanying sea level rises, all pose significant threats to the livelihoods of the poor, not least because of their economic dependency on agriculture. The consequences of natural disasters on the poor are also not solely limited to the short term, as the need to raise capital in periods of stress may lead the poor to sell assets they require for their livelihoods and long-term survival, including land, farming implements and bicycles. Falling farm incomes as a consequence of climate change may increase levels of poverty and force families to use any savings just to survive. The subsequent loss of food security and purchasing power will increase the likelihood of absolute poverty.

This low adaptive capacity to change is a consequence of a lack of resources and opportunities, including income, a lack of savings, low education levels, lack of land tenure and safety nets; for example, government support. The IPCC (2007a) recognises that it is in developing countries that people are most likely to suffer from the negative impacts of climate change as a consequence of both the economic importance of climate-sensitive sectors and their limited human, institutional and financial capacities to respond to the direct and indirect effects of climate change. Increased rates of illness and death are also predicted in Least Developed Countries whilst at a macro-economic level climate change will reduce government revenues and raise spending needs as climate-sensitive industries becomes less competitive and unemployment rises (Stern Report, 2006).

The vulnerability of the poor to climate change is also compounded by geographical location. The geographical areas that are most vulnerable to sea-level rises are found within the tropics, including the west coast of Africa, the north and eastern coasts of South America, south and south-east Asia; and small island states in the Caribbean, Pacific and Indian Ocean (IPCC, 2001). Low-lying coastal areas may also suffer a loss of agricultural land from sea-level rises and accompanying salinisation, whilst declining fish stocks as a consequence of climate change may threaten food security. It is also countries in the tropical and subtropical regions that are particularly vulnerable to a decrease in crop yields, threatening food security and exacerbating hunger (IPCC, 2001). Particularly at risk are countries in sub-Saharan Africa, where the threat of increased water scarcity poses a significant threat to agricultural production. Nor is it just the risk posed to agriculture and food security from climate change that has the potential to spread and deepen poverty. Threats to the supply of natural resources, including land and water heighten the likelihood for potential social unrest and for political conflict. There is a propensity for environmental refugees and mass migration in the future with accompanying political and economic issues of immigration that have become common in many developed countries.

The threats to the poor from environmental risk and the loss of ecosystem services is summarised in the Millennium Ecosystem Assessment authored by Duralappah (2004). Whilst substantial net gains in economic development and human well-being have been made since the middle of the twentieth century, these gains have been achieved at growing costs in the form of the degradation of many ecosystem services and a largely irreversible loss of biodiversity with an accompanying exacerbation of poverty. These problems, unless addressed, will substantially diminish the benefits that future generations obtain from ecosystems. The assessment also anticipates that the degradation of ecosystem services could act as a barrier to achieving the Millennium Development Goals (MGDs).

CLIMATE CHANGE AND THREATS TO THE TOURISM–POVERTY REDUCTION AGENDA

Tourism is a climate-sensitive industry and economic sector similar to agriculture, being reliant on the consistency of climate and the biodiversity of ecosystems to attract tourists and provide ecosystem services. Subsequently, climate change represents a potential threat to the longevity of the use of natural resources for tourism as part of poverty reduction strategies and a continued contribution to the MDGs. Whilst it is impossible to predict the consequences of climate change with complete certainty, it is highly probable that tourism as a climate-sensitive industry will have to adapt in the future to some degree of climate change. Melting ice caps, rising sea levels, reduced snowfall, loss of biodiversity and changing ecosystems will inevitably have implications for tourism and for the livelihoods of those who depend upon the industry.

Alongside the direct effects on the livelihoods of the poor who are dependent upon the tourism industry, the poor may also be further disadvantaged through the secondary effects of reduced tourism income. The economic multiplier effects of tourism were discussed in Chapter 2, and any reduced tourism demand as a consequence of climate change is likely to negatively affect the level of economic activity, including income and employment opportunities associated with the tourism supply chain. It is not just income to households that will be affected detrimentally but also taxation revenues paid to government from the formal tourism sector that can be used to improve infrastructure and services for the poor. Subsequently, there will be decreased levels of public resources available for investment in infrastructure improvements, including energy and transport, and in health and education provision, all of which represent vital developments for poverty reduction.

According to the WTO (2003), specific climate threats relevant to the tourism industry include: that sea-levels will rise threatening many coastal areas and small islands; temperature rises will change precipitation patterns, so water supply problems will be exacerbated; and climate change will increase the magnitude, frequency and risk of extreme climatic events including tropical storms and sea surges. More specifically it is probable that as sea-levels begin to rise there will be an increase in beach and coast erosion, a higher likelihood of coastal flooding, a loss of coastal ecosystems and a total submersion of some low-lying islands and coastal plains. The siting of much tourism infrastructure along the coasts of regions and islands magnifies the potential risk from sea-level rises and storms. The possible effects of climate change on a typical small island developing state (SID) is exemplified through Barbados in the Caribbean. Based on a study of the south and west coasts of the island to estimate the effects of a one metre rise in sea-level and a storm surge generated by a Category 3 hurricane, the Caribbean Planning for Adaptation to Climate Change (CPACC) agency commented that the: 'result is astonishing since most of the present day development, including the tourism infrastructure, is located within this inundation zone' (CPACC, 1999: 3, cited in Belle and Bramwell, 2005). A further potential consequence of a rise in sea-level is the intrusion of saline water into the fresh water aquifers that Barbados is dependent upon for water. Potential rises in sea-levels pose real threats to the tourism industries of low-lying islands such as the Maldives as highlighted in Box 3.5.

BOX 3.5 CLIMATE CHANGE AND THE MALDIVES

The Maldives are situated in the Indian Ocean and consist of 1,196 islands, many below an altitude of two metres, supporting a population of over 300,000. The natural beauty of the islands has made them into an attractive tourism destination, with tourism's 31.3 per cent contribution to GDP in 2011 emphasising the economy's heavy dependence upon it (WTTC, 2012). However, as a consequence of rising ocean levels as an outcome of climate change, most of the country will be flooded during the next 50 to 100 years (IPCC, 2007b). The problems of the islands have been accentuated as a consequence of the quarrying and dredging of coral offshore for its use as aggregate in the construction of hotels, roads and airports. Further damage to coral reefs caused by bleaching and pollutants has increased vulnerability and consequently has adversely affected their important function of protection against natural hazards, including tidal surges and beach erosion.

Ongoing annual rises in ocean levels have been recorded which threatens the continuing inhabitation of the islands in the long term. The implications for the tourism industry are also grave as the loss of beaches, the primary attraction for 70 per cent of tourists, would severely affect the local economy and 45 per cent of tourist resorts have already reported concerns about beach erosion (The Government of Madives, 2009). In an attempt to mitigate and adapt to the negative impacts of climate change on the Maldives, the Government of Maldives, the European Union (EU) and the World Bank signed a Memorandum of Understanding and established a Climate Change Trust Fund with a contribution of US$8.8 million from the EU which will aim at building resilience to climate change through funding priority projects (World Bank, 2010). Former President Nasheed (2008–12) was pro-active in raising awareness and taking actions to mitigate climate change, creating and hosting the first meeting of the Climate Vulnerable Forum, attended by 11 poor nations threatened by climate change. In 2009, President Nasheed also announced that the Maldives would become entirely carbon-neutral by 2020 but following his resignation this target is uncertain.

Source: after The Government of Maldives, 2009;
World Bank, 2010; WTTC, 2012

Besides their effect on the tourism industry, extreme weather conditions and natural disasters can have a significant impact on the broad economy, especially in small states where a single event can affect a large proportion of the country. Stressing the vulnerability of SIDS as a consequence of their geography UNCTAD (1983: 33, cited in Crowards, 2000) comment: 'Island developing economies are often particularly exposed to natural hazards for fundamental reasons of geography. Given the small size of individual islands and of island developing countries generally, the often overwhelming proportional impact of disasters in these countries justifies special concern by the international community.' A lack of economic diversification may also compound the threat from natural disasters in SIDS. The demand for tourism is highly reliant on a perception that destinations are safe places with a minimum degree of risk. Alongside outbreaks of wars, terrorism, civil unrest and high levels of criminality, natural disasters present a significant perceived threat to stability and safety. Whilst a downturn in tourism demand may prove to be short term, that is, two to three years, the consequences on the poor may be dramatic if livelihood opportunities provided through tourism are lost. The potential for economic hardship as a consequence of a downturn in tourism demand is particularly accentuated where there exists a high dependence upon it.

A further consideration of climate change's effect on tourism is how it may alter the spatial geography of tourism flows. The two most significant flows of tourism are from northern Europe to the Mediterranean and North America to the Caribbean accounting for tens of millions of tourists. Similar to the Mediterranean, tourism in the Caribbean islands is dependent upon the consistency of the qualities of climate and the beach, with its main market from North America escaping the cold winter. However, parts of the USA may become warmer, making them more attractive to vacation in, whilst rising sea-levels may threaten some of the Caribbean islands, damaging beaches and causing infrastructure damage (WTO, 2003). A predicted increased need for air-conditioning will also place pressure on the island's water and energy resources. All these developments would have profound implications for the poor of the Caribbean islands if the tourism industry is adversely affected by climate change.

The impact of climate change may also be felt on special interest tourism beside mainstream mass tourism. For example, the negative impact of climate change and human behaviour on coral reefs was discussed earlier in the chapter. It is the biodiversity of the reefs that makes them into natural attractions for tourism, with many reefs being located in developing countries. The destruction of reefs because of climate change, apart from removing their important ecosystem functions, would result in the loss of income and livelihood options not only from mainstream tourism but also niche markets such as diving. Other types of tourism, also dependent on a stable climatic and ecosystems – for example, wildlife and other types of ecotourism – could also be threatened by ecosystem changes and the loss of biodiversity. Whilst it is extremely difficult to forecast with accuracy the effects of climate change, even more so their impacts on tourism, an attempt to provide an overview of the likely effects across the continents housing the greatest numbers of the world's poor is given in Box 3.6. The fruition of these changes will ultimately depend upon the degree and depth of climate change that actually occurs but the findings suggest that whilst the urgency of the challenge of how to use tourism for poverty reduction may require short-tem responses, long-term strategies will need to consider best practices for mitigation and adaptation if tourism is to provide a sustainable tool for poverty reduction.

BOX 3.6 IMPLICATIONS OF CLIMATE CHANGE FOR NATURAL RESOURCES USED FOR TOURISM IN LATIN AMERICA, AFRICA AND ASIA

Continent	Threatened Natural Resources	Impact
Latin America	Biodiversity of fresh-water systems (home to 1,500 species of animals)	Highly sensitive to climate change
	Sea-level rises	Land loss and threat to coastal and island tourism infrastructure
	Mountain regions, e.g. Andes	Reduced snowfall and a gradual disappearance of snow and ice with a consequent threat to the longevity of the activity-based tourism market
Africa	Wildlife and ecosystems, especially in East Africa, including Kenya and Tanzania	Loss of biodiversity of fauna and flora that threatens ecosystems functions and the survival of wildlife, with subsequent negative economic impacts on the wildlife tourism market
	Increased water shortages, river flow changes, reduced water run-off and drying up of reservoirs	Decline in water-based activities; reduced water discharge may make natural attractions such as the Victoria Falls less attractive; the environmental quality and economic and business potential of many natural lakeside resorts would diminish
	Coastal zones and marine ecosystems (especially in Kenya and Tanzania)	Decline in marine-based tourism and the attraction of natural resources, e.g. coral reefs

Asia	World's highest mountain range the Himalayas	Reduced snow and ice; threat to ecosystems and loss of attractiveness; possible decline in the activity-based tourism market
	World's second biggest rain forest complex	Loss of biodiversity and attractiveness to tourists
	Over half of the world's share of coral reefs; Indonesia and Malaysia rank amongst the top countries for their biodiversity	Vulnerability of coral reefs to 'bleaching' caused by higher sea temperatures; loss of sand beaches in south-east Asia from sea-level rises all threaten tourism demand

Source: based on La Trobe, 2002; IPCC, 2007b

TOURISM STAKEHOLDERS' RESPONSES TO THE GLOBAL ENVIRONMENTAL CHANGE (GEC): POVERTY NEXUS

It is not the intention to provide an exhaustive account of how tourism stakeholders are beginning to respond to climate change and how they may in the future. For readers who are particularly interested in the science of climate change and tourism, there are texts dedicated to this subject; for example, Becken and Hay (2007) and Gossling and Hall (2006), which provide much more comprehensive analyses than are possible within the context of this text. The focus of this part of the chapter rests more on considerations of how tourism stakeholders may respond to the threats climate change poses to poverty.

It is evident that if tourism is to represent a viable long-term option for poverty reduction, tourism stakeholders need to address measures for mitigation and adaptation to climate change that accompany broader policy and management initiatives. As the chief coordinating body of stakeholders of global tourism, the UNWTO (2003) in the Djerba Declaration and in the Davos Declaration of 2007 (UNWTO, 2007a) acknowledged the need to integrate tourism with the objectives of the Kyoto Protocol and the United Nations Framework Convention on Climate Change (UNFCCC) to adapt to the global changes presented by climate change. Critically as the Davos Declaration observes with direct reference to the use of tourism for poverty reduction: 'Given tourism's importance in the global challenges of climate change and poverty reduction, there is a need to urgently adopt a range of policies which encourage truly sustainable tourism that reflects a "quadruple bottom line" of environmental, social, economic and climate responses' (UNWTO, 2007a: 2).

Within the range of actions to be taken by governments and international organisations, special attention is drawn by the UNWTO (2007a) to the need to provide financial, technical and training support to tourism destinations in developing countries, especially in LDCs and SIDS, with the aim of increasing the capacity for adaptive responses to climate change. From the evidence of how tourism-dependent destinations in the European Alps are responding to the threats of reduced snow cover, it is necessary to consider a range of options from technical improvisation to new product development and marketing strategies. However, such ability for adaptation is reliant on having financial resources and also the knowledge of tourism to be able to make suitable strategic decisions and plans. As the UNWTO (2007a) point out, there is a subsequent need to raise the capacity of tourism destinations in LDCs and developing countries to be able to respond to climate change. However, in cases where the whole geography of states is threatened by climate change – for example, the Maldives – the coping strategies that are necessary will lie beyond the remit of tourism, requiring holistic responses from supranational agencies that embrace collective responses.

There is an evident need for the tourism industry to continue with its efforts to mitigate the effect of and adapt to GEC. The UNWTO (2003, 2007a) draws attention for the need of the tourism industry to mitigate its GHG emissions, especially those from transport and accommodation. Alongside pollution from tourism superstructure – for example, hotels, attractions and restaurants – a major issue relates to the contribution of the transport element of tourism to global warming. For example, in the USA it is estimated that 76.5 per cent of tourism's contributions to greenhouse emissions is derived from transport, with the remainder coming from other tourist services – for example, accommodation, and restaurants (WTO, 2003). In the context of using international tourism for poverty reduction, the issue of aviation's contribution to climate change poses a particular challenge as it has become a focus of political conflict. Some climatologists claim that aviation is the fastest growing cause of climate change (Garman, 2006), although this view is discredited by pro-tourism organisations, including the UNWTO, WTTC and International Civil Aviation Organisation (ICAO).

The UNWTO itself recognises the need for tourists to be environmentally aware in their decision-making, calling for consumers to: 'be encouraged to consider the climate, economic, social and environmental impacts of their options before making a decision and, where possible to reduce their carbon footprint, or offset emissions that cannot be reduced directly' (UNWTO, 2007a: 3).

A conundrum therefore arises between the requirement for international tourism to play a significant role in poverty reduction and the contribution of aviation to climate change. A reduction in tourist flows from developed countries to LDCs potentially threatens tourism's viability as a tool for poverty reduction. One strategy to overcome the dilemma of balancing a reduction in the carbon footprint with a social agenda is for tourists to take fewer trips but stay longer in destinations, a situation that could benefit the poor if meaningful exchanges take place through tourism that actually lead to poverty reduction. Thus, whilst any decrease in demand for aviation would seem to threaten the potential use of international tourism for poverty reduction, this is not necessarily the case. The adaptation of tourists to a total fewer of trips but to remain longer in their destinations offers the potential to simultaneously reduce tourism's contribution to GEC whilst enhancing its use for poverty reduction.

SUMMARY

- Historically, there has been a strong human reliance on the natural resources of the surrounding environment to meet one's needs. However, the geographical inheritance of the place one is born into is not deterministic for development, as the world has become increasingly inter-connected since the beginnings of trans-ocean trade in the fifteenth century. More places have become integrated with each other through the forces of globalisation. Nevertheless, the world's poor remain either cut off from the benefits of this relationship or they are such that they exacerbate poverty. There are certain key characteristics that are common to many of the poorest countries, including being landlocked, having a small population, and a dependency on primary goods for exports. This combination of a lack of ocean access, small internal markets, and a reliance on primary goods that are highly vulnerable to volatile price changes in the world markets all limit opportunities for development.
- A reliance on the local environment is especially acute for the poor with a dependency on ecosystem services for well-being and poverty reduction. These services are determined by the quality of the ecosystem of which the poor are a part and include the meeting of 'provisioning', 'regulating' and 'enriching' needs. The poor are more heavily dependent upon the ecosystem services than the rich because they have less access to resources for coping strategies. Enrichment of people through the cultural services of ecosystems is important for the spiritual guidance of societies but its value is often overlooked by multilateral and government development agencies.

- The geographical characteristics of place and their differentiation are essential to the development of tourism and the willingness of people to travel from their home environments. The value of spatial variation in nature and 'authenticity' of culture are typically primary pulls for tourists to visit a particular place. Tourism is a process and system that integrates places into networks bringing the wealthier into contact with the poor. Whilst there are marked potential economic benefits from this relationship, there also exists potential cultural harm associated with aspects of the demonstration effect and acculturation, and negative environmental consequences from overuse.

- An increasing inter-connectivity of places and issues of political hegemony raise issues over the control the poor can have on directing development and livelihood opportunities. Issues of agency, structure and participatory approaches to development are important for ensuring that tourism policy reflects the needs of the poor and is tailored to overcoming barriers to their participation in the industry and fulfilling their aspirations. There is a need to recognise the epistemological differences of place and indigenous knowledge. Without rich and in-depth understandings of how poverty is experienced and interpreted, how the poor perceive that tourism can be used to enhance their livelihood opportunities and lift them out of poverty, there is a danger of externally imposed policy solutions failing because of a lack of awareness of localised and cultural interpretations of the poverty–tourism nexus.

- Global Environmental Change (GEC) of which climate change is a key driver, poses threats to the well-being of the poor as the ecosystem services on which they depend are threatened. It also poses a significant threat to climate-sensitive industries of agriculture and fishing in which the poor are traditionally employed. As a climate-sensitive industry, negative effects from GEC on ecosystems that attract tourists to countries and within countries, such as wildlife and coral reefs, will be detrimental to the use of tourism for poverty reduction. The issue of aviation's contribution to climate change has become a politically contentious one and raises key issues about how long-haul tourism can be best used for poverty reduction in a sustainable framework.

The global political economy and structural causes of poverty

4

This chapter:

- Critiques the importance of political economy for explaining patterns of poverty
- Analyses the processes of globalisation and their relevance to tourism and poverty reduction
- Evaluates the influences of free trade on tourism's use for poverty reduction

INTRODUCTION

The preceeding chapter focused on how the geography of place has relevance to explaining both patterns of poverty and the interaction of tourism and poverty reduction. It also emphasised how many places are becoming increasingly inter-connected and inter-dependent in economic relationships that are beneficial for some but not for others. This diversification of inter-connectivity and development is also reflected in lifestyles as described by Radcliffe (1999: 4): 'Cosmopolitan jet setters in São Paulo live one kind of development while women in sub-Saharan Africa walking for hours to collect water experience a completely different kind of development.' The lifestyles illustrated in this statement portray one that is highly global and inter-connected and one that is highly dependent upon the resources of place. The 'cosmopolitan and jet-setter' typology is indicative of an evident trend in international relations that emphasises an inter-connectivity of many places across economic, cultural and environmental spheres. This trend has been particularly evident in the culture and transport spheres since the 1960s and in those of economy and information technology since the 1980s. Inherent to this process of inter-connection, loosely termed 'globalisation', are issues of power and economic decision-making that affects the lives of hundreds of millions of people. Whilst globalisation has had a substantial impact on world economic development since the 1980s, the trend towards an interconnectedness of trade and the integration of national economies into a world economic system can be traced to the fifteenth and sixteenth centuries, as is explained in the next section of this chapter.

EARLY TRADE SYSTEMS

The encouragement of the development of trade was referred to in President Truman's 1949 speech as a way of aiding the re-building of the international economy in the post-Second World War period, and has been actively encouraged by the World Bank and neo-liberals since the 1980s, as was explained in Chapter 2. However, the emergence of inter-continental trade, along with the beginnings of European colonisation which would have a significant impact on global development, can be traced to the late fifteenth century. It was during this century that there began a shift in the European world perspective beyond its own geographical boundaries, which combined with small but significant technological advancements in sailing, notably in rigging and rudder technology, encouraged exploration. These advancements permitted the development and exploration of the oceans by Europeans and the discovery of 'new' territories (Beaudoin, 2007). They also heralded the changing of a European geographical perspective that previously had held Jerusalem as the world's centre and the Mediterranean as the world's most important sea.

This growth in exploration during the latter half of the fifteenth century, the 'Age of Reconnaissance', was also encouraged by the 'rediscovery' of Ptolemy's *Geography*, during the Renaissance period, which offered a view of the world that had been forgotten for nearly a thousand years (Roberts, 1995). Ptolemy, was an Alexandrian actually called Claudius Ptolemaeus, who in the third century AD compiled the coordinates of all the places in the known world at the time, approximately 8,000 of them. He used the sources of other geographers, military and administrative gazetteers, and seafarers' reports to compile the first World Atlas (MacGillivray, 2006). The extent of the world that Ptolemy mapped stretched from the Canary Isles in the west to China and Malaysia in the east, and from the Arctic Circle in the north to well below the equator in the south (ibid.). In the era of the internet and hyper-mobility, it may seem strange that a single text could inspire visions of travel and exploration. However, Europe in the Middle Ages was a place of short and limited geographical horizons, within which there were very limited opportunities to travel beyond one's immediate environment, the primary concerns for the majority of the population being to secure their survival and meeting their needs for food, shelter, family and community. The drive for the exploration and discovery of new territories was also driven by the financial desire of European princes for land and gold, which created opportunities for professional explorers and navigators.

The advancements in sailing technology led to the development of larger ships, which when combined with simultaneous developments in navigation techniques and cartography permitted exploration of the oceans. Towards the end of the fifteenth century, sea voyages were led by individuals that would change the knowledge of world geography and mark the beginning of economic and cultural interactions between different continents. These individuals included Christopher Columbus's voyage to the 'New World' of the Americas in 1493, Vasco de Gama's voyage to access the Indian Ocean in 1498 and Magellan's circumnavigation of the world in 1522. For MacGillivray (2006) this stage of early European exploration was the early step towards globalisation, when the stage and size of the globe finally became understood and a period of global competition between rival nation states began. The voyages were essential to an emergent inter-nation economic dependence that extended beyond Europe and by the early 1600s the roots of a trading system had become established that linked the nation states of western Europe with the unlimited resources of the 'New World' of the Americas (Heffernan, 2003).

Driven by the advancements in exploration and also in cartography, by the sixteenth century the first atlas had been produced, making navigation simpler, which in turn encouraged the expansion of trade. Thousands of boats left European ports in search of trade and profits in other continents during the sixteenth and seventeenth centuries. 'Discovery' would also be followed by conquest as a new world order emerged that has ramifications for today's global political economy and trade system. The incentives for European expansion embraced a mix of hegemonic, economic and religious influences, including authority over distant lands, the potential revenues they offered, and the opportunity to convert inhabitants to Christianity (Houston, 2001). The types of goods that were sought by the European adventurers and traders included spices and fine clothes from the Far East, and gold and silver from the Americas. Agricultural connections in the New World were established between producers and European traders who brought back tropical crops such as coffee, sugar, cocoa, tea and sugar cane, their popularity and demand in Europe leading to the establishment of their cultivation specifically for export to Europe.

Importantly for the development of commercial trade, the geography of the world was now understood to embrace great oceans, which provided trading routes and offered economic opportunities for those European countries bordering the Atlantic Ocean. These countries included Spain, Portugal, France, Holland and England, all of whom would progressively during the following centuries establish colonies and empires, an economic system that would have ramifications for the comparative levels of development between countries. The importance of this era for the expansion of trade and emergence of colonial links is emphasised by Mackinnon and Cumbers (2007), who attribute it as a contributory factor to the rise of capitalism in north-west Europe. European hegemony over trade was extended further in the seventeenth century with the founding of large trading companies, including the Dutch West Indies Company, the British East India Company, the Hudson Bay Company and the Royal African Company. Whilst British companies required a charter from the monarch, these companies conducted their affairs autonomously, and sometimes immorally, the most notorious practice being associated with the Royal African Company founded in 1672 and the pattern of 'triangular trade' established during the eighteenth century. This involved trans- porting cotton, sugar and other tropical products from America and the Caribbean across the Atlantic to the United Kingdom; the shipping of manufactured goods for sale from Britain to West Africa for sale and exchange for slaves, who were then shipped in horrendous conditions to work on the cotton and sugar plantations of North America and the Caribbean. According to some historians and econo- mists, it was the profits and vast wealth made from this trade that provided the capital to support the Industrial Revolution in Britain (Chamberlain, 1974).

Although the slave trade represents the most inhumane and barbaric aspect of European colonial expansion, the practice of importing raw materials from other countries, processing them and exporting them as manufactured goods back to their point of origin became established. The advent of the Industrial Revolution in the late eighteenth century compounded this process and wealth inequality between nations, with the GDP per capita of Western Europe, the richest part of the world at that time being no more than three times that of the poorest parts of the world, Africa (Sender, 2003, cited in Lines, 2008). As referred to in Chapter 1, the most prominent example of this was the exportation of cotton from India during the nineteenth and first half of the twentieth centuries to Britain, where it was manufactured into cotton goods and exported and re-sold in the Indian market. Even though this practice was to become a focal point for protests of the India National Congress and the leadership of Gandhi in bringing an end to British colonial rule in the twentieth century, it exemplifies a pattern of global trade that has left a contemporary legacy. For many of the LDCs whose main exports include primary commodities and agricultural products, it remains impossible for them to establish their own manufacturing industries in the face of the competition and economic tariffs imposed by the developed countries in the world markets.

Of direct relevance to the contemporary geographical distribution of poverty, the development of trade during from the sixteenth century laid the foundation for two key themes that were to emerge in importance during successive centuries. These are: (i) more places and people have progressively become reliant on world trade, subsequently poverty has become increasingly related to the world economy, rather than solely the natural resources of place; and (ii) different cultures have increasingly adopted a Western approach to poverty that no longer understands it as a natural state but rather as a problem that demands a solution. Whilst a progressive integration of the majority of the world's population into the world economy and the market system has undoubtedly led to greater opportunities and an overall increase in the standard of living for many, conversely as Hayter (1981) observes, it has also led to an increased dependency on people buying food which may not always be affordable.

WORLD ECONOMY AND COLONISATION

The advancements in cartography and map making from the sixteenth century onwards were important as they paved the way for later European military and commercial colonisation of the Americas, Asia and Africa. The importance of these developments in cartography is stressed by Heffernan (2003: 11) who comments: 'By representing the huge complexity of a physical and human landscape in a single image, geographers and cartographers provided the European imperial project with arguably its most potent device.' It was during the nineteenth century that European colonisation was to reach its zenith, the expansion being in part a reaction by European nation states to affirm their own power against perceived threats from their neighbours. Moral justification was also lent to colonisation by comparisons to the writings of Charles Darwin by 'social Darwinists', who argued that the principles of natural selection applied as much to the political arena of nation states as much as to individual species. The economic and power inequality that emerged between the world's regions and countries following the onset of the Industrial Revolution also led to new forms of racism and 'culturism', which subsequently provided an excuse for the exploitation of the poor through colonial rule, land acquisition and even slavery (Sachs, 2005).

This argument was also interspersed with the concept of 'environmental determinism', a form of scientific racism which advocated that Europeans and European settler communities in the Americas benefited from unique climatic and environmental circumstances that had created energetic and expansive civilisations. Conversely, the different and challenging climates and environments of the colonial periphery had created inferior societies and weaker civilisations. The economic hegemony and European dominance of most of Africa and large parts of Asia gave rise to the notion that this was the natural world order and the infamous term of 'white man's burden', that is, the right and obligation of European whites to rule the lives of others around the world to 'civilise' them (Sachs, 2005).

The economic system that was established under European colonialism facilitated divergent levels of development between the colonial countries and the colonies. The pattern that developed of raw materials being mined or agricultural produce grown in the countries of Asia, Africa and Latin America for transport to Europe and North America for transformation into high-value manufactured goods has left a legacy of trading patterns that continues today. The economies of colonies were left dependent on the production of low-value raw materials and agricultural products for export, including coffee, tea, cocoa, bananas, tobacco and rubber. In effect, colonisation transformed non-cash economies into ones that had to grow crops for sale in markets. A new system was established where people were forced to grow crops, including coffee, tea, cocoa, bananas, tobacco and rubber for sale, rather than for subsistence. According to Seabrook (2007), the outcome of this process was to make people vulnerable to price fluctuations in the world market, which at times of decline meant they have not the resources to buy back the nourishment they once provided for themselves. It is not difficult to draw parallels between colonialism and neo-liberalism, as in both systems peripheral countries to the developed ones can find themselves drawn into a system of having to produce agricultural products and raw materials for export.

Colonisation and empire thus became a process with which emphasis was placed upon ensuring a constant flow of raw materials, with white settlers being encouraged to colonise the new lands to develop them, and also the Christianising and civilising of indigenous people. Commenting on the effects of this process on African peoples, Maathai (2009: 39) observes that everything that was foreign and arrived with the colonial administration was associated as being: 'more advanced, closer to God's wishes, and in all ways preferable to their previous way of life and values'. The culture of Africa was further affected by colonisation following the Berlin conference of 1885 when the map of Africa was redrawn and split by the European powers into spheres of influence. National identity subsequently became an appendage to the tribal one as groups were 'civilised' and also divided across the new national frontiers; for example, the Maasi in Kenya and Tanzania and the Teso in Kenya and Uganda. These emergent nation states were subsequently given a name, flag and national anthem, to be ruled by Western-educated elites sympathetic to the colonial administration (ibid.) but in reality represented artificial creations of European hegemony.

The beginnings of the end of the colonial era came in 1945 at the end of the Second World War as a new world order was established, with the USA and Soviet Union as the new world military superpowers, and the USA as the world's economic superpower. A combination of influences converged to begin the process of decolonisation, including the weakened economic and military condition of European countries in the immediate post-Second World War period, an increased recognition of the guiding principle of the justice of national self-determination in international politics, and a growing sense of nationalism in many colonised countries. The myth of invincibility of European power had also been heavily challenged during the Second World War, not least by the surrender of the British, the largest empire of the time, to the Japanese during the battle for Singapore.

Whilst a new post-war reality was dawning on the European imperial powers, they sought to ensure that independence was granted on an economically and politically advantageous basis for themselves; for example, through the development of the British Commonwealth and French Union in Africa (Scott, 2005). Nor was the path to independence smooth for all countries. Whilst the British relinquishment of India was largely held to be a success, at least until the partitioning of the Punjab, which led to the deaths of tens of thousands of Muslims and Sikhs, in other countries there were armed conflicts between the colonial rulers and revolutionary groups. For example, there were conflicts with freedom fighters in Kenya between 1952 and 1956 and Malaysia between 1948 and 1960. Similarly, the French attempt to continue with colonial rule in Indo-China led to a prolonged guerrilla war and defeat to the Viet Minh, whilst the war for independence in Algeria between 1954 and 1962 caused up to 45,000 deaths.

Despite a hesitancy and reluctance on the part of the European powers to relinquish colonial territories on anything less than favourable terms, countries in Asia and Africa began to progressively gain their independence. Notable landmarks included India achieving its independence from British rule in 1949 and Ghana becoming the first country in Africa to achieve its political independence in 1957, later to be joined by many other countries in Africa and Asia who had been colonised by European powers. The gaining of independence was accompanied by a growing confidence to challenge the Western international system of political economy that affected their economies but excluded them from their management. It was during the second post-war decade that the developing countries began to find a voice that could be heard on the international stage. Particularly significant in this process was the first international conference of developing countries held at Bandung, Indonesia in 1955. This was the first time that a large bloc of developing countries had met in their own forum vis-à-vis meeting in institutions that were dominated by the North (Spero, 1985). This marked a significant juncture for the LDCs to become more numerous and more outspoken in their demands for international economic reform (ibid.).

GLOBALISATION

Whilst the principle of national self-determination brought at least a theoretical political independence for many countries, the economic dependency of LDCs on the West established during the colonial era retains elements of its legacy today, being transformed into a new format of hegemonic structure through the process of globalisation. The term 'globalisation' has become an increasingly familiar one in many spheres, from the economic to the cultural, particularly since the 1980s. The spread of economic inter-connectedness has been encouraged by neo-liberalism which has permitted an ease of movement of capital and finance across national frontiers for investment purposes. The rapidly increased flows of capital and financial movements have been accompanied by a revolution in information technology, making the technical transference of hundreds of millions of dollars between financial centres in different countries possible through little more than the press of a button, an example of what ex-USA president Bill Clinton meant when he referred to globalisation as the 'world without walls'.

Whilst an agreed definition may be beyond possibility given the divergence of political interests associated with the processes that underwrite globalisation, there are two basic themes of definition: 'the tight economic definition and the broader social definition' (MacGillivray, 2006: 4). The commonality of both trends lies in the multidimensional sets of social processes that are strengthening social and spatial interconnectedness. These processes are emphasised by Mackinnon and Cumbers (2007: 2): 'The term [globalisation] refers to the growing connections and linkages between people and firms located in different places, manifested in increased flows of goods, services, money, information and people across national and continental borders.' As was discussed briefly in Chapter 2 in the context of neo-liberalism, the support for economic globalisation was in part driven by the failure of previous development strategies, especially those that had relied on import-substitution and foreign aid (Stephan *et al.*, 2006). The rationale of import-substitution, implemented in many parts of Africa, Asia and South America in the 1950s was to satisfy the demand for foreign goods by replacing them with locally produced substitutes. It was hoped that this would kick-start industrialisation and lift developing countries from an economic dependence on agricultural goods. Just as import-substitution policy was seen as a failure, similarly the impact of foreign aid on economic growth had become increasingly discredited by the mid-1980s (Spero, 1985).

Central to globalisation is an increase in the inter-connectivity of places across space at a rate that has not been previously witnessed. This has been facilitated by the creation of 'space-shrinking' technologies' since the 1960s, particularly in the realms of transport and communications, reducing the distances between places in terms of time, in a process referred to as 'time–space' compression. The adoption of new innovation – for example, jet travel and mobile phones – by hundreds of millions of people has contributed to a process of mass market globalisation, increased competition and a subsequent reduction in price, intensifying and deepening processes of globalisation. The first era of a marked process of 'time–space' compression can be traced to the end of the nineteenth century through inventions that arose from the Industrial Revolution, including railways, steamships, telegraph and telephones. Advancements in infrastructure and technology during this time made round-the-world trips possible for rich Westerners and one-way trips for millions of working-class migrants from Europe to the United States also became a possibility (MacGillivray, 2006).

The influence of the railways in this first era of time–space compression in the nineteenth century had a marked significance for society and tourism. Besides being instrumental to the Industrial Revolution, by moving coal from the coal-fields to the factories to power the steam engines to drive industrial machinery, the railways were a major force in eroding localism and removing barriers to mobility, bringing together different regions of countries and eventually different countries within Europe. During the nineteenth century, the railways were also instrumental in developing tourism in Europe, the USA and Australia. As Hobsbawm (1962: 60) points out: 'No innovation of the Industrial Revolution has fired the imagination as much as the railway.' The construction of the railway system was vital to the development of coastal and mountain areas for tourism and also organised domestic and international tours, notably those associated with Thomas Cook.

Whilst there are similarities between the contemporary period of globalisation and the one at the end of the nineteenth century, the geographical reach of today's stage is significantly further, and the depth of relationships greater. The combination of the creation of a global economic market following the end of the Cold War and the rise of neo-liberalism, the rapid advancements in information technology since the 1970s, and the technology to support ever faster and mass travel or 'hyper-mobility' are transforming the world at a rate never witnessed before. It is particularly the micro-electronics revolution since the 1970s that has irrevocably changed the essence of human contact on Earth, shrinking distances and the sending of information increasingly quickly (Ellwood, 2001). New information and communication technologies (ICTs), notably the Internet, email and mobile phones, have taken the level of inter-connectivity of people and places to a new level. Alongside new freedoms of information sharing and communication they have also facilitated mobility; for example, airline and hotel reservations can be made from one's living room or bedroom. Accompanying the revolutionary developments in information technology has been the rapid expansion in aviation since the mid-twentieth century. The advent of the jet engine and the 'space-shrinking' that has accompanied it has offered people the chance to go to more places and more quickly than at any time in history. The importance of aviation for tourism cannot be overstated with 51 per cent of the 940 million international travellers in 2010 arriving at their destination by air (UNWTO, 2012).

The outcome of these economic and ITC processes is that many places in the world have become progressively integrated into an inter-connected system within which the economic and social changes of one place will induce changes in another place. There exists a common consensus that advances in transport and telecommunications has progressively made the world into a 'global village' that has integrated production, trade, finance, politics and culture. For Castells (1996) these developments signify the end of place, as space has become occupied by flows: flows of people, information and goods, increasingly breaking down the barriers that have previously made places distinct and different. There is then in Castells's (ibid.) and other commentators' view a trend towards a homogenisation of culture based on Western values, as Ellwood (2001: 9) puts it: 'Disney movies are children's fodder the world over. Barbie dolls, fast-food restaurants, hip-hop music and corporate driven, American style youth culture attract millions of new converts from the *bidenvilles* of Abidjan, Cote d'Ivoire, to the wealthy suburbs of Sydney.' Similarly Mowforth and Munt (2009) suggest that cultural globalisation is little more than a shorthand for a single global culture of consumerism defined by a US lifestyle.

However, there is another school of thought of the role of place in globalisation that emphasises that it is place differences that are the cause and effect of place inter-connectedness. This concept is certainly applicable to patterns of contemporary tourism in which a primary reason for travel is the difference in the character of place of the destination compared to 'home'. Closely associated with the theme of heightened inter-connectivity is heightened interdependency. The relevance of interdependency to world trade and inequalities between countries has been historically traced by Wallenstein in his world systems theory to the seventeenth century. Although a complex theory, in essence Wallenstein recognises the emergence of a new 'world system' from the sixteenth century onwards, within which the world consisted of four key groupings: the core, semi-periphery, periphery and external. In the expansion of global trade, the core states benefited the most and developed institutions to maximise the advantages of commerce, including bureaucracies and armies; for example, in England and France. The nations in the semi-periphery grew rich through the control of trade – for example, Spain and Portugal – but failed to develop the manufacturing industries that would have permitted them to retain their wealth. The role of the nations in the periphery was to provide the raw materials for the commerce that was controlled by the core, hence they had a strong dependency on the core nations. The last group of the external nations maintained a strong central state that led them to maintain their own relatively closed economic systems and be largely independent of the main networks of international trade; for example, Russia and China were archetypal of this category, that is, until the end of the Cold War and their progressive economic integration into the global economic system.

For Harvey (1989) the whole process of economic globalisation and compression of time and space is driven by a desire of capitalists to break down political and geographical barriers to permit them to expand their economic relationships to all parts of the globe. This desire was also evident in the imperialism of globalisation that marked the end of the nineteenth century, personified in the speech of Cecil Rhodes, one of Britain's most forthright imperial spokesman: 'We must find new lands from which we can easily obtain raw materials and at the same time exploit the cheap slave labour that is available from the natives of the colonies. The colonies [will] also provide a dumping ground for the surplus goods produced in our factories.' Thus geographic expansion can be understood as a pre-requisite for the continuation of capitalism, an ideology and economic system that requires new markets and suppliers of labour and raw materials. However, it is not purely the spread of geographical inter-connectedness of places that is a feature of globalisation but the growing intensity of these connections.

The strengthening of Western-centric global economic and political structures through supranational agencies and multinational companies gives rise to questions and debate about the extent that people can retain control and direction over their own lives. Multinational companies can move their production between nation states to places where they will gain a competitive market advantage – for example, through labour costs and workforce skills – as they wish. In the neo-liberal framework that emphasises the comparative advantage of countries and economic development, a great danger for the poor is that for some countries their comparative advantage becomes one of low labour costs and weak employee rights and legislation. The economic importance of multinational players on the world stage is underlined by statistics, that is, they account for 25 to 33 per cent of world economic output, 70 per cent of world trade, and 80 per cent of international investment (McGrew and Held, 2007).

For the world's poor, being agents of their own future is often difficult in the face of globalisation and neo-liberalism, as these processes have created a growing gap in inequality between regions of the world and within nations as was discussed in Chapter 1. An example of the barriers of political economy and difficulties of practice that a nation state can face in attempting to gain its place in world markets and develop its economies is given in Box 4.1, in a case study of Mali.

BOX 4.1 BARRIERS AND PROBLEMS TO ECONOMIC GROWTH IN MALI

The case of Mali illustrates the difficulty of LDCs becoming internationally competitive in export markets for products beyond traditional primary commodities, which stops them lending an added value to raw materials. A combination of factors have hindered economic development in Mali, including: (i) its geographical position as a 'landlocked' country with no coastal access to the sea for trade; (ii) health problems, including high levels of malaria, tuberculosis, HIV/AIDS; (iii) a geomorphology and climate, which with fragile soils and erratic rainfall contributes to low agricultural and food productivity; (iv) a lack of available fossil fuels that places a heavy reliance on imports; (vi) a small population means that the domestic market is very limited; and (vii) low levels of education and skills amongst its population restrict its attractiveness for inward investment.

The United Nations Development Programme (UNDP) suggest that Mali could become a successful garment exporter, processor of tropical agricultural products and tourist destination. However, to achieve success in any of these economic activities, including tourism, it is necessary to improve health, education and infrastructure, including water, sanitation, roads and power supplies. As a consequence of the country being far too poor to make these investments by itself, it is necessary that wealthier partner countries of the United Nations provide the financing and investment for economic development.

Source: after UNDP (2003)

The defence of growing wealth and social inequalities as an outcome of globalisation is weak; for example, a defense of a model of inequality is sometimes made on the basis that it is acceptable if those at the bottom feel they can also make it, having the aspiration and hope to reach the top (Bhagwati, 2007). Whilst this variant of the 'American Dream' may have appeal, for the majority of the poor at the bottom of the heap there is a lack of capacity and opportunity to make it to the top. The 'Dream' is an 'Illusion', within which they are disillusioned by the inequalities of globalisation. Proponents of globalisation often support it on the basis that wealth inequality does not matter if the people at the bottom are gaining materially, an absolute approach to poverty reduction, as is discussed in the pro-poor section of Chapter 5. Whilst this may have a justification for lifting people out of absolute poverty, it does little to promote civil harmony and values in society, an ideal that is often discussed as a criterion of a truly developed society.

Whilst neo-liberalists would argue that income inequality has fallen between countries since 1980, Shah and McIver (2006: 110) point out that this is purely due to rising incomes in China. They also highlight that China's approach to capitalism is anything but neo-liberal, as the state has actively invested in and created industries, protected them against foreign imports, and allowed them time to develop. Disputes also exist about the rates of economic growth that have been created by neo-liberalism. Whilst it is indisputable that during the last 40 years the majority of the world's population has become wealthier, the best average economic growth period within the capitalist system is disputed. For example, Shah and McIver (ibid.) observe that within the time-frame of a neo-liberal driven economy, the world's average economic growth rate has only been 1.5 per cent per annum, compared to the era of managed capitalism between 1960 and 1978 when global average economic growth per annum was 2.7 per cent. The sceptics of globalisation subsequently argue that it is a useful political myth to emphasise that free trade, an integral part of globalisation as is discussed in the next section of this chapter, can create prosperity and reduce poverty. In their perception it masks the reality of an increasing gap between the rich and the poor, within and between countries. For the critics, state intervention is essential to control the excesses of financial markets and to regulate multinationals, an argument strengthened by the global financial crisis of 2008.

It is evident that whilst globalisation may lead to increased levels of trade and create wealth, not every place or people within places are treated in a uniform or equal manner. The global flows of commodities, finance and people have and will affect places in different ways as they interact with local economies, cultures and communities. Whilst Friedman (2005) asserts that the advancement in information technologies helps to bring people together in equal terms through the opportunities it creates, the world has inherited inequalities of wealth. Thus the characteristics of place, including those of labour – for example, wage rates and skills – and culturally specific values and beliefs remain important in determining how a particular place will interact with the globalisation process. Economic development retains a geographic unevenness with uneven development being an internal feature of the capitalist economy, reflecting the tendency for growth and investment to become concentrated in particular localities. The use of tourism for poverty reduction displays similar properties, as the extent of its use as a means of economic development for the poor will vary between places, dependent upon the environmental, cultural and human characteristics of place and their strength to attract tourists.

The integration of people into a global market has also been criticised by opponents of globalisation. For example, Seabrook (2007) interprets this as a direct attack on the poor, to ensure that there is little opportunity for self-reliance outside the market system. Thus resource poverty is transformed into income poverty, removing control that people may have over their land and what they produce. Additionally, in the absence of land rights, the poor are vulnerable to unethical land capture by the more powerful, as exemplified in the case of the Kalpitya fishermen in Box 4.2.

BOX 4.2 KALPITYA FISHERMEN, TOURISM DEVELOPMENT AND RESOURCE LOSS

The issue of land 'grab' and capture is demonstrated by the case of the Kalpitya fishermen in Sri Lanka following the end of the civil war in 2009. Approximately 10,000 fishermen from the Puttlam district in north-west Sri Lanka reside or migrate to the 14 islands that are known as the Kalpitya islands that provide productive fishing grounds. After the tragic Asian tsunami in 2004, a Task Force for Rebuilding the Nation (TAFREN) was established, being composed mainly of key investment financiers in the tourism industry, who identified 15 new tourism zones of which Kalpitya was one. However, the planning of the development has taken place in the absence of the consultation and participation of regional and local stakeholders. The proposed development involves acquiring 1,200 hectares of land and the building of 17 hotels with a total of 10,000 beds, the main market being for weekend breaks from Singapore, with a typical itinerary having tourists arriving on a Friday, playing golf and watching a cultural dance on a Saturday, then after an Ayurvedic treatment returning to Singapore on Sunday.

According to Tourism Concern (2012), the decision to develop has not involved the participation of local officials, politicians, religious leaders, cooperatives or local communities, including the fishermen, having been taken by central government. This has caused disquiet amongst local politicians and the effect on the local fishing communities is exemplified in this voice of discontent: 'We do not know anything about these developments. People come from outside and claim the land belongs to them. They want to build tourist hotels here. What will happen to us? What will happen to our children? What will happen to our livelihoods? Where should we go when we lived here for generations? Who is responsible for this type of development?'

The fishing communities are worried about being displaced from their traditional lands and the loss of their customary rights as a consequence of tourism development. Three of the islands have already been leased for 99 years to developers and tenders have been put out for a further five. The effect on the fishing communities has already been felt, with tourism developers having encroached onto some of the islands and erected barbed wire fences, meaning the fishermen cannot operate their beach seines [fishing areas]. One fisherman commented: 'I cannot go to my beach seine as the tourist developer says it is within his territory. We have been here for genera-tions. My father and forefathers were engaged here for beach seine fishing. These newcomers say this land belongs to them.'

The National Fisheries Solidarity Movement (NAFSO) is helping the fishermen to lobby the government in an attempt to defend their rights and also for environmental protection. For example, one of the proposals involves building a five-star hotel on a mangrove swamp where fish spawn, which besides threatening the future of the fish stocks also threatens the ecosystem services of mangroves that act as barriers to tsunamis and other associated climate threats. The tourism development is also threatening cultural and religious prac-tices with reported cases of access to the sea, mosques, temples and churches having been lost. The seriousness of the situation is underlined by threats to local people from the military, the National Intelligence Bureau and the police.

A further example of this type of land capture can be traced to the 1980s, when the Malaysian government decided to develop the island of Langkawi off the west coast of peninsular Malaysia as their flagship tourism destination. A decision was made to develop a tourism complex at a beautiful bay named Tanjung Rhu for a total cost of US$1 billion in 1980s prices. The bay was chosen because of its outstanding beauty, including casuarina trees, a high-quality beach, crystal clear lagoons and waterways (Bird, 1989). The effect of this development upon one local farmer is narrated by Seabrook (2007: 56) who recounts the farmer's view of how his land was taken by compulsory government purchase for a golf course development: 'The only people in the world who are truly free are those who can grow their own food. My land has yielded a harvest ever since anyone can remember. Next year it will give its last harvest – a handful of dollars. After that it will be barren and my family will be poor.' In the case of Langkawi, the tourism development scheme failed as the development company went bankrupt, leaving a trail of environmental destruction in its wake.

Critics of economic globalisation suggest that an international mobile elite has gained from globalisation but for the majority globalisation has not been so posi-tive, with a core of people having been excluded from market benefits entirely as exemplified through the case of Langkawi. For Lines (2008) the extent of this marginalisation embraces both poor countries and the poorest people in other countries. Criticisms have also been made of a downward suppression on wages and the conditions of employment for workers. The global workforce has doubled in size through the entry of China, India and the former Soviet Union into market capitalism. Whilst opportunities for people to be part of a global labour force are to be welcomed if they help lift them out of poverty and improve livelihoods, without protection of their rights, a global system of free and easy movement of capital is open to exploitation by the controllers of capital. In this system, multi-national companies are free to locate to where there is a pool of skilled labour with the lowest wage costs in an attempt to maximise their profits. In countries where there exists a lack of employment legislation or protection of workers' rights, the work force will be open to exploitation by the controllers of capital. Not only may they face poor working conditions, long hours and low pay but there is a knock-on effect of the loss of employment opportunities in countries where better working conditions and higher wage levels have been achieved after decades of political struggle for equality. The resultant effect is that the divide or gap between the wealthy and the poor will increase, even if the workforce in developing countries experiences an increase in actual income.

TRADE LIBERALISATION, FREE TRADE AND TOURISM

A central component of globalisation, and certainly one that has created heightened political controversy over its effects on development and poverty, is 'free trade', based on the principles of a free market system and neo-classical economics. As a central part of economic globalization, there is a consequential belief in the unbridled role of the market system by its proponents, a type of 'market fundamentalism'. The central argument of free trade is one that is drawn from the classical economists of David Ricardo and Adam Smith, based upon concepts of specialisation, comparative advantage and the free movement of goods. The basis of the argument put forward by Ricardo of comparative advantage is that every country in the world has an economic advantage of some kind in which they should specialise, leading to an optimal utilisation of scarce resources (Holden, 2005). The aim of free trade is to secure the benefits of international specialisation (Pass *et al.*, 2000), with each country specialising in a certain number of economic activities for which it possesses the best natural and human resources. In theory, specialisation enables an economy to make the most efficient use of its scarce resources, thereby producing and consuming a larger value of goods and services than would otherwise be the case (ibid.), benefiting the maximum number of people.

Through trading, each country could specialise in what they are best able to do and maximise their resources, rather than trying to produce everything they need. Using the analogy of the family, Mankilis (2001) points out that although families are competitive with each other – for example, for employment or shopping – it is unlikely a family would be better off by isolating itself from other families and markets. If it did, they would have to grow their own food, build their own shelter and make their own clothes. Hence, it is advantageous for the family to trade with others to meet their needs and wants. In theory, trade allows each individual to specialise in the activity they do best and most efficiently, whether as a car mechanic, window cleaner, doctor or farmer. Similarly, it can be argued that as international tourism demand for the natural and cultural resources of LDCs is growing faster than for other countries, they should specialise in tourism. Whilst there is a logic in this argument, it is the framework of liberalisation and conditions for free trade that arouses most controversy and criticism. Liberalisation encourages the removal of any measures that a national government may wish to pursue to protect its own industries, such as tariffs, quotas or foreign exchange controls, and encourages the deregulation of its economy, removing any restrictions on the foreign establishment, ownership, employment of personnel, and remittances.

The aim of liberalisation and deregulation is the creation of a 'free market' that operates at a global level, in the case of tourism, this will mean that foreign-owned and -run companies will have freer access to domestic markets under the same trading conditions that exist for local companies of the host country. Whilst the concept of a global society maximising its scarce resources may seem beneficial, the opening of a country's tourism industry to unlimited inward investment and foreign control raises a range of economic issues, not least where the majority of the economic benefits will rest, as was illustrated in the case of neo-liberalism and Kenya's tourism industry in Box 2.2. As Badger *et al.* (1996: 14) point out: 'Yet, whereas an export-led trade such as tourism does have potential for economic growth, the accrued benefits for the host nation will depend on where the profits go, who controls the tourism industry, and what is perceived by those in power as the crucial indicator of economic growth: either another development of a casino hotel for tourists or a clean and efficient water supply for local residents.' It can be argued that the issue of control of resources is more acute for tourism than for other industries because the resources being traded are a country's natural and cultural resources.

The issue of the control of resources revives the debate of external hegemonic power inherent to dependency theory. Whilst colonialism may have disappeared, the role and power of multinationals is often equated to a new variant of it with the role of multinationals in tourism being evident through hotel chains, airlines and tour operators. They become involved in tourism in LDCs in different ways, including direct investment and ownership, equity participation, hotel leasing and through management contracts. Tour operators may occasionally own hotels in a destination but more frequently lease rooms from a hotel for a certain period of the year. As Badger *et al.* (1996: 22) comment: 'Power is increasingly resting in the hands of these large northern-based companies, who can direct flows of international tourists to particular destinations because of their high-tech globalised reservation systems. An estimated 80 per cent of all tourists travel with a tour operator package, so it is easy to appreciate the power of the tour operator vis-à-vis the host country.' Although there has been a strong market trend towards independent travel since the time of Badger's (ibid.) critique of the tourism industry, control of international transport systems, hotel ownership and reservation systems, and additional services such as car rentals remain in the hands of companies of the developed countries.

Other economic problems can arise from economic specialisation at a national level, particularly if an over-dependency on one sector is created. In the discussion of tourism's contribution to GDP and employment generation in Chapter 2, it was noted that an over-dependence upon tourism creates a high degree of vulnerability in an economy given tourism demand's susceptibility to external events such as economic recession, political upheaval and natural disasters. Bhagwati (2007) similarly draws attention to the dangers of over-dependence of a country upon one economic sector. He argues that whilst an outward-trade orientation helped the Far Eastern economies of Taiwan and South Korea in the post-war years to export labour-intensive goods, which added to employment and reduced poverty rapidly, there is the possibility of 'immiserizing growth'. The basis of Bhagwati's argument is that export-led economies with a high reliance on one export may increase production to a level which eventually leads to a depression in the international price, as supply outpaces demand. A parallel can be drawn with tourism, where an over-supply of accommodation will result in decreased prices in the destination if increases in demand fail to keep pace with increases in supply. Over development may also result in environmental problems which will depress demand and prices even further.

Bhagwati (ibid.) subsequently emphasises the need for economies to diversify their economic base to avoid an 'economic mono-culture'. In the case of tourism and its economic relationships with the poor, serious consideration needs to be given to its use as an additional economic activity from which to gain income, rather than a replacement for traditional industries such as fishing and agriculture in which the poor have traditionally been most heavily employed. As the earlier example of the farmer in Langkawi who had lost his land to tourism development illustrates, the poor have a strong reliance for their survival upon the reliability of being able to grow their own crops for food. Alongside a differentiation of place there is also likely to be a differentiation of benefits between people in communities that develop tourism. Those individuals with access to capital and the ability to invest in the tourism industry are likely to benefit whilst people who are working in the peripheral (informal) businesses may be marginalised, seeing little economic benefits from tourism as they are denied access to the tourism market. This is often the case where the poor get little access to tourists when their movements are highly regulated by larger tourism businesses and operators.

Similar to globalisation there are significant criticisms of the free trade system. The political criticisms of the benefits for the multinationals have been referred to and similar criticisms relate to its consumer-driven approach. For example, Gilpin (2001: 198) stresses that the emphasis of neo-liberalism is to benefit the consumer by reducing price and increasing consumer choice, which in turn should increase levels of economic demand and growth. An evident issue is the sustainability of such a model in a finite world of natural resources, and the scientifically proven inability of the earth's environmental systems to cope with the pressure of dealing with the quantities of waste materials and products that a consumer-driven system generates. Ethical issues of consumer benefits within this system are also well versed, relating to workers' rights and conditions in developing and LDC countries.

Criticisms also relate to the present rules of a world trade system that ensures that poor countries have to open their markets to rich countries but not vice versa (Shah and McIver, 2006). Stiglitz and Charlton (2007) argue that the world trading system requires wholesale reform, not least in the developed countries that permit protection of their own industries, particularly agriculture. They point out that the United States government subsides the production of cotton in America by several US$ billions per annum instead of importing it from Africa at half the price. Similar allegations can be laid against the agriculturally subsidised products of the European Union which subsidises its sugar beet industry when sugar can be produced much more cheaply in warmer climates. The subsidies of the production of this crop encourage the production of a surplus which is subsequently placed into the world market for sugar, reducing prices and consequently reducing the economic and financial benefits for producers in LDCs.

There are further criticisms of the duplicity of trade liberalisation measures taken by developed economies. In essence this relates to developed countries having negotiated reductions in the tariffs and subsidies for the goods for which they lack a comparative advantage but have failed to implement the same for goods and services where developing countries have the advantage. This means that it is easier for developed countries to sell their goods and services in the markets of developing countries than it is for the developing countries to sell their goods and services in the markets of developed countries. This stance ironically makes it difficult for the production of agricultural exports by developing countries, often something that has been adopted by LDCs to meet the terms of SAPs, as this activity is, however, hampered by tariff and non-tariff barriers applied by developing countries. As the IBRD (2009: 75) comment: 'But rich countries often impose their highest barriers specifically on the exports of developing countries, especially agricultural products. In addition to tariff production, they provide subsidies and often forms of support to domestic producers.' In the case of tourism, there are far fewer restrictions or trade barriers to the involvement of developing countries in the world trade system compared to manufactured and agricultural goods. However, it is difficult for any country to enter into the international market given the force of control of the international tourism industry by multinational players as was exemplified in the case of Fiji in Box 2.4.

SUMMARY

- The origins of a recognisable international trade system and enhanced inter-connectivity of places can be traced to the fifteenth century, as a changing European world perspective, combined with advances in shipping technology, led to an age of voyages, discovery and the formulation of a world geographical image. This advancement culminated in the production of the first world atlas in the sixteenth century and an understanding of how the world's land masses are linked by great oceans. This had ramifications for an emergent world trade as sea-faring nations such as Spain, Portugal, Netherlands, France and England constructed trading links with parts of the 'New World'. Patterns of world trade were established between agricultural producers and European traders who brought back tropical crops such as coffee, sugar, cocoa, tea and sugar cane.

- Geographical exploration became linked to the rise of large trading companies, capitalism and colonialism. By linking places through trade, an inter-dependency has been created based on the exchange of goods and services and more people have been integrated into international markets. Subsequently, poverty has become increasingly related to the world economy, rather than solely the natural resources of place; and different cultures have increasingly adopted a Western approach to poverty that no longer understands it as a natural state but rather as a problem that demands a solution. The European colonisation of large parts of Africa and Asia led to a system of trade where colonised countries exported raw materials to European countries which were used to manufacture goods that were then exported back and sold in the countries producing the raw materials. This led to marked differences in levels of development between the countries of Europe and those of Africa and Asia, and established a trade pattern that still exists today.

- Since the beginnings of the end of colonialism in the aftermath of the Second World War, the processes of globalisation have become much stronger. At least two main strands are recognisable: economic and cultural globalisation. The spread of economic inter-connectedness has been encouraged by neo-liberalism which has permitted an ease of movement of capital and finance across national frontiers for investment purposes. This has been accompanied by the creation of 'space-shrinking' technologies, particularly in the realms of transport and communications, reducing the distances between places in terms of time, in a process referred to as 'time–space' compression and given rise of the concept of the 'global village'. However, there is another school of thought about the role of place in globalisation that emphasises that it is place differences that are the cause and effect of place interconnectedness. This concept is certainly applicable to patterns of contemporary tourism in which a primary reason for travel is the difference in the character of place of the destination compared to 'home'. The adoption of new innovation – for example, jet travel and mobile phones – by hundreds of millions of people has contributed to a process of mass market globalisation, increased competition and price recession, intensifying adoption and deepening processes of globalisation. Critics of economic globalisation suggest that an international mobile elite has gained from globalisation but for the majority globalisation has not been so positive, with many people having been excluded from market benefits.

- Whilst globalisation may lead to increased levels of trade and create wealth, places and people are not treated in a uniform or equal manner. Global flows of commodities, finance and people affect places in different ways as they interact with local economies, cultures and communities. The characteristics of place, including those of labour – for example, wage rates and skills, – culturally specific values and beliefs, remain important in determining how a particular place will interact with the globalisation process. Economic growth retains a geographic unevenness, an internal feature of the capitalist economy, reflecting the tendency for growth and investment to become concentrated in particular localities. The use of tourism for poverty reduction displays similar characteristics, as the extent of its use as a means of economic development for the poor will vary between places, dependent upon the environmental and cultural characteristics of place and their strength to attract tourists.

- A central component of globalisation and certainly one that has created most political controversy over its effects on development and poverty is 'free trade'. The aim of free trade is to secure the benefits of international specialisation, with each country specialising in a certain number of economic activities for which it possesses the best natural and human resources. Whilst the concept of a global society maximising its scarce resources may seem beneficial, the opening of a country's tourism industry to unlimited inward investment and foreign control raises a range of economic issues, not least where the majority of the economic benefits will rest. It can be argued that the issue of control of resources is more acute for tourism than for other industries because the resources being traded are a country's biodiversity and cultures.

5 Critiquing tourism and poverty reduction

This chapter:

- Reviews tourism and poverty reduction policy initiatives
- Evaluates pro-poor growth, pro-poor tourism and ST-EP
- Analyses how tourism can impact on the poor

INTRODUCTION

For tourism to be used as an effective means for poverty reduction it is essential that it overcomes barriers of place, geography or political economy that may arrest the integration of the poor into the process of economic development. The key aim of this chapter is to subsequently review and evaluate the key policy initiatives that have been taken to date to integrate tourism into the poverty reduction and alleviation agenda. Reflecting on how the tourism industry may or may not offer economic benefits to the poor, Nobel Peace Prize winner, and unfortunately now deceased, Wangari Maathai gives an interesting insight through her own observation of tourism and poverty in Yaoundé in Cameroon. As the Goodwill Ambassador for the Congo Basin Forest Ecosystem, she was visiting the Commission for the Forests of Central Africa (COMIFAC), staying in a luxury hotel on one of the hills overlooking the city. She describes looking across from the hotel to observe a group of farmers on a hillside, farming on a very steep slope using methods that would result in soil erosion when the rains arrived. Reflecting on this situation, she comments: 'I wondered how much of the revenue of the hotel – which was owned by a foreign corporation – was making its way into the government coffers, and then, in turn, how much of that money the government was investing in its agricultural sector, including in an extension service, that could educate the woman and assist her in farming more sustainably' (Maathai, 2009: 15). This poignant observation of Maathai's highlights key issues and questions of how tourism can be best used as part of a strategy for poverty reduction and how it may play an active role in capacity building and creating livelihood opportunities, a similar situation to that of the disjuncture between tourism and poverty that exists in Cape Town as discussed in Box 5.1.

BOX 5.1 TOURISM AND POVERTY IN CAPE TOWN

Cape Town in South Africa has been voted the world's top tourist destination, possessing beautiful beaches, fashionable suburbs and great cuisine. However, the millions of tourists that arrive through the smart airport are quickly exposed to the shanty towns that flank the motorway to Table Mountain. The marginalised situation of the poor led Xola Skosana, a political activist, to go on hunger strike for a month to protest about their living conditions and the inequality of the society. In direct relevance to the relationship between tourism and poverty, he commented: 'It is interesting to me that a woman would make up a bed in a five star hotel then come home to sleep on the floor . . . or cook the best meal for someone else and come back to live off a slice of bread.' The conditions of the poor are those that typify poverty, including flimsy dwellings with no electricity, no running water and no sanitation. As one of the residents living in Khayelitsha, Cape Town's biggest township, commented: 'There's been no change since 1994 [the end of apartheid]. We're still hungry, we are still living in a dirty place', whilst another resident commented: 'Cape Town is largely for the benefit and entertainment of tourists.'

Source: after Smith, 2011

The need for the tourism industry in LDCs to provide benefits for the poor is similarly emphasised by Seabrook (2007: 21) in the following passage:

> The world which the rich make their play-ground is crafted to the picturesque and scenic; even some of the poorest countries now promote themselves as tourist destinations. The Gambia, Tanzania, South Africa and Kenya are promoted for their clear waters, dramatic wildlife and stunning scenery. These are also places where millions are dying of AIDS, where violent crime is commonplace and pitiless social injustice prevails. But this does not impinge upon the enjoyments which the well-to-do purchase for themselves.

In the scenario of the model of tourism portrayed by Seabrook, tourism is likely to bring few benefits for the poor, instead segregating and marginalising them to ensure that environments are not spoilt for tourists. Nevertheless, the desire of some of the poorest countries to promote themselves as tourist destinations is reflective of a now established awareness that tourism has the potential to help achieve economic growth and development. Progressing beyond securing macro-economic benefits from tourism, any government that has the moral conviction and political desire to provide opportunities for its nation's poor and reduce the incidence and indecency of poverty needs to rationalise how it can utilise tourism in a positive manner to progress human development and address the types of social problems exemplified by Seabrook (ibid.).

Given the comparative advantage of the natural and cultural resources for tourism in many LDCs, and the emphasis for the World Bank and IMF on Poverty Reduction Strategies (PRSs), governments need to identify how to utilise tourism development to maximise its positive impact for creating livelihood opportunities for the poor (Roe *et al.*, 2004; UNEP/UNWTO, 2005; Goodwin, 2006; Novelli and Hellwig, 2011). As was commented on in Chapter 2, tourism's potential to reduce poverty is supported by its economic importance in LDCs, being the primary source of foreign exchange earnings in 46 of the 49 poorest nations (UNWTO, 2009: 1). However, whilst the measurement of tourism's macro-economic impacts permits a comparative analysis with other economic sectors, there is an absence of empirical data to demonstrate its contribution to poverty at the micro-level, the traditional praxis resting upon an assumption that local people will automatically benefit through conventional systems of the trickle-down and multiplier processes (Roe *et al.*, 2004).

As was referred to in Chapter 2, the linking of tourism to poverty reduction is a recent addition to the development debate, becoming a policy consideration since the start of the millennium. Whilst this is in part a consequence of a lack of understanding of the potential role of tourism in poverty reduction, it is also attributable to a perception of the characteristics of conventional tourism development, including control by local elites and transnational corporations, negative environmental and social impacts, and high economic leakages (Torres and Momsen, 2004). However, the World Bank policy shift at the end of the 1990s away from SAPs to PRSs has refocused thinking on to tourism as a tool for poverty reduction. The evolution of a policy framework for tourism's use for poverty reduction can be attributed to three key sources. It has been advocated through the United Nations World Tourism Organisation (UNWTO) 'Sustainable Tourism – Eliminating Poverty Program' (ST-EP); the United Kingdom's Department for International Development's (DFID) 'Pro-Poor Tourism' (PPT) policy; and the work of the Netherlands Agency for International Development (SNV). Within both PPT and ST-EP, emphasis is placed upon putting the poor at the centre of the development process (Scheyvens, 2002, 2003; Sofield, 2003; Easterling, 2005; Sharpley, 2009). As a key agency in placing tourism within the poverty reduction agenda,

DFID developed the construct of PPT towards the end of the 1990s, building on the concept of 'pro-poor growth', which symbolised the re-orientation of development towards Poverty Reduction Strategies. From the concept of pro-poor growth emerged 'pro-poor tourism', which was first used by the management consultancy firm of Deloitte and Touche in a report for DFID on sustainable livelihoods in South Africa at the end of the 1990s. Both pro-poor growth and PPT are indicative of a changing paradigm in development thinking which is explained and evaluated in the next section of the chapter.

PRO-POOR GROWTH AND PRO-POOR TOURISM

Similar to the concept of development, as to what 'pro-poor growth' is and how it should be achieved is a hotly debated issue (Kakwani and Pernia, 2000). Since the dominance of the 'trickle-down effect' in development thinking in the 1950s to 1960s, the poor have had an absent or at best indirect place in development policy. As Kakwani and Pernia (2000: 2) comment, trickle-down theory is built on the premise of a vertical income flow from the rich to the poor, a process that 'happens of its own accord'. They also observe that the poor are at the bottom of the food chain, thus 'the proportional benefits of growth going to the poor will always be less' (ibid.: 2).

The failure of trickle-down theory and neo-liberalism to lift the bottom 1 million out of poverty has necessitated a re-think in economic approaches to development. Unmanaged laissez-faire economic development, operating within the existing structures of society, in the spirit of the free market and Adam Smith's 'invisible hand', has bypassed bringing benefits to the chronically poor. Unmanaged economic growth may increase poverty by marginalising the poor even further. For example, affluent farmers may increase their grain production by purchasing new seeds which in turn may result in lower grain prices in a situation of over-supply. The effect on the more marginal farmers who do not possess the resources to attain the seeds is that their static grain yield produces even less income (Bhagwati, 1988, cited in Kakwani and Pernia, 2000).

The significant difference in pro-poor growth compared to traditional development strategies is that economic growth is orientated towards the poor, rather than assuming they will eventually be beneficiaries of economic growth per se. This approach is summarised in the definition of pro-poor growth by Kakwani and Pernia (2000: 3): 'as one that enables the poor to actively participate in and significantly benefit from economic activity'. DFID (2004) similarly stress the usefulness of the concept because of its emphasis on aligning economic growth with positive changes in the well-being of the poor, combining both 'pro-growth' and 'pro-poor' policies. They also emphasise the benefits of the duality of this relationship, as whilst increased growth can help to reduce poverty, reducing poverty also helps to increase growth though improving people's capabilities and making them more productive members of the workforce. This sentiment is summarised in the following statement from DFID (2004: 2): 'giving the poor access to assets and markets contributes to growth for the simple reason that it allows more of a country's resources – its people – to become more productive. Pro-poor growth strategies therefore enable poor people to participate in, as well as benefit from, the growth process.'

Whilst there is little dispute about the ethos of PPG, that the poor should be active in and significantly benefit from economic development, there is a divergence of views upon the prioritisation of either 'absolute' or relative benefits that are accrued by the poor. This is not surprising as these two types of benefits can be interpreted as reflecting different political ideologies and world-views about the importance of the equity of distribution of resources in society. A relative para-digm is centred upon a comparison of the changes in the incomes of the poor compared to those of the non-poor. Within this definition, growth can only be held as being pro-poor when the distributional shifts accompanying income growth favour the poor, that is, the incomes of poor people are growing faster than the rest of the population, leading to a subsequent reduction in income inequality within society. By contrast, in an 'absolute' definition economic growth is considered to be pro-poor if poor people benefit in absolute terms, against an agreed measure of poverty, typically income. In this scenario, the extent to which growth is held to be pro-poor depends on the rate of change in poverty as measured by how fast the incomes of the poor are rising. This absolute definition is the one operationalised by the World Bank on the rationale of 'maximising poverty reduction' (World Bank, 2012: 1), and also by DFID on the rationale of 'emphasising growth in the incomes of poor people' (DFID, 2004: 2).

The World Bank's rationale for selecting an absolute definition of pro-poor growth over the relative one is that focusing on inequality in wealth distribution could lead to sub-optimal households, that is, economic growth may not be fully realised because of a policy emphasis on the distribution of wealth. It is argued that a government or society prioritising a relative definition of pro-poor growth could favour a lower overall rate of economic growth provided that poor house-holds were benefiting proportionally more than average, making poor households worse off in real terms. For example, if a strategy for pro-poor growth was achieving an average income growth rate of 2 per cent and the average income growth of poor households was 3 per cent, they would be worse off than in a scenario where average growth was 6 per cent but the income of poor households grew by only 4 per cent. The first scenario would fulfil the principle of the relative definition of PPG, even though poor households would be materially worse off than in the second scenario, within which they are becoming relatively poorer to the rest of the society.

The two schools of thought on what constitutes pro-poor growth are reflective of complex philosophical, political and economic arguments and positions. The relative definition would appear to have a stronger element of social justice in its emphasis upon reducing economic inequality in society. However, according to the absolute school of thought, this pursuit of social justice could be detrimental to raising levels of income for the poor and implicitly lifting them out of poverty. It is also possible to interpret different political paradigms operating within the two schools of thought. The relativist school could be understood as one that favours a degree of political management of the economic system in an attempt to ensure equality. An absolute definition could be understood as favouring laissez-faire, unbridled, market-driven development, in an attempt to push economic growth rates to their maximum – an approach synonymous with the principles of neo-liberalism. Whilst the absolute school would appear to make a compelling case that a relativist approach to PPG could actively disadvantage the poor from achieving higher incomes, it is difficult to assess the extent to which this represents a sound economic theory or is little more than a political manoeuvre to prioritise unbridled capitalism and neo-liberalism. More credence and acceptance could be given to this approach if empirical support were lent to it through case studies of where a relative approach to PPG has actually suppressed economic growth and economically disadvantaged the poor.

The importance of these definitions in the evaluation of whether growth may be considered pro-poor or not is demonstrated in Figure 5.1. The figure illustrates inequalities between the growth in income for the poor vis-à-vis other citizens for selected countries. The y or vertical axis of the graph measures the percentage income growth rates per annum for the poor whilst the x axis measures the overall income growth rate in income per annum.

The selection of countries is based on available datasets and traverses different periods of economic growth between the countries: Bangladesh (1984–2000), Brazil (1985–96), Chile (1987–98), Ghana (1987–97), India (1983–97) and Zambia (1991–98). The 45 degree line in the diagram represents the position of where the poor's incomes are changing at the same rate as for the average per capita of their country. Using a relative definition of pro-poor growth, only Ghana would meet the key criteria of the rate of increase in the income of the poor having surpassed the overall average of the rest of the population. This is despite income having risen only 1.6 per cent in Ghana, compared to 3.2 per cent in India and nearly 5 per cent in Chile. All the other countries experienced a rise in inequality, although the incomes of the poor rose in all countries except Zambia. Thus using an absolute definition, pro-poor growth was achieved in Brazil, Bangladesh, India and Chile, alongside Ghana. Whilst the graph suggests that the poor will benefit from higher rates of economic growth if it is sustained for a decade or more, it is also evident that the poor may benefit less than the rest of the population if they

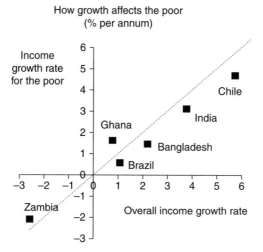

Figure 5.1 *Income growth rates for the poor in selected countries*
Source: taken from the DFID briefing sheet, February 2004

are not given a priority in development strategies. The example of Ghana, where the growth of income of the poor was higher than in Brazil and Bangladesh despite a lower overall growth rate, suggests that the political and policy environment of growth can determine the relative increase in income for the poor.

PRO-POOR TOURISM

Given that the potential of tourism for realising macro-economic benefits in developing countries has been recognised since the 1960s, it is unsurprising that as the development agenda began to shift from SAPs to PRSs at the end of the 1990s, the concept of pro-poor tourism (PPT) should represent a logical development of the pro-poor paradigm. As the title infers, PPT suggests an orientation of the tourism system and industry to generate net benefits and livelihood opportunities for the poor. This approach is emphasised in one of the earliest definitions of PPT as: 'specifically taking the needs of the poor into account in tourism development' (Ashley *et al.*, 2000: 1). The United Kingdom's Department for International Development (DFID, 1999) stresses that such consideration does not necessitate an expansion of the tourism sector but does require a tilting to unlock the opportunities for the poor from tourism. This represents an important acknowledgement as it implies that the focus of beneficiaries from the tourism industry is of as much importance as growth in its size, the key challenge being to identify mechanisms for unlocking opportunities for the poor (Ashley *et al.*, 2001; Scheyvens, 2007). A more recent and fuller definition of PPT is the one offered by the Pro-Poor Tourism Partnership (2012) as: 'tourism that results in increased net benefits for poor people. It enhances the linkages between tourism businesses and poor people, so that tourism's contribution to poverty reduction is increased and poor people are able to participate more effectively in product development.'

The orientation of this definition is towards an absolute definition of pro-poor tourism, as no explicit reference is attributed to the relative distribution of wealth. Whilst Mitchell and Ashley (2010) make reference to the absolute definition of pro-poor growth as being politically undemanding, they also observe that a restrictive definition of economic growth as being pro-poor only when it is presumed to reduce inequality would exclude most of the tourism industry from involvement in PPG. A relative approach to PPT also necessitates the availability of empirical data to demonstrate the impact of tourism on poverty reduction and the distribution of income in society. However, there is a current lack of empirical evidence of the beneficial impact of tourism on poverty reduction. This lack of data is also a problem in lobbying governments for support for the use of tourism in PRSs in LDCs, especially in countries where public resources are relatively small and face a variety of competing demands. As Mitchell and Ashley (2010: 10) comment: 'of concern to policy makers and practitioners in the field is not so much how to label their tourism, but how – and how much – to invest in developing tourism; the likely impact on poverty; and how to enhance the poverty reduction effect'.

Despite the political and definitional problems that characterise PPT, there is a consensus view that it is not a specific product or niche of the tourism market but an 'approach' to securing an increase of the net benefits for the poor from tourism, through ensuring that it contributes to poverty reduction. Whilst there may be a variety of different types and ways that tourism can make an active contribution to poverty reduction – for example through philanthropic tourism, volunteer and community-based tourism (CBT) – to make a significant contribution the focus must be on the mainstream tourism industry to enhance linkages between it and poor people. Any type and size of company can be involved in pro-poor tourism – for example a small lodge, an urban hotel, a tour operator or an infrastructure developer – provided it aims to supply benefits for the poor. The inclusion of the last player, an infrastructure developer, is indicative that the benefits for the poor from the tourism industry do not only arise directly, but in this example they arise indirectly from improved services including roads, sanitation and utilities. The targeting of opportunities for the poor may also be actively pursued in the supply chain of tourism, a concept that is developed in the final chapter.

Although PPT sounds like a new kind of alternative tourism, understanding that it is an approach and not a product, and that it can be applied to mass tourism as well as post-Fordist models of tourism, helps to distinguish it from other types of alternative tourism, e.g. sustainable tourism (ST), ecotourism (ET) and community-based tourism (CBT). A further key difference is that whilst PPT may share characteristics of these alternative forms of tourism – for example, they may al seek to challenge the existing structures of political economy of tourism, including an agenda to support wealth distribution and intra-generational equity, democratic participation, women's rights, and natural resource conservation – PPT is the only approach to have poverty as its key focus. The geographical focus of PPT is also more closely defined than for other types of alternative tourism, focusing exclusively on developing countries (Ashley *et al.*, 2001).

The centralisation of the poor as the key focus of PPT ensures that they should receive economic benefits directly as an outcome of a successfully implemented strategy targeted to their needs. The prioritising of the needs of the poor contrasts to the other forms of alternative tourism whose strategies may prioritise nature conservation and target economic benefits to the local population or community, rather than specifically the poor. The emphasis of PPT is one that re-orientates the use of tourism to lift people out of poverty, a possible outcome being that through the provision of sustainable livelihood opportunities from tourism there is a lessened propensity for environmental degradation as a consequence of poverty. In contrast to ST or ET, environmental and natural resource conservation is secured as a positive benefit of the prioritisation of tourism for poverty reduction, rather than a reduction in poverty being a positive secondary outcome of the prioritisation of nature conservation. Thus although in some cases strategies for PPT, ET and ST may result in similar outcomes, their priorities and routes for achieving them may be different.

Similar to the evolution of PRSs, it is evident that PPT does not necessarily represent a radical challenge to the status quo of the existing political economy. It can operate as a concept within existing political structures, including neo-liberalism, provided that the benefits of tourism include and target poor people. Referring to the two types of pro-poor growth outlined in the last section and recognised by the World Bank (2012), an absolute definition of PPT would not need to involve any re-distribution of wealth provided that income levels of the poor rose through direct or indirect engagement with the tourism industry. Within this absolute paradigm, as Mitchell and Ashley (2010) observe, almost all types of economic growth have the potential to be pro-poor, even if the main beneficiaries are the non-poor and growth is associated with rising inequality. An evident restriction of this approach is its sole focus on income as a measure of poverty, ignoring other issues of poverty including empowerment, democracy and rights of citizenship.

In contrast, if PPT is operating within the 'relative' pro-poor paradigm, tourism could only be recognised as being pro-poor if it is contributing to a distributional shift in income growth that favours the poor vis-à-vis the rest of the population. This would result in a decrease in income inequality and proportionally increased resources for the poor, a process that should also lead to their subsequent empowerment. However, as was commented on in the general context of PPG, there is a potential danger that in pursuing a relative agenda for PPT that opportunities for economic growth from tourism are not taken if poor households incomes are benefitting proportionally more than the average. Thus the somewhat ambiguous nature of PPT along with its moral imperative means it is open to political hijacking (Macbeth, 2005) and criticisms have also been made of its lack of political definition. Perhaps as Chok *et al.* (2007: 40) observe, unless existing structural inequalities are addressed in the wider political economy, PPT is unlikely to 'reap significant and long-term benefits for the already marginalised'.

SUSTAINABLE TOURISM – ELIMINATING POVERTY (ST-EP)

Alongside PPT, the other main initiative for the use of tourism to combat poverty is the 'Sustainable Tourism-Eliminating Poverty' (ST-EP) campaign created by the UNWTO. This initiative is explicitly linked to sustainable tourism development, having been launched at the World Summit for Sustainable Development in Johannesburg in 2002. The link between sustainable development and poverty reduction is made clear in the following statement from the UNWTO (2007b: 15): 'The project, called ST-EP (Sustainable Tourism – Eliminating Poverty) seeks to refocus and incentivise Sustainable Tourism – social, economic and ecological – to make it a primary tool for Eliminating Poverty in the world's poorest countries, particularly the LDCs: bringing development and jobs to people who live on less than a dollar a day.' The initiative was an agreement between the then WTO and the United Nations Conference on Trade and Development (UNCTAD) to implement a new framework to assist developing countries and LDCs to use tourism for poverty reduction. The explicit reference to sustainable development embedded in ST-EP is an evident difference to PPT. It has a direct aim of helping to fulfil the objectives of the MDGs as highlighted in Box 1.1, summarised in the following statement from Kofi Annan, the former United Nations Secretary General: 'ST-EP will promote socially, economically and ecologically sustainable tourism, aimed at alleviating poverty and bringing jobs to people in developing countries . . . these objectives are fully consistent with the goals set out in the Millennium Declaration' (ibid.).

The ST-EP programme has a global perspective on the use of tourism in poverty alleviation that recognises the spatial dimensions of the international tourism system, and the need for tourism to be adopted by supranational agencies and national governments of both developing and developed countries in partnership as a tool for poverty reduction. Five major areas have been identified for global action by the UNWTO, summarised as: (i) for developed countries to formulate pro-development strategies to encourage tourism to the world's poorest countries to enhance economic well-being, social development and mutual understanding; (ii) for less developed countries to recognise the economic potential of tourism and make it a central focus of their Poverty Reduction Strategy Programs; (iii) for all countries to help poor countries to use tourism services to fight poverty and promote sustainable development; (iv) to build a pro-poor development element into tourism strategies; and to recognise the use of tourism in building under-standing between people and enhancing global security; and (v) for International Development Agencies to place tourism amongst their key priorities for infra-structure and entrepreneurial support; and for all tourism stakeholders to embrace the MDGs and pursue sustainable and responsible practices (UNWTO, 2007b).

Integral to these five areas is the need for partnerships between stakeholders in developed and developing countries and international agencies. This would include governments, international and bilateral development agencies, multina-tional corporations and civil society. There is also a clear statement of intent to move tourism beyond just a tool for economic development to one that directly embraces poverty reduction. The UNWTO also stress that tourism should be attributed a higher priority in development assistance programmes and poverty alleviation strategies. The explicit relationship between sustainable development, poverty and tourism is to develop holistic sustainable tourism that embraces social, economic and ecological aspects whilst specifically alleviating poverty. Such a noble aim is unlikely to attract much opposition, however, similar to PPT, criticisms have been made of ST-EP that it lacks both reflectivity on the tourism system and political evaluation, seeking little more than to promote a positive image of tourism as being pro-environmental and pro-poor (Scheyvens, 2007; Gossling *et al.*, 2004).

Although both PPT and ST-EP are open to criticisms of as lacking a radical polit-ical agenda for distributive justice, the placing of the 'poor' as a key focus of both initiatives, exemplified in the UNWTO (2007b) recommendations to build pro-poor development from tourism into both poverty reduction and tourism strategies, re-orientates the emphasis of tourism development policy to addressing poverty alongside macro-economic targets. It is part of a wider recognition that the global political agenda cannot afford ethically, economically, environmen-tally and politically to permit 1 billion people to remain isolated from the economic opportunities increasingly available to the rest of the global population. This paradigmatic shift for the use of tourism to directly combat poverty is representa-tive of a more holistic view of tourism's economic agenda and a realisation that a strategic macro-economic focus will not necessarily ensure benefits for the poor.

While pro-poor proponents highlight the potential significance of tourism's contri-bution to poverty reduction, a key challenge is how to identify indicators that reflect the core issues of poverty reduction. Although traditional macro-economic indicators of the success of tourism, including numbers of tourist arrivals, foreign exchange earnings, GDP, employment, stock of facilities and revenues provide a useful means for comparison between countries and economic sectors, they contribute little to assessing tourism's impacts upon poverty reduction. According to Goodwin (2006), the evaluation of 'success' is a central challenge for tourism and poverty analysis, as there is a requirement to identify indicators that reflect the core issues of poverty reduction. These need to include ones that are identified by the poor and not just those imposed by external agencies.

More recently, the pro-poor value chain has aimed at providing a way to assess the level of contribution that tourism can offer to the poor in a destination. The pro-poor value chain has its basis in the commodity chain approach, which involves an assessment of several components including institutions, actors, modes of production, the movement of materials needed for production, the distribution of products, marketing and consumption dynamics. The application of this approach to the tourism value chain, however, remains problematic as it is composed of a complex mix of goods and services that are often not measurable due to their intangible nature. When attempts have been made to quantify the contribution of tourism to poverty reduction, they have been criticised on the basis of a weak and ineffective mechanism of data collection that reveals little about the conditions of the poor and fails to provide a basis for informed policy-making (Roe *et al.*, 2004; Goodwin, 2006). There is therefore a central challenge to be creative and innovative in the creation of rigorous and robust quantitative indicators that are capable of assessing tourism's contribution to poverty reduction. Alongside the need for a quantifiable assessment of tourism's impact on poverty reduction, there is a need for interpretive research to produce richer and more complex understandings of the experiences of the poor and also their perceptions of tourism as a means to improve their livelihoods. Localised and culturally specific in-depth understandings of the experiences of poverty are required as a basis for policy decision-making on how tourism can be used for poverty reduction. In the absence of these it is difficult to target any type of economic development including tourism to meet the requirements of the poor.

CONSIDERATIONS AND CHALLENGES OF THE USE OF TOURISM IN COMBATING POVERTY

Although PPT and ST-EP are significant policy initiatives, the utilisation of tourism to combat poverty faces significant challenges, which has led to a questioning of the extent that tourism can actually alleviate poverty and assist poor people to have improved livelihoods. These limitations are exemplified in Box 5.2 which considers the use of tourism for poverty reduction in the case of Humla in Nepal. The basic tenet of tackling poverty through tourism rests upon ensuring the economic involvement of the poor in the industry. To achieve this requires enlightened political leadership, philanthropy from the private sector and tourists, access to resources and the ability to establish meaningful partnerships between different stakeholders. As the major player influencing tourism investment and the distribution of its benefits, the willingness of the private sector to adopt an ethos of providing opportunities for the poor will be critical to the success of PPT and ST-EP initiatives.

Although governments have the power to influence the tourism industry, they are unable to legislate that private investors must provide non-commercial benefits for the poor. Nevertheless, the success of any poverty reduction strategy is dependent upon visionary leadership by government and, critically, they must recognise the potential of tourism as a means of alleviating poverty. Similarly, international donor agencies such as the World Bank, and the Asian and African Development Banks need to be aware of the potential and be willing to support poverty reduction strategies using tourism. Government and international development agencies also have a key bridging role in attempting to establish meaningful links and cooperation between the established industry and the poor in attempts to give them access to participation in tourism. In meeting this objective, policy frameworks determined by governments have a significant role to play in facilitating the involvement of the poor in tourism. This would include the allocation of resources for training, micro-loans for enterprise development, and fairtrade strategies. Examples of such initiatives undertaken by the Netherlands Development Organisation (SNV) and United Nations Development Agency (UNDP) are given in Boxes 5.2 and 5.3.

BOX 5.2 PRO-POOR TOURISM IN HUMLA, NEPAL

Humla is one of the most remote and under-developed regions of Nepal, situated in the north-west corner of the country on the border with Tibet and ranked as the fourth poorest region in Nepal with a human population of approximately 50,000. The people in the area suffer from severe food deficits and occasional disease epidemics. Development options are severely limited by its cold mountainous terrain, only 1 per cent of the land being suitable for agriculture, and its poor infrastructure, even the district capital of Simikot is ten days walk from the nearest road. Lack of opportunities for women is an evident issue as Humla is the lowest ranking region of Nepal in terms of women's empowerment.

Given the poor infrastructure, the Netherlands Development Agency (SNV) has been active in improving trails and foot suspension bridges within the area. Besides aiding the movement of people and facilitating the transport of goods by animals – including mules and yaks – the main Hilsa-Simikot trail is now of a standard to permit trekking tourism. However, the numbers of tourists trekking on the route is in hundreds per annum, meaning that tourism makes a limited contribution to economic and social development in the region. This limited effect is compounded by economic leakages with much of the tourism revenue resting with trekking agencies based in Kathmandu who sell the trips to the trekkers.

The majority of the people live below the World Bank poverty line, very few have regularly paid jobs and some are 'landless', struggling to produce even one month's worth of food. A problem in developing stronger tourism linkages within the area is the limited availability of local products and services for the outside agencies to use; for example, many of the trekking agencies bring all their food with them from Kathmandu. It is subsequently proposed to develop a multiple-use visitor centre for the region, where different tourism stakeholders could meet and exchange services, products and information. This would permit the coordination of services such as transportation, guides, portering equipment and agricultural produce – for example, vegetables, fruit and poultry – with the aim of maximising opportunities for the access of the poor to the tourism market. However, one of the problems faced in developing meaningful links between the private sector agencies and the poor is a cultural and political problem. Trekking companies have already established relationships with the local 'elite' who operate a monopoly on trekking in the area and control market competition and access.

Alongside helping to develop the infrastructure, the role of the SNV is also to act as a facilitator for pro-poor tourism through the District Partners Programme (DPP), which aims to provide an institutional environment for sustainable economic development initiatives for women and men. This involves acting as a coordinator of stakeholders, including village committees, the private sector and NGOs who are working in the area. Emphasis is placed on participatory planning, stakeholder involvement and capacity building for the poor to work in the tourism sector. This capacity building includes aspects of product development, marketing strategies and the establishment of linkages with outside trekking agencies. Having identified the potential feasibility of tourism in Humla, training has been given to the District Development Committees and NGO staff operating in Humla in aspects of sustainable and pro-poor tourism. The sourcing of funding for micro-tourism enterprise development is also another important role for SNV.

The practical outcomes of the project to date include improved sanitation (over 400 toilets have been built on the trail); community support funds for the development of micro-enterprises have been approved; a tax of US$2 per tourist is now being levied; and one community campsite has been developed. Ultimately, how successful the scheme proves to be depends upon political will, stakeholders' partnerships and available resources. The vulnerability of tourism to external factors has been demonstrated by the recent civil war between the Maoists and the then government, which caused a decrease in tourism demand to Nepal, a situation that is now hopefully fully resolved.

Source: after Saville, 2001

BOX 5.3 NEPAL: TOURISM FOR RURAL POVERTY ALLEVIATION PROJECT (TRPA)

This project was funded by the United Nations Development Project (UNDP) and illustrates the use of tourism for development across several government ministries. Its aim was to tackle poverty through the creation of a sustainable tourism development project in line with Nepal's Ninth National Development Plan (NNDP) for the period 2000–2005. A holistic approach that integrated the poverty alleviation objectives of other economic sectors including health, transport, agriculture and environment was taken. The aim of this strategy was to demonstrate how tourism could be used for poverty reduction and at the same time complement the wider objectives of other government ministries. For example, an objective of the Ministry of Health was to provide clean drinking water to all communities and improve the levels of sanitation. This objective would need to be met through the TRPA project, because without a water supply and a suitable level of sanitation, sustainable tourism would not be possible. A further objective of the NNDP was to improve the biophysical environment of Nepal, and more specifically to remedy the environmental problems arising from the existing economic and social conditions, especially poverty. The TRPA was seen to have a significant role in achieving this objective.

A range of pilot projects were established in impoverished districts of Nepal in 2001, the basis for identifying the selected geographical areas being a series of indicators developed by the United Nations Development Programme (UNDP). These included life expectancy and health standards, literacy levels, remoteness and lack of public infrastructure, gender inequality, and per capita income. Six districts were chosen, from which target groups were identified to maximise the impacts tourism could have on alleviating poverty and aiding the poor. By 2006, tourism ventures had been established with 48 Village Development Committees (VDCs) in impoverished parts of Nepal.

Inherent to the approach of TPRA was the participation of local communities in tourism ventures. Thus emphasis was placed upon impoverished village communities undertaking self-assessment in terms of their capabilities and resources for tourism. The extent to which the scheme has been successful is unknown as it awaits detailed assessment. However, it has brought together three levels of government – national agencies and ministries, District Development Committees and VDCs with industry stakeholders – and facilitated community empowerment. Examples of practical projects include the construction of a Sherpa porters' shelter at Namche for 60 porters with beds, toilets, washing facilities and a kitchen. Prior to this, there were no facilities for porters – injuries and the death of porters being a major concern of trekking tourism in Nepal. Another project was the establishment of a micro-hydro energy project in Phortse village in Lower Sagamartha that helps to supply electricity to households and tourist lodges. This is an area that has substantial tourism but has suffered a major energy crisis resulting in deforestation. A further initiative is capacity-building training workshops including environment and waste management, biodiversity, lodge management and accountancy.

Source: after Rossetto *et al.*, 2007

The case study of Humla (Box 5.2) vividly illustrates the challenges that are faced in geographically isolated regions of countries, in this case a landlocked country, which is one of several contributing factors to the underdevelopment that characterises Nepal. The role of SNV as a facilitator and coordinator has been important for bringing various stakeholders together with interests in tourism. The second case study in Box 5.3, the 'Tourism for Rural Poverty Alleviation Project' is significant because of its ambition to link tourism into achieving the priorities and objectives of several government ministries. This is important as the political ranking of ministries of tourism may be relatively low compared to other ministries, including agriculture and health, just as International Development Agencies may find themselves in low position relative to other government departments. Through being able to demonstrate how tourism can make a positive contribution to opportunities for health and education within an integrated planning approach across government ministries, tourism's chances of playing an active part in achieving targets such as MDGs and improving the poor's well-being are enhanced.

Yet, tourism cannot have a universal geographical application in combating poverty in developing countries and there are several challenges to its use for poverty reduction as shown in Figure 5.2. Scale and resources of place are important variables in the likely prioritisation of tourism for poverty reduction. An evident pre-requisite for tourism development is that there is an asset base of natural and cultural resources that is attractive for tourists. Consequently, tourism's use in combating poverty will

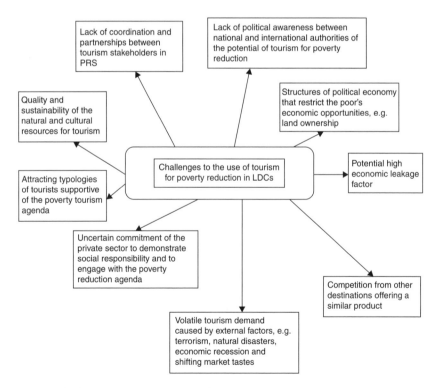

Figure 5.2 *Challenges to the use of tourism for poverty reduction*
Source: after UNWTO, 2006b

be restricted to specific regions and locations, and subsequently not all LDCs and regions of developing countries will be able to benefit equally. In Ricardian terminology, some places will possess the natural and cultural resources that lend them a much stronger comparative advantage than others. Geographical scale also influences the intensity of the impacts of tourism on poverty reduction. As Ashley *et al.* (2001) comment, whilst poverty reduction through PPT may be significant at a local or district level, its national impacts would vary according to the relative importance of tourism to the national economy.

The characteristics and hegemonic relationships of political economy will also be influential in determining the success of tourism and poverty initiatives. Local tenure and land-ownership issues will be important in deciding not only which land is used for tourism but also the extent to which poor people have access to resources for their livelihoods. Where poor people lack ownership rights, they are vulnerable to development decisions which may act directly against their own interests. In contrast, tenure over land, wildlife or other tourism assets can give the poor market power, enabling them to play an active participatory part in decision-making and secure benefits from tourism (Ashley *et al.*, 2000). There is also a need to educate policy makers about tourism. Whilst governments have become more aware of the macro-economic benefits that can be gained from tourism as explained in Chapter 2, there is a lack of awareness of how tourism can be used for poverty reduction. As the UNWTO (2006b: 5) point out: 'it is often believed that tourism can develop and bear fruits for the host society solely through the action of private investors, which in the case of most LDCs is mostly foreign', a perspective which has been shown to be wrong, as the economic, environmental and social costs of inappropriate tourism development have become more evident.

Partnerships between the different tourism stakeholders will be essential to the success of tourism poverty reduction schemes. Beside an enlightened approach from national governments to incorporate tourism into PRSs where viable and a political will to empower the poor through capacity building and opportunity creation, all the stakeholders in tourism will need to adopt an informed and philanthropic approach to how tourism can be used to help the poor. Issues of ethics and collective working for a greater social good vis-à-vis an emphasis on the individual benefit of an organisation will determine the success of any poverty strategy. For example, hotel owners and tour operators need to work with local communities and local government to develop a model of tourism that actively presents the poor with livelihood opportunities. The private sector also needs to evaluate its supply chain linkages to local suppliers, attempting to develop and maximise these where possible to multiply income and employment opportunities for the poor.

A further key tenet of poverty reduction is the strengthening of inter-sectoral linkages with tourism to enhance economic benefits for the poor and reduce high economic leakages from tourism. One sector of the economy for which this is particularly important is agriculture. As Torres and Momsen (2004) note, agriculture remains the livelihood of most of the poorest people in developing countries and tourism has the potential to create extra demand for local agricultural produce. However, the development of this backward linkage is dependent upon the tourism industry being willing to facilitate communications and negotiations with local farmers, and they, in turn, having the ability to supply produce of a quality and regularity that is demanded by the industry.

A further reason for the necessity to develop linkages to other economic sectors such as agriculture is that without it, there is a danger that a polarised form of development based upon tourism may take place (Brohman, 1996). Subsequently, as tourism becomes more successful, the rest of the economy fails to follow, causing a disparity of wealth between tourism and other types of economic activity (Torres and Momsen, 2004). The medium- to long-term effects of this are for more natural and human resources to be used for tourism as it becomes more financially beneficial than other economic sectors. The ultimate effect may be to create an economic over-dependency upon tourism and a subsequent threat to livelihoods and social well-being if demand falls. The threat of a decrease in tourism demand, combined with the vulnerability of tourism demand to external factors, is a significant challenge to the use of tourism as means for development or tackling poverty. Events such as terrorism, natural disasters, economic recession and changing market tastes all threaten tourism demand. Even if it may seem that prioritising the use of tourism for poverty reduction lends a moral authority to a right for the success of a tourism destination market competition from other destinations will remain. The use of tourism for poverty reduction does not bestow an automatic right for success on a destination; its success will depend on marketing and the quality of the product just as for any other tourism destination or type of tourism.

HOW TOURISM CAN IMPACT ON THE POOR

If the focus of tourism policy is to be on poverty, and tourism is to be used as a component of PRS, there is a requirement for understanding how tourism can positively benefit the poor. However, there is little data that inform us of the beneficiary impacts of tourism development on the poor. Existing data tend to be micro-level in scope, focusing on a single enterprise or a community, which are typically analysed through a combination of sustainable livelihood analysis (SAS) that includes micro-economic analysis and non-financial impacts on how people live (Mitchell and Ashley, 2010). In the absence of empirical data from tourism policies that have directly targeted the poor, Mitchell and Ashley (ibid.) suggest that there are three key pathways through which the impacts of tourism, both positive and negative, are transmitted to the poor. These categories have similarities to those recognised in economic multiplier theory: the direct, secondary and dynamic impacts. However, they have been modified and re-focused to the poor, also incorporating positive and negative environmental and social changes that may affect their livelihood opportunities, and are summarised after Mitchell and Ashley (2010) as:

1. *Direct effects*. Incorporated into this category are positive and negative direct effects from tourism development on the poor. The creation of employment opportunities for the poor in the tourism industry and informal sector and micro-enterprises are an important and obvious example of a positive direct effect on livelihoods and income. However, other direct effects of tourism on the poor that may improve their well-being may be less obvious. For example, the poor may directly benefit from the improvements in infrastructure required for tourism development, providing access to telecommunications, clean water, energy supplies, sanitation and roads, which may enhance both the standard of living and other livelihood opportunities. Conversely, tourism development could have a negative effect on livelihood opportunities; for example, resulting in a reduced access to beach resources as a consequence of their privatisation for hotel development. The development of tourism may also change a household's exposure to the risk of poverty. It may be reduced if tourism provides a diversification of income streams or increased if a culture of over-dependency on tourism is created exposing households to a downturn in demand. In terms of having the greatest positive impacts on livelihoods, creating employment opportunities for the poor in the tourism industry should be the key target of policy.

2. *Secondary effects*. In this pathway, emphasis is placed on the indirect and induced effects of tourism development on the poor. In an economic context, indirect effects occur when a change in tourism expenditure impacts on the non-tourism economy. Other sectors of the economy that are stimulated by investment and expenditure in tourism typically include construction, agriculture and fisheries but also embrace handicraft production, an economic sector that may be especially significant for the creation of livelihood opportunities and the empowerment of women. For tourism to create demand in these economic sectors, it is essential that the supply chain of the tourism industry is linked to them to reduce the effects of economic leakages and create employment opportunities. It is also critical for the success of PRS that the secondary industries have policies and directives to incorporate the poor into their operations so that they benefit from increased levels of economic activity. The geographical impacts of these secondary effects are also important to tourism's use in poverty reduction as they have a further spatial reach than the direct impacts that occur primarily in the destination, subsequently benefiting households over a larger geographical area. Owing to the diversity of the industries involved in the supply chain, the indirect effects also benefit a larger number of households compared to the direct, albeit

with smaller earnings per household. There is also the additional but significant environmental benefit of a reduced carbon footprint as the transport distances of supply chain produce for the tourism industry are minimised.

Important for conceptualising economic impacts of tourism on the poor is the economic multiplier model as was discussed in Chapter 2. The basis of this model is that expenditure on tourism and the stimulation of extra demand in its supply chain and linked economic sectors means money begins to circulate in the economy. For example, employees in the tourism industry and the secondary industries that supply it will spend some of their wages on goods and services that in turn induces extra demand in the economy, which in turn may create extra employment opportunities for the poor. Theoretically, the initial tourism investment could circulate indefinitely in the economy but it does not, as in each round of expenditure there are economic leakages, thereby removing it from circulation. This occurs for a variety of reasons including repaying interest charges on foreign loans for tourism development; imports for the tourism industry – for example, kitchen equipment for hotels and food, drink and beach products; the repatriation of profits by foreign travel and tourism companies; the employment of foreign workers who may send money home to their relatives; and the paying of taxes to the government.

3. Dynamic effects. The focus of this pathway is how tourism impacts on the wider structure of the economy over time. Whilst the effects are less tangible than for the previous two pathways, they can be significant for the poor. Examples of dynamic changes could include the integration of women into economic networks, which may induce social changes on the perception of the role of women in society. As well as bringing direct benefits, the development of infrastructure may offer dynamic benefits for the poor by opening up access for opportunities that previously had not existed; for example, being able to physically access education that had previously been geographically remote. Such opportunities will provide dynamism to the economy and result in economic growth. Conversely, economic changes following the success of tourism may also occur in the economy that may have a negative impact on other economic sectors upon which the poor rely for employment. For example, a strengthening national economic profile based on a boom in tourism may raise the value of the national currency against foreign currencies making agricultural exports more expensive, leading to a reduction in foreign demand. This would adversely affect the livelihoods of the poor, as agriculture is a sector of the economy that employs and interacts with many poor people. It is subsequently evident that the use of tourism in PRSs needs to accommodate various scenarios of how tourism could potentially impact longitudinally on other sectors of the economy upon which the poor are reliant.

These three pathways are indicative of how the poor could potentially be affected by tourism. Whilst there appear to be potential benefits and livelihood opportunities that can be created through tourism for the poor, the theory means little in terms of reducing poverty unless it is possible for the poor to access these opportunities. Instrumental to the creation of opportunities is the necessity for the implementation of a range of measures ranging from focusing on the poor in macro-policy to raising the knowledge and skills capacity of the poor to work in the tourism industry or to develop their entrepreneurial skills. Careful consideration also needs to be given to how to create opportunities for the poor in the tourism supply chain, including industries in which they are traditionally employed, e.g. agriculture and fishing. Alongside offering a means to help countries to meet a reduction in poverty as one of the MDGs, tourism may also play an important role in the creation of opportunities for women, perhaps for the first time. Not only is this important for the individuals but also wider policy objectives to empower women and give them a larger voice in the running of societies.

TOURISM AND POVERTY INITIATIVES REVIEW

As was stated in the last section, a major challenge that is faced by proponents of the use of tourism for poverty reduction is a lack of research and published data to support their case, as Mitchell and Ashley (2010: 1) observe: 'Despite the voluminous research outputs of economists, anthropologists, sociologists, geographers and a range of development practitioners, there is little understanding and no consensus on what impact tourism has had on poverty in the developing world.' To an extent this is not surprising as large data gaps exist throughout the development agenda on the impacts of the tourist industry. As a sector of the economy that is often difficult to define because of the complexity of its composition, impact research is often challenging and costly. In the case of its use for poverty reduction, the paradigm is relatively new and subsequently initiatives are limited and relatively short in duration.

In their careful review of the limited available data and from direct practice in the field over a decade, Mitchell and Ashley (2010) reached the conclusion that no single type of tourism can lay claim to having a monopoly on being pro-poor. This is an important statement for PPT policy, as it has often been assumed that alternative forms of tourism – for example, ecotourism, CBT or independent travel – would be more pro-poor than mass tourism. They also infer that there has been a stereotyping of aspirations about the relationships of types of tourism to the poor that favours the alternatives and niche to mainstream and large scale. As Mitchell and Ashley (2010: 134) comment: 'Just because a tourism segment is based on culture or wildlife does not mean it is pro-poor. And just because it is built around business tourism or large-scale leisure resorts does not mean it is not pro-poor.'

In an attempt to get an overview of the extent that different types of tourism could benefit the poor, a comprehensive review was undertaken by the UNWTO

(2006a), asking its member states to present case studies of projects, businesses or other tourism activities that had effectively contributed to poverty reduction. An eclectic range of projects were included that were deemed to be representative of how tourism could make an active contribution to poverty reduction. These included: rural and agro-tourism programmes; community-based hotels, restaurants and eco-lodges; tourism micro-entrepreneur networks; village tourism; community-owned tour operators; natural parks or protected areas; guide training programmes; regional development based on tourism; and handicraft development programmes.

The limited amount of available data and retained activity in the field of tourism and poverty reduction is reflected in only a total of 26 projects from 20 different countries being included in the report, 17 of which had commenced their activities in 2000 or later. It is also evident from the selection of projects that there is not necessarily an evident cohesion of project types, although the majority are skewed towards alternative types of tourism development including rural, village and community-based programmes. The scale of operation is also varied, from a focus on an individual enterprise to regional development. An evident absence is the identification of projects that involve the mainstream tourism industry, the process of 'tilting' the industry to meet the needs of the poor that characterises PPT.

The small scale of the projects that characterise much of the tourism and poverty initiatives has drawn criticism of their limited impact on the poverty reduction agenda. In reference to the UNWTO ST-EP programme, whilst recognising the importance of its establishment, Goodwin (2009) observes that it remains a programme with small-scale schemes that have not engaged with the tourism industry. Based upon the 26 case studies presented in the UNWTO (2006a) report, it is not easy to characterise the direct employment generated through the schemes, as the character of employment varies from one project to another and is affected by seasonality. The poor were typically employed in guiding services, catering, reception of tourists, entertainment, waiter services, cleaning, sale of products, handicraft production and in a few cases for administration and management purposes. Emphasising the need for participatory research with the poor to gain a clear understanding of how tourism should be developed to provide positive impacts, it was found in many cases that whilst training and capacity building is needed for many of these positions, tourism employment and the jobs themselves were often interpreted as part-time activities for the families involved, as they have to deal with other obligations, notably the growing of food.

The importance of the supply chain in generating secondary and dynamic effects from tourism on poverty reduction was emphasised in the last section of this chapter. In the review of the selected projects, the UNWTO (2006a) found that two main problems were experienced in strengthening the supply chain through the use of local suppliers to reduce economic leakages. The issue of a lack of quality and an ability of local suppliers to meet tourist expectations was overcome by some of the tourism businesses setting up training programmes for the local suppliers to help them understand the demands of hotel businesses and tourists. The second problem related to the capacity of local enterprises to ensure a regular supply of produce, a problem which requires an increase in technical capacity and some degree of investment to overcome.

Despite the lack of evidence of engagement of the mainstream tourism industry in poverty reduction, the United Kingdom tourism industry has been instrumental in establishing the charitable organisation of the Travel Foundation, whose aim is to improve the livelihoods of peoples working in developing countries. An example of one of their projects is described in Box 5.4, which demonstrates how participatory approaches to gain a richer understanding of the problems faced by the poor combined with the establishments of partnerships, in this case the local community with the Kenyan Association of Tour Operators (KATO), can improve the economic benefits of tourism for the poor.

BOX 5.4 DEVELOPING AND MARKETING A SUSTAINABLE MAASAI VILLAGE TOURISM EXPERIENCE IN KENYA

Whilst examples of the private sector taking a leading role in the use of tourism for poverty reduction are sparse, one initiative is the creation of the Travel Foundation in the United Kingdom, a charity that works closely with the tourism industry to make tourism more sustainable and enhance the livelihoods of the poor through running destination projects. One of these projects was the 'Kipas Maasai Village Tourism Experience' located in the Mara Triangle of the Maasai Mara game reserve in Kenya, where the aim was to transfer the tourism product into a sustainable model for tourism. The 'Experience' is based on the visitation of tourists to five villages located within the area to learn about the Maasai culture. The trips were organised by tour operators to the villages and the tourists were transported by driver guides. The Travel Foundation scheme had four key objectives related to: an enrichment of livelihood opportunities for the Maasai; an increased authenticity of cultural exchanges between the village people and tourists; the provision of outbound and destination tourism operators with a sustainable cultural tourism excursion to offer their clients; and to disseminate lessons of good practice learnt from this scheme to other community tourism ventures to improve the sustainability of their businesses.

After exploratory meetings with the villagers it was found that the economic benefits from tourism actually reaching them was minimal, as the driver guides who were taking tourists to the villages were taking 96 per cent of the visitor entry fees. The way this issue was overcome was with the joint support of a partnership of the Kenya Association of Tour Operators (KATO) and United Kingdom outbound tour operators, and the facilitation of dialogues between the tour operators and the local community. Discussions with driver guide representatives also took place, as there was high level of hostility to any changes in the arrangements of the excursions that would financially disadvantage them. This hostility was overcome through the support of the tour operators and the travel industry at large, the action and threats of media exposure of the driver guides' actions in taking such a high percentage of the tourist entry fees, and the disciplining of disruptive guides by their employers. The drivers were also awarded 10 per cent commission on the sales of tickets for the village excursion and tours through KATO.

The successes of the scheme have resulted in better governance and management of the tours, with a vast increase in economic benefits for the local people of the villages. Received fees from the entry permits by the villagers have increased by 800 per cent and a transparent payment system for the collection of visitor fees has been implemented. The scheme also emphasises the value of participatory mechanisms and dialogue to bring stakeholders together – for example, between the local community and destination tour operators – and to help in enhancing the understandings by other stakeholders of the experiences and problems that are faced by the villagers, including marginalisation and exclusion from the industry and decision-making. A further positive outcome has been that visitor satisfaction has increased with the tours, which bodes well for the continuing use of the villages by tour operators.

Source: after The Travel Foundation, 2012

In an attempt to embrace the tourism industry into a wider network, one strategic initiative that has been taken at a national level is the development of a Fair Trade programme for tourism in South Africa. The concept of Fair Trade arose from the concerns over the imbalances in world trade within the free trade framework that had led to the accumulation of the staggering levels of debt by LDCs, causing the well-publicised mass protests at the WTO (World Trade Organisation) ministerial conferences in Seattle in 1999, Prague in 2000, and the G8 summits in Genoa in 2001 and Cancún in 2003. In essence, whilst there exists no definitive definition of what fair trade is, it can be understood as an attempt to redress the imbalances that exist in global trade which favour established producers in developed countries over those in developing countries. Emphasis is placed upon securing a fair wage for the production of products that are then sold in the global market. The movement is in essence a collective international one with a common aim to attain a fairer deal for producers in LDCs and has typically been associated with the production of primary agricultural products; for example, bananas, coffee, tea and chocolate. Although the concept of fair trade has gained more publicity since the millennium it is not new, with its origins dating from the 1970s when aid agencies began working with craftspeople in developing countries to satisfy a growing demand for ethnic produce in the households of developed countries, being taken forward by niche trading groups (Ransom, 2001).

In attempting to give an explanation of what fair trade is and how it is different in its orientation to the inequalities that are a part of the free trade system, Ransom (2001: 20) asks a range of questions: 'Can it [fair trade] be made to work for, rather than against, impoverished community producers in the South? Can the process of production be democraticised, ownership shared, organised labour encouraged, child labour made unnecessary, environmental sustainability and human rights promoted? Can consumers be induced to think – and pay – more than they currently believe is necessary?' The questions contain strong ethical issues about the nature of the relationships of the developed countries with the developing, the relationship of consumerism with production, and about how global trade may be compounding poverty.

A key component of fair trade is subsequently that whilst goods have a slightly higher price than comparative non-fair trade produce, as they are not mass produced and the system is dealing with smaller stakeholders, the revenues are returned to the producer at source. The advantages of this system is that the extra revenues gained by small-scale agricultural producers in an LDC can provide the means to realise the opportunities for children to attend school or gain access to improved health care. To date, the Fair Trade System has been primarily applied to commodities with little application to the service industries including tourism (Cleverdon and Kalish, 2000). One country that has taken an initiative in establishing a fair trade policy is South Africa with its development of a Fair Trade Tourism South Africa (FTTSA) as is explained in Box 5.5.

BOX 5.5 FAIR TRADE TOURISM SOUTH AFRICA (FTTSA)

The issue of LDCs gaining access to global markets to be able to trade on a level playing field with developed countries is a central one and the emergence of the loosely allied concept of Fair Trade, which guarantees a just renumeration to the producer – for example, coffee and tea farmers – is one way of attempting to combat discriminatory practices and imbalances in trade. To date, the Fair Trade ideal has had little application in tourism but one country that has attempted to develop a Fair Trade tourism system is South Africa, the only country to have an independent certification scheme for tourism. The normal process in Fair Trade schemes is to have an independent third party who will provide assurances to the consumer that a product or service meets ethically defined requirements, including sustainable development and community participatory approaches to development.

The key aim of Fair Trade Tourism South Africa (FTTSA) is to enhance black participation in decision-making and reduce poverty in post-apartheid South Africa. The history of the Fair Trade movement in South Africa dates to its instigation in agriculture in the 1990s as the Fairtrade Labelling Organisation (FLO) certifying cooperative and commercial farms meeting their criteria. Tourism was identified as a priority economic sector for development in the South African Government's 'Tourism White Paper' of 1996 and also through PPT as a means for poverty reduction. A key feature that emerged to be embedded into the FTTSA certification scheme, and one that runs central to development and the pro-poor agenda, was good governance that recognises human rights, sustainable development and the empowerment of the poor.

FTTSA particularly focuses on the certification of black or community-owned businesses and employs approximately 2,000 staff of which 80 per cent are black. It provides an environment to help with the poverty reduction agenda, the advantage for tourism businesses being that the certification offers an enhanced credibility and access to niche markets, augmenting their visibility, viability and sustainability. The effects will also be beneficial to their supply chain and associated economic sectors; for example, agriculture, which is the main employer of the poor in LDCs. To date, FTTSA has certified over 50 businesses in the accommodation sector and associated services, including bed and breakfasts, safari lodges, township tours, shark cage diving and eco-adventures. The scheme has helped to prioritise the needs of those who have previously been discriminated against and marginalised in the apartheid system, and the poor who were capable of engaging with national and international markets but required support to do so. The overall success of the scheme to date in empowering poor communities and reducing poverty has led to the FTTSA now providing support to Madagascar and Mozambique to develop their own FTT certification schemes.

Source: based upon Boluk, 2011

SUMMARY

- Given the comparative advantage of the natural and cultural resources for tourism in many LDCs, and the emphasis for the World Bank and IMF on Poverty Reduction Strategies (PRS), governments need to identify how to utilise tourism development to maximise its positive impact for creating livelihood opportunities for the poor. The evolution of a policy framework for tourism's use for poverty reduction can be attributed to three key sources. It has been advocated through the United Nations World Tourism Organisation's (UNWTO) 'Sustainable Tourism Eliminating Poverty Program' (ST-EP); the United Kingdom's Department for International Development's (DFID) 'Pro-Poor Tourism' (PPT) policy; and the work of the Netherlands Agency for International Development (SNV). A key concept related to the use of tourism for poverty reduction is pro-poor growth (PPG), which was a term first used towards the end of the 1990s. However, similar to the concept of development, as to what 'pro-poor growth' is and how it should be achieved is contested. The debate between 'relative' and 'absolute' PPG reflects complex philosophical, political and economic arguments and positions.
- Pro-Poor Tourism represents a logical development of the Pro-Poor paradigm and although it sounds like a new kind of alternative tourism, it is an approach and not a product. As the term infers, PPT suggests an orientation of the tourism system and industry to generate net benefits and livelihood opportunities for the poor. It can be applied to mass tourism as well as post-Fordist models of tourism, and is the only tourism policy to have poverty as its key focus. The geographical focus of PPT is also more closely defined than for other types of tourism, focusing exclusively on developing countries. Similar to the evolution of PRSs, it is evident that PPT does not necessarily represent a radical challenge to the status quo of the existing political economy. It can operate as a concept within existing political structures, including neo-liberalism, provided that the benefits of tourism include and target poor people.

- An evident pre-requisite for tourism development is that there is an asset base of natural and cultural resources that are attractive for tourists. Consequently, tourism's use in combating poverty will be restricted to specific regions and locations, and subsequently not all LDCs and developing countries will be able to benefit equally. In Ricardian terminology, some developing countries and regions will possess the natural and cultural resources that lend them a much stronger comparative advantage than other places. Although PPT and ST-EP are significant policy initiatives, the utilisation of tourism to combat poverty faces significant challenges, which has led to a questioning of the extent that tourism can actually alleviate poverty and assist poor people to have improved livelihoods.

- There is a lack of data on the beneficial impacts of tourism development on the poor. Existing data tends to be micro-level in scope, focusing on a single enterprise or a community, which are typically analysed through a combination of sustainable livelihood analysis (SAS) that includes micro-economic analysis and non-financial impacts on how people live. Typical impacts include 'direct', 'secondary' and 'dynamic' effects. To date, the small scale of the projects that characterise much of the tourism and poverty initiatives has drawn criticism because of their limited impact on the poverty reduction agenda and small-scale character. Through being able to demonstrate how tourism can make a positive contribution to opportunities for health and education within an integrated planning approach across government ministries, tourism's chances of playing an active part in achieving targets such as MDGs and improving the poor's well-being will be enhanced.

6 ▌ A way forward

This chapter:

- Identifies and evaluates emergent paradigms and challenges relevant to the tourism and poverty reduction agenda
- Analyses necessary changes in development to induce poverty reduction
- Explores strategies for how tourism can be used for poverty reduction

INTRODUCTION

The three key themes of the book have focused on the interaction of tourism, development and poverty and this chapter attempts to consider the relationship between them in the context of emergent paradigms and the associated challenges and opportunities that have direct relevance to the use of tourism for poverty reduction. The preceding chapters of this book have been written on the premise that poverty is an economically and socially created condition and is subsequently solvable if the political will exists to do so. To an extent this is demonstrable in the advances that have been made in terms of reducing the percentage of the world's population living in extreme poverty but there still remain approximately over 1 billion people experiencing chronic poverty. Chronic and absolute poverty remain an entrenched problem in particular regions of the world, notably sub-Saharan Africa, the East Asia and Pacific region, and also South Asia.

Poverty affects not only today's generations but also future generations where people are caught in a 'poverty trap'. There are also pressing issues of demographic change in the LDCs where the majority of the populations are under 35 years of age, which creates its own political and social tensions and challenges. There are pressing economic, environmental and social problems linked to poverty, which the poor have to face and deal with on a day-to-day basis, but that have implications for us all. It is evident that economic growth, if appropriately targeted, can create livelihood opportunities for the poor. However, as has been stressed in the previous chapters, after six United Nations development decades, global economic development is still failing to have relevance and make positive links to hundreds of millions of the world's population. It is therefore imperative that ways are found to ensure that economic growth continues on a sustainable basis and critically becomes fully inclusive of the poor. This entails understanding development as a participatory process that is able to fulfil the poor's aspirations rather than as being defined by the prescriptive doctrines of supranational agencies and multinational players. Whilst this may be interpreted as idealistic, without ideals there is little chance of economic and social progress, and creating opportunities for the poor.

New systems and processes have to be found to promote economic and environmentally sustainable growth that prioritise the poor in the LDCs and other developing countries. This will not be achieved without the meaningful participation of the poor in the development process. Human freedoms, rights and opportunities, whether in tourism or any other type of economic development are essential components for good governance and civil cohesion as opposed to poor governance and social division. The growth of tourism to LDCs theoretically offers the potential for the creation of livelihood opportunities and improvements in well-being for the poor. This is not an easy task but is one that is achievable with political will, good governance and productive partnerships between the private sector, government, NGOs and, critically, the poor. Chapter 5 evaluated the two most significant developments in this direction to date, PPT and ST-EP. Whilst these do not directly challenge the existing political economy, they are highly significant initiatives in recognising tourism's potential for poverty reduction, although it is also evident that there is a vast amount of work to be done in making tourism a realistic option to operationalise within the economic growth–poverty reduction nexus. A part of this is to ensure that approaches to tourism and poverty reduction embrace emergent paradigms in development and political change as is discussed in the next section of this chapter.

EMERGENT PARADIGMS AND CHALLENGES

A green economy

There are emergent social and economic trends in society that are and will have an important relevance to how tourism is used in development and for poverty reduction. A central one of relevance is the increasing debate of the purpose of economic growth, how to achieve it in a sustainable way, and also a questioning of what are the 'developed countries' evolving to and what is development for. Such questioning has a philosophical bias related to the meaning we attach to life, our relationships to each other and our surroundings. Whilst this may seem esoteric or perhaps avant-garde, to have any real chance of alleviating poverty and achieving a balance with our surroundings into the future, it is necessary to have a clearer definition of what development is. Without addressing this key issue, global society will be on a constant 'economic growth is good' treadmill, which will eventually stop running as environmental resources can no longer support its operation. Cultural differences are also evident in the perspective of what development is for. Whilst in the West it is typically seen as a means of LDCs catching up to the living standards of the West, in Africa development is interpreted more to do with well-being, happiness and community (Commission for Africa, 2005).

This train of thinking has led to the emergence of the post-development paradigm, critics who condemn the development project itself as creating mass poverty under an illusion of social improvement based upon Eurocentric economic paradigms of advancement, which interpret the problems of the 'Third World', including poverty as being only able to be fixed by Western 'know how', ignoring the needs of local people. Oswaldo de Rivero (2001) terms this the 'Myth of Development' that rests upon a premise of Western civilisation's ideology of progress and the association of happiness with material progress. Sachs (1999: 7) is similarly damning on the whole concept and processes of development, expressing an opinion that it has led to increased inequality rather than less and is increasingly focused on global security. This opinion was stated before 9/11 and the case for understanding 'development' as a process for global security has become even stronger given the links between poverty, a lack of education and terrorism. Commenting on the political expediency of the concept, Sachs (1999: 7) writes: 'Development thus has no content but it does possess a function: it allows any intervention to be sanctified in the name of a high evolutionary goal.' The central theme of post-development thinking is the questioning of what is being done in its name and what is hoped to be achieved through its pursuit. Although post-development thought has been criticised as 'romantic', it raises important issues and reflections on what the human race is aspiring to achieve, individually and collectively.

Environmental constraints have also emerged as a challenge to a pattern of development driven by natural resource usage. Human desires are insatiable and it is a myth to assume that economic growth can fulfil not just the need but the 'wants' of everyone without leading to an environmental catastrophe. Two decades after the Earth Summit in Rio de Janeiro, what may have seemed far-off concerns have now become reality, including climate change, loss of biodiversity, desertification and land degradation. In 2011, the United Nations Environment Programme (UNEP) published a seminal report 'Towards a Green Economy: Pathways to Sustainable Development and Poverty Eradication: A Synthesis for Policy Makers', indicative of the United Nations' evaluation of the future direction of global economic and environmental policy. Although not a radical political manifesto for revolutionary change, the report is highly significant for laying down a pragmatic agenda for the 'greening' of economic development. In particular it calls for 2 per cent of global GDP to be ring-fenced for its use in greening ten central sectors of the economy in order to shift development and unleash public and private capital flows onto a low-carbon, resource-efficient path. UNEP (2011: 9) define a Green Economy as: 'one that results in improved human well-being and social equity, while significantly reducing environmental risks and ecological scarcities'.

Other concerns have also been raised about the direction of our economic progress and calls been made for a new political economy embracing a wider perspective of economic development to include concerns of wealth and income distribution, well-being and happiness, and environmental sustainability (Shah and McIver, 2006). The emphasis of economic growth subsequently shifts from the achievement of an end state – for example, mass consumerism – to become a process that provides a sustainable and socially just route to a better quality of life and equality that extends beyond a material measurement. Such reflections raise questions of the type of growth and development we want and the trade-offs we are prepared to make as a society for economic production to meet our needs and wants.

As a part of the move towards a green economy, tourism is recognised by UNEP (2011) as an economic sector that has an important role to play in a sustainable future. Whilst recognising the environmental challenges of tourism, including GHG emissions, high levels of water consumption and damage to biodiversity, the report emphasises that when tourism is 'well designed' it can both interact beneficially with the local economy and reduce poverty. Somewhat optimistically it suggests that tourists are driving the greening of the sector, although there is limited empirical evidence to support this claim. Whilst the tourism industry has undoubtedly become more environmentally aware, and made valid contributions across the sector – for example, through corporate social responsibility and charters of responsible tourism – the evidence that this is consumer driven is largely circumstantial. Recognising that the interaction between the tourism industry and the consumer in the market will be crucial for deciding the outcomes of tourism's relationship with nature, Holden (2009) in a review of available empirical data of consumer behaviour found that the influence of an environmental ethic on tourism consumption was to date marginal.

The report emphasises the employment multiplier effect of tourism, highlighting that it is estimated that one job in the core tourism industry creates about one and a half additional or indirect jobs in the tourism-related economy. Progress towards the greening of the sector should reinforce the employment potential of the sector with increased local hiring and sourcing. Similar to the proposals of the UNWTO (2012) and Pro-Poor Tourism Partnership (2012), UNEP (2011: 19) stress opportunities for the poor: 'In greening the tourism sector, increasing the involvement of local community, especially the poor, in the tourism value chain is essential to developing the local economy and reducing poverty.'

This call for a move towards a green economy is symbolic of a widespread disillusionment with our prevailing economic paradigm, a sense of fatigue emanating from the many concurrent crises and market failures experienced during the first decade of the new millennium, epitomised in the global financial and economic crisis of 2008. It also builds on underlying conscious and subconscious anxieties about how human activity is affecting the environment, its effects on ourselves and future generations, the world's ecosystems and individual species. Whilst since the 1980s the size of the world economy has quadrupled, benefiting hundreds of millions of people, approximately 60 per cent of the world's major ecosystem goods and services that underpin livelihoods have been degraded or been used unsustainably (UNEP, 2011). The environmental base of the economic growth of recent decades is not sustainable as stocks of natural resources have not been allowed time to regenerate, causing widespread ecosystem degradation and loss.

As was explained in Chapter 1, the geographical focus of the extra couple of billion people added to the global population by 2050 will be in LDCs. This will place extra pressure on natural resources; for example, water stress is projected to increase with water supply satisfying only 60 per cent of world demand in 20 years (UNEP, 2011). There is also a need to respond to the changing demographics that will shape the course of the twenty-first century and to find a balance between meeting people's needs and sustaining the natural environment. Issues of food security, freshwater supplies and clean drinking water are key challenges to the improvement of the lives of the poor. The projections of increases in the populations of geographical regions where many of the world's poorest countries are found suggest that there are going to be even greater challenges to the poor's well-being in the future and to achieving the Millennium Development Goals (MDGs). However, a young population – for example, in Africa two-thirds of the population are under 25 – presents great opportunities in terms of potential dynamism of a growing workforce and a consumer market. The history of development, including most recently the dynamic growth of China, points to the importance of large internal markets. To realise this potential requires a combination of the provision of educational opportunities for the majority of the population and investment to create employment and income-earning opportunities.

Persistent absolute poverty is the most visible form of social inequity, related as it is to unequal access to education, health care, income opportunities and secure property rights, denying the ability for individuals to play a full role in society. A key feature of a green economy is that it seeks to provide diverse opportunities for economic development and poverty alleviation without liquidating or eroding a country's natural assets. It is in essence putting sustainable development into practice that embraces intra- and inter-generational equity. This is particularly necessary in LDCs, where ecosystem goods and services are a large component of the livelihoods of poor rural communities and provide a safety net against natural disasters and economic shocks as was discussed in Chapter 3. As an industry based on climate sensitivity and natural resources, tourism has the potential to play a major role in achieving sustainable development that includes elements of pro-poor growth, distributive justice and resource conservation. However, despite the preaching of a similar doctrine during the last two decades, evidence suggests only limited achievements can be made if the dominant wider political economy does not promote or engage with a progressive social agenda toward equality of income and opportunity, which neo-liberalism and free markets have failed to do.

A changing political economy

A second major trend to accompany the changes in environmental pressures and demographics is a changing political economy. As several commentators (Pieterse, 2010; De Rivero, 2001) have stated, neo-liberalism, especially the style of Anglo-American capitalism that manifested itself in the Washington Consensus, is crumbling from its own excesses. The global financial crisis of 2008 has led to a questioning of its merits and calls for greater state intervention and regulation, particularly of financial markets that act as a key driving force of globalisation. This recognition for an increased role at least at a national level to direct economic development is partially reflected in the shift of the World Bank and IMF from SAPs to PRS, within which tourism has a significant role in many LDCs.

An increased role for the state in directing economic development provides opportunities for it to be pro-active in developing policy for the use of tourism for sustainable economic growth and poverty reduction. This is important, as for tourism to play a serious role in poverty reduction strategies it needs recognition and careful planning to produce a holistic approach in place of *ad hoc* schemes that have only a local economic impact on the poor and can only help limited numbers of people. Ideally, nationally strategies for the use of tourism for poverty reduction need to be integrated with the priorities of other ministries; for example, health and agriculture as was exemplified in the case of Nepal in Box 5.2. Besides such an approach proving the worth of tourism as a tool for poverty reduction to government, it also demonstrates to rural communities and the poor that tourism can offer them wider benefits than purely employment and income opportunities, to include, for example, health and education provision.

A changing political economy encompasses a changing geographical paradigm of hegemonic core areas. Whilst the rise of the NICs represented a significant demonstration of the economic and industrial development possibilities outside the USA and Europe, it is particularly the economic rise of countries with large internal markets that is re-positioning the cores of economic power in the first half of the twenty-first century. Whilst the USA and Europe will continue as significant global economic players, the impressive economic rise of China since the 1980s, notwithstanding the environmental problems and human rights issues that have accompanied its growth, adds a new dimension to global economic investment patterns. China's economic growth is accompanied by an increase in South–South relations in trade and the growing economic and political importance of the 'BRIC' countries, that is, Brazil, Russia, India and China (Pieterse, 2010). It is in the newly industrialising countries of Asia, Latin America and eastern Europe that the world economy is being driven forward, with economic growth in the global south being higher than in developed countries, even in Africa, the so-called 'basket case' of twentieth-century development (ibid.). Concurrent to the growth in the economic importance of the South has been an increased economic and political instability in Europe and the USA following 9/11 and the 2008 financial crisis.

Development progress has been made in the first decade of the twenty-first century in many African countries, with many of the continent's wars having ended or been scaled back and many countries seeing economic growth at their highest levels since independence, accompanied by a decline in many fatal diseases including Aids, TB and malaria pandemics (Sachs, 2010). One of the key drivers for progress in the African countries has been the role of China, which is ubiquitous in its presence on the continent and alongside an investment in infrastructure and industry has also been instrumental in fighting the spread of AIDS. Emphasising the contemporary and future importance of major Southern economic powers in global investment, Sachs (2010: 31) suggests: 'Where China is today, India will follow soon.'

Africa is undergoing large-scale foreign and domestic investments in mining, banking, agriculture and information technology, with an increasing number of investors regarding the social investments in education and health as areas in which they can and should participate. Besides China, the business organisations of other BRIC countries are investing heavily in many countries in contrast to established Western economies (Clayton, 2012). The attraction is a potential high return on investments even if the risks are also comparatively high in relation to other parts of the world. Some of the world's fastest growing economies are now in Africa: Ghana was the fastest growing economy in the world in 2011 and Africa as a whole has the fastest growing middle class in the world, expected to rise from approximately 300 million to nearly 1 billion by 2022 (ibid.).

The significance of the shift towards increased inward investment in African countries also offers an opportunity for the creation of entrepreneurial activity and the potential to lift millions of people out of poverty. This is important as the potential for the creation of independent livelihoods through increased financial investment is likely to be substantially higher than through aid programmes. The combination of political stability and inward investment in several African countries will be likely to offer an environment for potential tourism investment provided infrastructure barriers can be overcome, which if tilted to include the poor within PRSs will offer livelihood opportunities. An interesting example of the debate of the potential role of tourism investment as a catalyst for development and poverty reduction in Sierra Leone is given in Box 6.1.

BOX 6.1 'TOURISM WILL NOT BE A QUICK FIX FOR SIERRA LEONE'

This is the headline from an article in a British newspaper in response to the United Kingdom's ex-prime minister Tony Blair's (2009) column in the same paper entitled 'Sierra Leone rises again' in which he states that the end of the civil war in the country means that the natural resources of the country, including unspoilt beaches, beautiful tropical islands, world-class fishing and diving, and a rich cultural and historical legacy linked to its role in the slave trade, can now be used for tourism as a catalyst to economic development. He refers to the optimism and ambition of the plans of entrepreneurs in Freetown, including the construction of new hotels and facilities in anticipation of the increase in tourist demand over the next few years. Alongside its natural and cultural resources, Blair (ibid.) suggests that the country's inclusion in the influential guide book series *Lonely Planet* as one of its top ten countries to visit and the availability of direct air routes to Europe that take just six hours are instrumental to driving a growth in tourism demand. Referring to the commodity dependency of Sierra Leone's economy on diamonds, Blair (ibid.) suggests that tourism has the potential to overtake diamonds as the country's largest foreign exchange earner.

Writing in response to Tony Blair's vision that tourism will rescue the national economy of Sierra Leone, Forna (2009), a Sierra Leonean, points out some realities of the challenges that face the development of tourism in her country. One is the lack of infrastructure, a problem that is common to many LDCs. She refers to the airport being sited on a peninsula with no connection to Freetown other than by a: 'hair-raising helicopter ride or – intermittently – an ancient ferry, which sometimes runs aground, forcing local fisherman to rescue passengers'. In reference to the optimism of the hotel entrepreneurs, she comments that they face problems of a lack of water and electricity, with hotels being forced to rely on their own generators and bring in daily bowsers of water, adding that despite billions of dollars having been given in foreign aid, the country's infrastructure remains scarcely improved. In contrast to Blair (ibid.), Forna (ibid.) advocates that the agricultural sector offers a real long-term sustainable future for the country not tourism, pointing out that Sierra Leone was once a rice-exporting country but now is reliant on rice imports. Critically, she also points out that very little economic development and growth can be achieved in any economic sector without a working infrastructure. A further criticism that can be made of Blair's vision is that a growth in tourism development and the realisation of macro-economic benefits will not necessarily reduce poverty unless it incorporates the poor into the industry and markets that drive it. The application of trickle-down theory does little to alleviate poverty, there is a need to tilt the mainstream tourism industry to incorporate the poor and develop alternative forms of tourism to provide opportunities for the poor.

In a further addendum about the economic development of Sierra Leone, President Ernest Bai Koroma writes about the tragedy of the waste of the country's natural resources during 60 years as a consequence of previous government corruption and the descent of the country into a tragic civil war. He talks now of a desire to use the wealth of the natural resources of the country, including gold, iron ore, bauxite, palm oil, sugar, offshore oil and diamonds to improve the lives of Sierra Leoneans. To achieve this he recognises the need for improved governance and the need for foreign investors to open their supply chains to local small and medium-size enterprises. In a strategy to give an added value to these raw materials and boost Sierra Leone's economic growth and exports, he stresses the need for more processing of these resources in the country. Focusing on the price disparity between the primary commodity and processed material, he comments: 'a ton of iron ore currently sells on the world market for less than a fifth of the price of a ton of steel. If Sierra Leone can start to process more of our iron ore into steel, it could add 20 to 40 per cent to our GDP by 2035' (Koroma, 2012: 9).

Source: after Blair, 2009; Forna, 2009; Koroma, 2012

Alongside increased inward investment, a further range of factors is also contributing to improved rates of economic growth in Africa. These include an increasing use of information technology, which has spread providing enhanced communications and networking. The development of the information technology and telecommunications industry is emphasised by Maathai (2009) as being critically important to the future economic development of African countries. She cites the countries of Kenya, South Africa and Ghana as examples of the enormous potential markets in sub-Saharan Africa for the telecommunications industry. Importantly, she stresses the potential that the development of this sector makes in terms of opportunities for Africans to increase their standard of living, expand intra- and inter-African trade, and for economic development that extends beyond the extractions of primary resources and commodity exports.

Accompanying the adoption of IT across the continent is the development of the air transport industry which will play a pivotal role in increasing the inter-connectivity of places between and within African countries in the future. The development of an air transport sector is vital to increasing flows of tourists between African countries and the orientating of tourism towards PPG and poverty reduction. A reflection of the growing confidence to invest in Africa is the plan to develop Africa's first budget airline, Fast Jet, which will operate primarily on east to west routes, linking Kenya, Tanzania, Ghana and Angola (Lea, 2012). With an emergent middle class in the continent, the potential for air travel is emphasised in a comparison of capacity with the United States, with there being presently one aircraft seat for every 13,000 Africans compared to 2.5 aircraft seats for every one American (ibid.).

Critically, there has been improved governance in many of the African states attributed in part to the influence of the collection and publishing of data on progress towards the targets of the MDGs, which has induced competition between countries on grounds of improvements in environmental and social welfare (United Nations, 2011). Fundamental to ensuring the effective and equitable use of tourism for poverty reduction is good 'governance', which establishes the framework for economic, social and environmental progress through participation, transparency and accountable processes. The concept of governance and its importance for development is emphasised by the IBRD (2009: 60) as: 'the way public officials and institutes acquire and exercise authority to provide public goods and services, including education, health care, infrastructure, and a sound investment climate. Good governance is associated with increased citizen participation and improved accountability of public officials. It is fundamental to development and economic growth.' The necessity of good governance to create the right economic, social and legal frameworks to encourage growth and allow poor people to participate in it is also stressed by the Commission for Africa (2005). It points out that reductions in poverty do not occur without economic growth which is driven by the private sector. Subsequently, it is the role of government to create the climate in which: 'ordinary people – whether they be small farmers or managers of large firms – can get on with their daily tasks untroubled, and feel that it is worthwhile investing in their future' (ibid.: 28).

Conversely, 'bad governance' embraces corruption and the abuse of public office for private gain, which undermines the legitimacy of government and reduces the availability and quality of public services, if financial resources are instead misap-propriated for private use. Corruption may also take the form of excessive bureaucracy that can make it necessary for unofficial payments, a euphemism for bribes, to get things done. Alongside undermining faith in institutes, this system-atic corruption may also prevent the poor from starting small enterprises. For example, Holden *et al.* (2011) observed in Elmina in Ghana that a significant barrier to the development of tourism micro-enterprises by the poor was the necessity to pay multiple incentives to officials to attain the necessary permits for their operation as is described in Box 6.5.

BEGINNING THE DEVELOPMENT CHANGE

> If the poor are to gain directly from growth and participate fully in the development process, new institutions and policies are needed to achieve redistribution of productive resources to the poor, generate rapid expansion in jobs and income-earning opportunities and provide social and economic services on a mass basis. A shift of development strategy to achieve these ends will depend on political will, efficient economic management and effective mobilisation of resources.
>
> (Brandt, 1980: 128)

This statement, calling for radical change and shift in policy and development strate-gies to provide an agenda for poverty reduction through participatory processes, reads as though it could have been written today. Somewhat depressingly, it was written over 30 years ago as the outcome of the 'Independent Commission on International Development Issues' established by Willy Brandt, the former chancellor of the then Federal Republic of Germany. The 'independence' was stressed as a freedom from the agendas of international organisations and the commission was: 'to present recom-mendations which could improve the climate for further deliberations on North–South relations' (ibid.: 293). Including Brandt, the Commission had 17 members, with ten coming from developing countries. Whilst not acted upon at its time of publication, many of its recommendations for policy and action, including the prioritising the needs of the poorest, abolishing hunger, the stabilisation of commodity prices, the end to developed countries' protection of their industries, controls of transnational compa-nies, new approaches to development finance, and power sharing, have a remarkable resonance with the contemporary political agenda and several of the MDGs.

Whilst progress has been made in reducing poverty over the last 30 years, it is evident that there still remains a considerable amount of work to be done in achieving a reduction in poverty and improving human development in its widest sense of incorporating democracy and social justice. It is also evident that the paradigms, principles and procedures of political economy that have dominated since the 1980s are inadequate to meet the needs of the poor and alleviate poverty totally. There is a subsequent need to change the 'rules' of the global economy to ensure that they are favourable to development in the LDCs and critically to the poor within those countries. The important institutes for setting the parameters of global governance remain those established through Bretton Woods, that is, the World Bank and International Monetary Fund. Despite having reportedly placed poverty reduction at the centre of policy design through the PRSs, the simultaneous pursuit of neo-liberal ideals has meant that many developing countries remain pressurised into opening their markets to multinational and foreign companies, cutting state support of farming and industry, and deregulating their financial sectors. There is little evidence to suggest that these measures have been beneficial to those in chronic poverty.

The institutions and purpose of the IMF and World Bank themselves, created over 60 years ago in a different economic and political era in the context of post-Second World War economic reconstruction, require re-evaluation and reform. A signifi-cant step forward would be for an enhanced voting power of the LDCs and devel-oping countries in the governing structures of the World Bank and IMF; for example, sub-Saharan countries comprise 27 per cent of the member countries but have only 8 per cent of the votes in the Division of the World Bank dealing with loan appro-priations (Green and Allen, 2008). The African perception of both the World Bank and the IMF is that they are highly rigid organisations with harmfully prescriptive approaches to development and one in need of a stronger African voice in decision-making and increased responsiveness (Commission for Africa, 2005).

There is also the issue of leadership and presidency of the World Bank and IMF. The process of choice is hardly openly democratic, with the USA always choosing the head of the World Bank, always an American, and Europe selecting the head of the IMF, always a European. The confidence of the voice of the political South was raised in 2012 with a call for the Nigerian finance minister, Ngozi Okonjo-Iweala, to become the first African female director of the World Bank. Whilst she was unsuccessful in her candidature, it will be increasingly difficult in the changing global political economy of the rise of the South's economic power during the twenty-first century for the directorship of the World Bank and IMF to remain respectively in the hands of American and European 'elects' indefinitely.

Simultaneously, the rules of the World Trade Organisation also need reform to shift them away from the protection and interests of developed countries and to help protect those of developing countries. A change to the conditions of trade are necessary, to ensure that trade tariffs, that is, taxes on imports, are not used by rich countries to ban exports from LDCs, whilst at the same time generous subsidies are given to agricultural production in the developed countries. This practice of subsidy allows farmers in the USA and the European Union to export their produce at approximately half the economic cost of production, undercutting developing-country producers (Green and Allen, 2008), a situation that is compounded through the removal of trade barriers that permit large Western agribusinesses to dominate productivity. Beside the general undermining of the agricultural sector in developing countries, which is the most significant economic sector in which the poor are employed, this practice also poses a challenge to strengthening the links between the tourism industry in LDCs and local agricultural producers if it is cheaper for tourism enterprises to purchase imported agricultural products from the developed countries. An inability to strengthen this supply chain link with local agriculture substantially reduces income and employment opportunities for the poor.

There is a subsequent evident need for a re-orientation of development policy at global and national levels, one objective being to ensure that poorer countries have more power to determine their own economic policies. For this to happen will need a conceptual leap by many of those who hold power and the emergence of a new generation of leaders who are willing to tackle conservative mainstream paradigms and thinking. For Sachs (2005: 2), the approach to tackling global poverty extends beyond just government leaders and those of global institutions to become a collective one, as he eloquently comments: 'This task is a collective one –for you as well as me. Although introductory economics textbooks preach individualised and decentralised markets, our safety and prosperity depend at least as much on collective decisions to fight disease, promote good science and widespread education, provide critical infrastructure, and act in union to help the poorest of the poor.' Implicit in Sachs's statement is the level of inter-connectedness of today's global society, that even if for no other reason than for our own self-interest, poverty is not an issue that can be ignored as it threatens everyone's security. His vision also emphasises stakeholder partnerships and a wider social responsibility towards the world's poor. Chapter 5 evaluated the initiatives being taken in the pro-poor tourism arena, and the targeting of the poor within the private and public sectors is evidently a key part of the use of tourism for poverty reduction. Other initiatives taken by individuals – for example, philanthropic tourism and volunteer tourism – are indicative of a wider collective direct action that Sachs (ibid.) is referring to.

Sachs's (2005) emphasis on collective action as an approach to tackling poverty has resonance to global security and the ability of individuals to be able to have and take opportunities to develop their own lives in a peaceful and secure environment. World history emphasises that poverty is a contributory factor to times of social upheaval, including political extremism, terrorism and wars over resources. Creating structures of political economy that accommodate poverty reduction and the levelling of wealth inequalities is therefore in the interests of global society besides the poor. Against a backdrop of a world that is running low on natural resources, including water, oil and productive agricultural land, and faces an uncertain future from climate change at a time of increasing wealth inequalities within and between countries, it would be either foolish or brave to ignore this inflammatory cocktail of shaken social spirits.

A key part of this re-orientation of development policy is to ensure the poor have enhanced representation in development decision-making at a local besides global level. Just as the Commission for Africa (2005) have advocated greater representation in the World Bank and IMF, at a local level the poor need to be included in decision-making and not marginalised and excluded. Included in this re-orientation is a need to respond to the environmental pressures that are faced by the poor. As was explained in Chapter 3, the environment and resources of place typically provide the poor with their livelihood resources they depend upon for their well-being but many of the ecosystem services the poor rely upon have been placed under threat from ecosystem degradation. One approach to mitigating the likelihood of poverty is thus to arrest environmental degradation through resource conservation, combined with democratic participatory approaches to planning and development, and the use of environmentally renewable technologies.

The aims of this greater representative and participatory processes should be to develop a rich understanding of the poor's economic aspirations and to raise the capacity of local people to realise them through sustainable resource usage. This combination of actions lends the poor substantially more power to be able to adapt to livelihood challenges and opportunities through giving them legal protection of access and control of use of the natural resources they require. Whilst an inclusive voice in the development decision-making process at a local level is important, the spatial geography and political resonance of this voice needs to extend beyond the local to the regional and national levels as decisions made at these levels have repercussions for local development, as is illustrated in Box 6.2 in the context of sustainable tourism development in the Annapurna region of Nepal.

BOX 6.2 ISSUES OF PARTICIPATORY DECISION-MAKING IN TOURISM DEVELOPMENT IN ANNAPURNA

Whilst a participatory and inclusive voice for the poor in the development decision-making process at a local level is important, the spatial geography and political resonance of this voice is also critical. Local and community based decision-making may be undermined by decisions that are made beyond localised boundaries, exemplified in the case of planned infrastructure development juxtaposed to the Annapurna Conservation Area (ACA) in Nepal, a country that is regularly ranked in the lower quartile of the United Nations Human Development Index (HDI). Nepal's comparatively poor level of human development may be attributed to a combination of factors, including poor governance and its geophysical characteristics. The challenges presented to infrastructure construction by Nepal's topography have contributed to its restricted development, whilst the harsh climatic conditions and difficulties in communications make livelihoods marginal and vulnerable. Yet the geomorphology of the Nepal Himalaya that has traditionally exacerbated this undeveloped state is simultaneously a strong magnet and draw for tourists, as in the case of ACA. Given the topography and lack of transport infrastructure (there are no roads within ACA), the tourism industry is characterised by trekking, that is, mountain and hill walking.

The ACA has thousands of people who live in its boundaries and consequently integrates aspects of development, conservation and tourism management, coordinated under the auspices of the Annapurna Area Conservation Project (ACAP). Emphasis is placed upon the participation of village peoples in the development decision-making to help realise self-directed opportunities, leading to the eventual self-management of ACA. Partnerships between ACAP and village representatives have subsequently been established; for example, with village development committees (VDCs), lodge management committees (LMCs) and women's development committees (WDCs). This 'bottom-up' philosophy of tourism planning and development based upon principles of participatory approaches, community empowerment and local governance has led to ACAP being cited extensively as an example of successful community development through tourism. The scheme has received various international agency, governmental and industry awards; for example, the British Airways 'Tourism for Tomorrow' Award in 1991 and the World Wide Fund for Nature Conservation Merit Award in 2000.

The future of ACA is uncertain as the construction of a major new road linking the settlements of Jomson and Beni that has recently been completed follows the principal trekking route of the Kali Gandaki valley, follows with the potential for the extension of the road beyond Jomson to the Chinese border. If this happens, the Kali Gandaki valley could again become an important trade route between China and India, bringing increased development opportunities to Annapurna, but also changing the character of tourism as Annapurna loses its remoteness. Local lodge owners consider that macro-political forces beyond ACA have had a major influence on its development, as exemplified by this statement: 'The road has been in the envelope for the last 30 years – it is a big political game between China and India – the power is not with the village development committees; it is more with what China and India want.' Tourism to ACA had also been adversely affected by the civil war in the country, which, whilst now finished, demonstrated the vulnerability of the industry to events that were beyond the control of local development decision-making. Several lodge owners thought of tourism as a 'young' industry and less sustainable than traditional agriculture, one that was not necessarily economically secure for the long term.

In the face of these external political forces, planning for sustainable tourism development was viewed as being relatively inconsequential by the lodge owners, characterised in the following statement: 'The future of tourism as we know it has a deadline– so long-term planning doesn't have a future.' There existed a consensus that once the road was opened, efforts to control access and development into the ACA would be difficult. There was also concern over an absence of previous government consultation and the lack of consideration of the road's impacts upon their livelihoods. Whilst they perceived the road as being beneficial for development, bringing increased trade and domestic tourism, they thought it would also cause a significant decline in the more lucrative Western tourism market as Annapurna loses its remoteness and authenticity.

Source: after Holden, 2010

The necessity to achieve a sustainable resource usage model for natural resources that makes the poor active participants in development is also a theme of Maathai's (2009) analysis of the required steps to create the environment in which African countries can alleviate poverty. She uses the analogy of the 'traditional African stool' to define three legs of support that are required. Whilst drawing upon the post-imperialist experiences of African countries and having a strong cultural context, the principles have a symbiotic relation to key concepts of sustainable development, human development and the green economy. The first leg is the creation of good governance, what she refers to as 'democratic space' in which individual rights are respected, including human, women's, children's and environmental. This includes equitable access to resources, rather than them being apportioned by political leaders amongst themselves, their friends and their supporters. The need for governmental reforms has been dramatically demonstrated by the mass protests and changes in governance that swept through several North African countries and the Middle East beginning in spring 2011, possibly marking a seminal point in demand for change from autocratic to democratic governance.

Addressing the lack of capacity to design and deliver policies for sustainable development and poverty reduction is the theme of the second leg of Maathai's stool, which is based upon the sustainable and accountable management of natural resources to ensure their continuance for present and future. An important dimension to the sustainable agenda is an emphasis on the intra-generational equity of resource usage across all age groups and classes in society, as Maathai (2008: 56) puts it: 'in a manner that is just and fair, including for people on the margins of society'. To achieve this will require some degree of a political and economic restructuring of society and the development of participatory processes, and the ensuring of access to resources and the benefits of development for the poor. The third leg of the stool rests on the creation of 'cultures of peace', which encompass fairness, respect, compassion, forgiveness, recompense and justice. Maathai is also keen to emphasise that the three legs are not separate but interconnected. As she puts it: 'Just as the African stool is made out of a single block of wood, each leg or pillar, is reinforced by the others and formed from the same gain, so the issues must be addressed together and simultaneously' (ibid.: 57).

These three legs form the solid support for the stool's seat, which can be visualised as the place and space in which development can take place. If a country's citizens feel that their country is founded on secure democratic principles that permit an equitable distribution of resource across cultural, ethnic and social groups, and has transparent accountability of government, there is a much greater opportunity of a culture of peace within which people can be educated, productive, and creative; a space within which they can realise their potential. A notable further advantage of the creations of a 'secure seat' is that it provides a much more attractive environment for inward investment from the private sector and global agencies. Subsequently, if the stool can be created, not just in African countries but in other LDCs that also suffer from poor governance, there is an opportunity to concentrate resources into strategic areas to help communities climb out of extreme poverty.

One major initiative that has been taken forward that combines many aspects of Maathai's 'stool' is the Millennium Villages Project (MVP) in ten African countries to demonstrate how the MDGs can be achieved as is described in Box 6.3.

BOX 6.3 MILLENNIUM VILLAGES PROJECT (MVP)

The Millennium Villages Project (MVP) is a partnership between the Earth Institute at Columbia University, Millennium Promise and the United Nations Development Programme (UNDP), which aims to demonstrate that even the poorest and most remote communities in rural sub-Saharan Africa can escape poverty traps and attain the Millennium Development Goals (MDGs). Poverty is understood within the MVP as being multidimensional to include hunger, education, access to health care, water resources and environment. Emphasis is placed on tackling the root causes of poverty in partnerships between governments, civil society and businesses with the purpose of empowering communities and providing them with solutions to lift themselves out of poverty. Project staff work in the villages with the local communities to meet their specific needs and to design action plans that will help them achieve the MDGs. Simple solutions, such as the use of high-yield seeds, fertilisers, and anti-malarial bed nets, combined with infrastructure improvements of key public facilities, such as clinic and schools, and capacity building at the local level are employed to combat extreme poverty. The project wants to demonstrate that through low-cost investments in agriculture, education, health, business development and infrastructure, greater changes can be made to fight extreme poverty, hunger and diseases.

To date the MVP has benefited almost 500,000 people in 14 sites located across ten African countries (Ethiopia, Ghana, Kenya, Malawi, Mali, Nigeria, Rwanda, Senegal, Tanzania and Uganda). The sectors covered by the project are: food, water and energy, environment, technology and innovation, gender equality, mother and child health, education, and business entrepreneurship. The four key pillars of the MVP are: (i) increasing sustainable agricultural crop production; (ii) improving food and nutrition security; (iii) farm diversification for income generation; and (iv) underpinning sustainability by restoring and conserving the natural resource base. Since the project started there has been a decrease by 30 per cent in the levels of chronic under-nutrition and a fall of 50 per cent in the proportion of under-weight children below two years of age across the villages. Supporting rural economies in their transition from subsistence farming to commercial agriculture is also a crucial element of the project, including facilitating access to loans and providing links between farmers and farmer cooperatives. A successful case was the organisation of banana farmers in Ruhiira in Uganda into producer groups, which increased the benefits of sales to almost twice the price for their bananas, compared to when they were sold individually. The overall aim of the Millennium Villages Project is to develop capacity-building within the communities so that these initiatives can be continued and a solid foundation provided for sustainable growth into the future.

Sources: http://www.millenniumvillages.org/;
http://www.unmillenniumproject.org/mv/index.htm

'TILTING TOURISM': THE USE OF TOURISM FOR POVERTY REDUCTION

The emergent trends towards a green economy and the shifting geographical dynamism of the global political economy presents opportunities for the comparative advantages of the natural and cultural resources of many LDCs to be used in a sustainable approach to tourism that can reduce poverty. A major consideration in tourism's use for poverty reduction is its geographical scale and the political economy within which it operates. To play an effective role, tourism policy targeting poverty reduction needs to be able to work within different development paradigms. One is the alternative development paradigm – a typical type of low-scale development project that would fulfil many of the criteria inherent to this paradigm, described in Box 6.4, on tourism development in Kerala in India.

BOX 6.4 THE DEVELOPMENT OF *GOODEARTH* COMMUNITY-BASED TOURISM IN KERALA, INDIA

Renowned for their beauty, cruising the backwaters of Kerala on houseboats has become a popular tourist activity with hundreds of boats transporting tourists around the lagoons, canals and rivers. The development of the industry has led to negative environmental and social effects, including the pollution of the waters from engine and toilet waste. Several of the boats are also multistorey affairs blasting music through the beautiful scenery that first attracted tourists.

In 2011 four villages – Vayalar, Chenganda, Perumbalam and Kodamthuruthu – established the Keyal Gramodhaya (Backwater

Self-help Group) in conjunction with the ecotourism specialist Village Ways, to create an ecotourism and community-based tourism project. The villagers constructed a houseboat called the *Goodearth* that they run, working as crew and guides whilst other local people provide services such as laundry, and women make meals for the guests on the boat. Village Ways provided a grant and loan repayable over 30 years to fund the initiative. The *Goodearth* is a small boat with a small environmental footprint; for example, whilst there is an engine, there is no air-conditioning, which greatly reduces energy consumption compared to other boats. All the toilet waste and used water is held in tanks and discharged safely on shore. The trip involves tourists visiting the villages and having direct contact with the villagers and the revenue from the boat's guests is used for village projects, including bridge and path repairs.

Source: based on Eilers, 2012

The case study presented in Box 6.4 illustrates an image of the type of project that is often envisaged in an alternative paradigm of how tourism can be used for poverty reduction. It is small scale and exhibits many characteristics that are symptomatic of sustainable development and social justice; for example, partnerships between the private sector and local communities, participatory approaches, the taking of tourists directly to the market, employment of local people, revenue-sharing schemes and good environmental practices. Whilst to paraphrase the title of the highly respected economist Schumacher's bestselling book 'Small is Beautiful', and to recognise that the impacts of community-based ecotourism projects on the poor may offer significant livelihood opportunities at a local level, at the more macro-economic scale of poverty alleviation, projects of this scale can only ever have a limited and localised impact.

To make tourism effective as a development activity that can reduce poverty on a macro-scale, there is a need for LDCs to identify the opportunities for the use of tourism at a national level for poverty reduction. Whilst requiring a re-think of tourism's role and function in society, this is hardly a new proposal, having been proposed by Ashley *et al.* (2001) over a decade ago, but it is yet to manifest itself in a meaningful way in the policies of nation states. Tourism for many LDCs offers a viable and sustainable economic development option and if it is managed with a strong focus on poverty alleviation, it can directly benefit the poor through the generation of direct, indirect and dynamic benefits as were discussed in Chapter 5. Whilst there are opportunities for action-based approaches as described in the example of Kerala, structural influences of the wider political economy will continue to influence the relationship that tourism has with the poor and also other sectors of the economy. Subsequently, the reforms to the World Bank and IMF to lend a larger voice and weight to the development perspectives of the LDCs and the poor, as discussed in the last section of the chapter, are as necessary to benefit the poor through tourism as for any other economic sector. Besides the impact of the political economy, a range of other barriers exist that challenge the use of tourism for poverty reduction, as is highlighted in a detailed interpretive analysis of the barriers to the poor's involvement in the tourism industry in Elmina in Ghana in Box 6.5.

BOX 6.5 CASE STUDY OF ELMINA: BARRIERS TO THE POOR'S PARTICIPATION IN TOURISM

Ethnographic research was conducted with the 'poor' to provide in-depth understandings of their experiences of poverty and the barriers to participation in the tourism industry in Elmina in Ghana. The tourism market is primarily based upon the cultural experiences of the diaspora from the United States of America and United Kingdom who return to this former slave port to rediscover their roots. Two major annual special events are hosted to commemorate the history of the slave trade – Emancipation Day and the Pan African Historical Festival (PANAFEST) – whilst the forts of Elmina and St Jago represent the primary cultural 'attractions', their main function being to inform and educate visitors about the trans-Atlantic slave trade. Attempts to quantify the economic and livelihood opportunities created by tourism development in Elmina is difficult given the inconsistencies and lack of statistical data, hence any trickle-down effect to the poor is unknown.

A widespread perception held amongst the poor was that as a consequence of their lack of education, their opinion accounted little on economic development, including tourism, in Elmina. There was a strong desire amongst the female participants to have a voice in decision-making, especially as in many families they are the chief income earners, ascribing their exclusion to cultural norms which are patriarchal. In the understandings of poverty, the centrality of a lack of income was stressed in the following statements: 'Poverty is not having a job to earn regular money' and 'it is about not feeding your children, not buying fuel for the fishing boats and firewood to smoke the fish'. The lack of opportunity to secure a regular income was associated with the decline of the traditional industries, especially fishing as expressed in the following statement: 'The fishing industry is the umbilical cord of the people . . . and anything that happens to it leads to the quenching of the fire in our homes.'

Whilst tourism was perceived as offering possible income earning opportunities, a range of barriers were identified by the poor that restricted their involvement in the industry. These included a lack of access to regular income which stopped enterprise opportunities, exemplified in the following statement: 'How can I buy a taxi to take tourists between Elmina and the Cape Coast [regional capital and also a tourist destination] when I don't have enough money to pay for my rent, buy water to drink and food to feed my family?' The inability to save income was compounded by a lack of access to credit facilities, as the poor do not have the collateral to secure loans from banks. A further barrier to entrepreneurship is the necessity to secure several different permits from various government departments to run a business. The process is costly and many of the government departments are situated outside Elmina and respondents claimed that 'incentive' payments have to be paid to officials to process their applications. A lack of education and skills was also a major barrier to gaining employment in the formal tourism industry. The restrictive practices of the tourism industry and market was a further barrier, as tour operators typically have contracts with large hotels, restraints and selected handicraft shops, which restricted tourist purchases to these outlets, giving the poor little market access. A common complaint amongst the poor was a lack of consultation with them about tourism development and their non-participation in decision-making.

Source: after Holden *et al.*, 2011

As the case study of Elmina illustrates there are a range of barriers to overcome that embrace the macro- and micro-levels of policy and practice in tourism. In an attempt to give a structure to how tourism should be used for poverty reduction the UNWTO and SNV (2010) have established ten key guiding principles as shown in Box 6.6.

BOX 6.6 TEN PRINCIPLES FOR PURSUING POVERTY ALLEVIATION THROUGH TOURISM

1. All aspects and types of tourism can and should be concerned about poverty alleviation.
2. All governments should include poverty alleviation as a key aim of tourism development and consider tourism as a possible tool for reducing poverty.
3. The competitiveness and economic success of tourism businesses and destinations is critical to poverty alleviation – without this the poor cannot benefit.
4. All tourism businesses should be concerned about the impact of their activities on local communities and seek to benefit the poor through their actions.
5. Tourism destinations should be managed with poverty alleviation as a central aim that is built into strategies and action plans.
6. A sound understanding of how tourism functions in destinations is required, including how tourism income is distributed and who benefits from this.
7. Planning and development of tourism in destinations should involve a wide range of interests, including participation and representation from poor communities.
8. All potential impacts of tourism on the livelihood of local communities should be considered, including current and future local and global impacts on natural and cultural resources.
9. Attention must be paid to the viability of all projects involving the poor, ensuring access to markets and maximising opportunities for beneficial links with established enterprises.
10. Impacts of tourism on poverty alleviation should be effectively monitored.

Source: UNWTO and SNV, 2010

This list of principles offers a useful framework for consideration in defining tourism policy for poverty reduction; however, many of these principles have to date received little serious consideration in policy and practice. They are also representative of an attempt to establish an agenda for tourism that is built on a sustainable policy and involves meeting political, environmental, social and cultural goals. The emphasis is on trying to tilt the tourism industry and market to work efficiently in the interests of the 'poor'. In the first two principles there is a strong emphasis on the importance of tourism for poverty alleviation and to make it a key aim of tourism development. The role of government is recognised as essential for establishing a national framework for the inclusion of tourism in poverty reduction strategies. There is a requirement for tourism-specific knowledge in government of its potential for poverty reduction, including its supply chain, to ensure the inclusion of the rural population in tourism development. To achieve this more empirical data are required to demonstrate how tourism can make a practical and real contribution to poverty reduction, including the contributions of different types of tourism; for example, mass tourism, domestic tourism, community-based tourism and ecotourism. The problem of a lack of data on poverty, however, is not restricted to tourism – the World Bank (2008) bemoans the lack of available statistics on poverty in many of the poor countries, which makes the ability to assess who is in poverty problematic. Similarly, there is a dearth of data that are relevant to the experiences of poverty. As the World Bank (ibid.) points out, when governments are faced with a lack of resources to provide and maintain the most basic services, record-keeping and the gathering of statistical data may not always be the most urgent priority. However, when statistics and data are unreliable or absent, the decisions of how resources are allocated may be poor and ineffective.

Principles three and four recognise the requirement for the success of market competitiveness of destinations and businesses and the involvement of the private sector if tourism is to be successfully used as a tool for poverty reduction. In Figure 5.2, competition from other destinations was recognised as a challenge to the use of tourism for poverty reduction. There is a need for even the most philanthropic-orientated business to be successful in the market to ensure a robust tourism demand function and its financial sustainability to be able to provide livelihood opportunities for the poor in the future. Therefore, market competitiveness at a destination level, alongside that of an individual organisation, is an essential pre-requisite for any tourism poverty reduction strategy to be operationalised. Marketing strategies also need to attract typologies of tourists that are supportive to enhancing the livelihoods of the poor, particularly those who like to visit markets and pursue tourism experiences based upon nature, culture and everyday life that are likely to be provided by the poor (UNWTO, 2007b). The propensity for this uptake can be enhanced by attracting domestic tourists, who are more likely to have shared cultural values and practices of local people, and are more likely than international tourists to frequent the tourism services offered by the poor in the informal sector. The use of organised markets in prime locations can also greatly facilitate local sales to tourists (Ashley *et al.*, 2001). For example, women craft sellers have sites within some wildlife parks in KwaZulu Natal in South Africa, while at Gonarezhou National Park in Zimbabwe, one of the demands of local communities is for a market at the park entrance to access incoming tourists to the park.

If tourism is to be used to alleviate poverty for large numbers of the poor, it is essential that the mainstream tourism industry as the major investor and holder of capital, the principal creator of economic opportunities, is engaged as the key player in pushing the agenda forward as is suggested in the fourth principle, with the tilting of the mainstream tourism industry towards a pro-poor orientation being especially important. The scale of engagement with the private sector needs to range from the larger multinational operators down to the small and micro-businesses. They should be encouraged by global agencies, multinational agencies, government and NGOs, to deliver benefits to the poor, through employment practices, local linkages and a pro-poor tourism focus as initiated by the Travel Foundation described in Box 5.4. This approach should be combined with working at the local level within communities in order to engage with and reach the poor, to fully understand and address their needs, and to create opportunities accessible to them. This must, however, relate properly and professionaly to the wider practicalities and realities of the tourism market to create feasible and sustainable livelihood opportunities.

The principle of businesses seeking to benefit the poor through their actions builds on concepts such as Corporate Social Responsibility (CSR). Whilst CSR has become a part of the tourism industry at a corporate level, the emphasis has rested primarily upon environmental issues rather than social responsibilities (La Trobe, 2002). The need for businesses to establish better links with the poor and contribute to human development is also a focus for the UNDP (2008), through their 'Growing Inclusive Markets Initiative' that seeks to realise the potential resources of the poor by encouraging the private sector to engage in business with them, as is explained in Box 6.7.

BOX 6.7 UNDP: 'DOING BUSINESS WITH THE POOR'

A necessity for businesses to establish better links with the poor and contribute to human development is defined within the UNDP's 'Growing Inclusive Markets Initiative' that seeks to realise the potential resources of the poor and contribute to human development and the MDGs by encouraging the private sector to engage in business with them. There are three central aims of the initiative as defined by the UNDP (2008: v):

- Raising awareness by demonstrating how doing business with the poor can be good for poor people and good for business
- Clarifying the ways that business, governments and civil society organisations can create value for all
- Inspiring the private sector to action.

Relating the need to do business with the poor to reduce poverty, the UNDP (2008) highlight that 2.6 billion people are living on less than US$2 per day, more than 1 billion lack clean water, 1.6 billion lack electricity, and 5.4 billion lack access to the Internet. They also point out that the poor have a huge 'potential for consumption, production, innovation and entrepreneurial activity that is largely untapped' (ibid.: 1), adding that business with the poor can create value for all. The scale of the potential market is large, especially when the market at the 'bottom of the income pyramid' is considered. For example, there is a total market of 4 billion people living on an income of less than US$8 per day, representing a combined income of approximately US$5 trillion, equivalent to the gross national income of Japan. This market is willing to pay for goods and services but often suffers a 'poverty penalty', which ironically means sometimes the poor can end up paying more than the rich for essential goods and services. For instance, the poor of Jakarta, Manila and Nairobi pay five to ten times more than the people of the affluent areas of these cities for clean water, and more than residents in London or New York. Similar disparities extend to credit, electricity and health care. Whilst recognising that market-based approaches cannot help all people escape poverty, there exists a strong financial incentive to develop inclusive business models that embrace the poor as consumers which can offer these services at a lower price whilst offering profits to the companies providing them.

Alongside providing a market, the poor also offer a large source of labour, which based upon their local knowledge and connections may mean they are well placed to serve other poor consumers. Inclusive and participatory approaches between businesses and the poor have the potential to offer enhanced life opportunities as the poor's resources are translated into opportunities. However, to achieve this requires a business model that does not harm society and exploit natural and cultural resources, as has often been the case. There is a subsequent need for an ethical rather than exploitative approach from business to their interactions with the poor based upon models of social business, alongside legal legislation and workers' organisations to protect the poor from exploitative practices. Two examples of where tourism businesses have been actively involved in creating socially based business models are the Mt Plaisir Estate Hotel in Trinidad and Tobago and the Siwa Sustainable Development Initiative led by the private sector in Egypt. In the first case, over a period of 14 years the Mt Plaisir Estate Hotel has played a major part in transforming a poor rural village into a vibrant and self-sustaining community though empowerment and capacity building. The Siwa Initiative was kick-started by a Cairo-based environmental consultancy, EQI, that began to invest in community-based initiatives in the late 1990s. The scheme emphasises the employment of the local poor, the use of traditional systems of building with local materials and also the use of environmental management. It is a scheme that relies on inherited local knowledge and practice and has led to the creation of three tourist lodges, a female artisanship initiative, organic farming and the creation of community art projects. Seventy-five Siwans are employed full time in the initiative and typically several income-generating opportunities are created each month.

Source: after UNDP, 2008

Principles five and six relate to destination strategy and research on the performance of tourism. The concept of tourism strategies having poverty alleviation as a key aim represents a radical addition to the traditional one of focusing on market growth and competitiveness. This radicalism is also evident in principle six that hints at a relativist stance to the pro-poor debate by emphasising an understanding of how tourism income is distributed amongst social groups. In the context of social equity, this is an important area but one in which we lack knowledge. Whilst economic multiplier studies in tourism have given a much clearer understanding about income and employment generation, and economic leakages, there exists a vacuum of data on income distribution amongst the social strata of destination communities. One approach to this is suggested by DFID (2004) which stresses the importance of household surveys to assess the distribution of income at the beginning and the end of the survey periods, which must be adjusted for inflation during the period to measure real incomes. In the context of using a household survey to provide data on poverty, a poverty line must also be decided upon, the use of which permits identification of the number of households living in poverty at the beginning of a set period. The poverty line can be set on different comparisons, depending upon the purpose of the calculation; for example, if the purpose is to compare countries, then it would make sense to use the international US $1.25 a day line, or if it is one for an individual country, it would make sense to use a national poverty line.

Principle seven extends the vision of participatory approaches that are inclusive of the poor beyond poverty reduction to their active encouragement and facilitation of destination planning and development strategies. For this principle to have any real meaning it is essential that it extends beyond tokenism to encourage a process in which the aspirations of the poor in the tourism industry are listened to and barriers to their involvement are understood, as exemplified in the case of Elmira. It is through the comprehension of these issues that strategies can be developed to include the poor in the industry. Principle eight calls for consideration of how tourism impacts on the livelihood of communities, including natural and cultural resources. This is a complex task to undertake, as it will require an identification and evaluation of impacts that are directly attributable to tourism in the environmental and cultural spheres. This is difficult as it not always straightforward to attribute environmental and cultural changes to tourism vis-à-vis other causal factors that may also be inducing change. For example, changes in culture can be caused by the influences of satellite television and the internet, whilst environmental changes can be caused from other sources that are spacially detracted from the destination.

The theme of the poor having viable business projects is central to principle nine, which suggests that market access and project viability are key considerations for any PRS that seeks to include the poor. Key issues in this principle relate to aspects of raising capability levels of the poor and providing access to capital and loans. The final principle re-emphasises the need for data collection on the impacts of tourism on poverty reduction and the need to establish a monitoring system for how tourism impacts on the poor. This would embrace social, cultural and environmental considerations, including issues such as restrictions in access to natural resources and cultural changes. There is also a requirement to formulate criteria to identify whether pro-poor growth can be judged as successful or not, an issue that encompasses the purposes of development debate and how to assess human well-being. Kakwani and Pernia (2000) comment that ideally the measurement of pro-poor growth should incorporate all capabilities that enhance human well-being but in reality this is not feasible given the limited amount of available data, therefore the most important culturally specific capabilities should be selected as outcomes of full participatory processes with the poor. For each capability, indicators should be developed that reflect different aspects of life and against which progress may be measured. For example, if as a consequence of economic growth there is an improvement in poor people's use of health services, or reductions in child labour and an improvement in education, then growth may be regarded as being pro-poor (Kakwani and Pernia, ibid.).

Moving from principles to laying down a conceptual framework for tourism and poverty reduction, Zhao and Ritchie (2007) have developed a model as shown in Figure 6.1, which incorporates many of the UNWTO and SNV (2010) principles. Their choice of conceptual title to express the use of tourism for poverty reduction is 'anti-poverty tourism' (APT).

At the base of their model are the stakeholders that are integral to the tourism poverty agenda. These include: the poor; government; private sector; tourists;

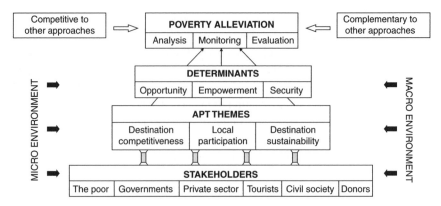

Figure 6.1 *An integrative framework for anti-poverty tourism*
Source: from Zhao and Ritchie, 2007

civil society; and aid donors. These stakeholders represent a consortium of players that can set the agenda and influence how tourism is used for poverty reduction. There are evidently inherent power imbalances between them; for example, the poor have much less control to influence the use of tourism for a poverty reduction agenda than the private sector or government. These imbalances will need to be addressed for meaningful participatory opportunities that are fully inclusive of the poor and lends them an influential voice in development decision-making. As has been stated, without a rich understanding of the issues, problems and barriers the poor face, there is a high propensity for the design of ill-conceived and ineffective policies and strategies for the use of tourism as a tool for poverty reduction. It is absolutely essential that partnerships between the different stakeholders in tourism are formed so that policies and practices are created that will orientate the industry towards poverty reduction as one of its business goals.

Zhao and Ritchie (2007) advocate three key themes of an ATP strategy that encompass the mix between tourism and poverty reduction, integrating industry requirements with economic, social and environmental processes. Their three key themes are: (i) a requirement for the destination to be market competitive; (ii) local participation; and (iii) destination sustainability. Market competitiveness has previously been discussed within the context of the UNWTO and SNV (2010) principles. Beside the maintenance or enhancement of the quality of the surrounding environment to attract tourists, of equal importance is the conservation of natural resources for their ecosystem functions, sustaining the meeting of the needs of present and future generations. The third key theme relates to a requirement for the participation of the poor in the tourism industry. To re-iterate the point, it is essential that the poor are included into the tourism economy, otherwise the industry is unlikely to produce benefits for them and may create negative impacts on their livelihoods. Alongside the creation of economic opportunities for the poor, their participation is also likely to enhance the fostering of positive attitudes towards tourism development amongst the local population. The model can therefore be interpreted as advocating participatory processes that will determine how the poor understand the potential of tourism to enhance their livelihoods and the barriers that arrest the opportunities to realise them.

The 'determinants' identified in the model closely reflect the conceptual frameworks for development as advanced by the World Bank. The creation of opportunities as was discussed in Chapter 2 is critical for the poor to have the chance to change not only their own lives but also those of future generations by breaking free from the 'poverty trap'. The requirement for political empowerment of the poor to accompany economic advancement is also essential to ensure that they do not remain marginalised but are brought more into the mainstream of their societies as active citizens. The third component of 'security' relates to the reduction of vulnerability of the poor to external shocks through the development of coping mechanisms and adaptation. At a political level, one example would be the development of a social security system directly targeted at the poor, similar to those established in most developing countries. Finally, as was advocated in the last UNWTO and SNV (2010) principle, it is essential that the effects of tourism on the poor are monitored, analysed and evaluated to allow for decisions by government and other stakeholders on resource allocation and strategy adaptation to maximise the potential of tourism for poverty reduction.

To move concepts and principles into practice, it is necessary to develop strategies and mechanisms for their implementation to overcome the barriers faced by the poor to gain access to the tourism industry and market. As exemplified in the case study of Elmina in Box 6.5, there are several barriers that are faced by the poor, which are related to deep-rooted denial of opportunities that typify poverty; for example, a lack of education and a lack of income earning opportunities. Based upon the work of the UNWTO (2006b), Pro-Poor Tourism Partnership (2012) and UNWTO (2012), a range of mechanisms to reduce poverty through tourism are shown in Figure 6.2.

The mechanisms rely upon government and private sector action and partnerships. It is essential that as part of a wider move towards good governance, there is a removal of the 'red tape' of needing to acquire numerous permits to start a formal sector tourism enterprise, a process which not infrequently involves bribery and corruption. Enterprise is a key driving force for economic growth and it is essential that the poor also have access to capital to start their initiatives. A major barrier to the involvement of the poor in the tourism industry is their lack of access to finance, compounded by the demands of traditional lenders for collateral against the security of loans, resources the poor do not have; and the problems

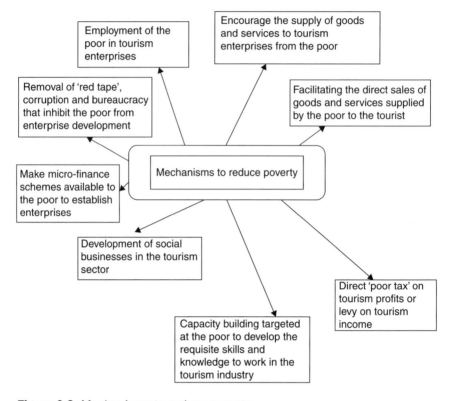

Figure 6.2 *Mechanisms to reduce poverty*

of illiteracy that dictate against completion of the requisite application forms. This lack of access to finance presents a major problem for the poor in accessing the tourism industry through the establishment of small enterprises. One type of scheme attempting to overcome this barrier is micro-credit and instrumental to its use as an alternative system of finance for the poor has been the work of Nobel Prize winner for economics Mohammed Yunus, the founder of the Grammen Bank. The bank lends expressly to the poor, at rates of interest that are lower than commercial banks and certainly money lenders.

Yunus (2007) has also gone beyond the notion of micro-credit, making a call for the introduction of new type of business, which he terms a 'social business'. He refers to existing companies as 'profit-maximising businesses' (PMBs), whose objective is purely profit, a key problem being that in this paradigm of operation businesses remain incapable of addressing many of our most pressing social problems. To correct this, there is a requirement to a subsequent evolution of 'social businesses', whose criterion for the evaluation of their success is based upon the social benefits that are created. Social businesses are in essence 'cause-driven' vis-à-vis 'profit-driven', with the potential to act as change agents for the poor's lives that they come into contact with. The basis of the idea is that whilst the company would earn profits, investors who support it will only recoup their investment over a period of time. The objective of investors who put capital into the business is therefore largely philanthropic, in Yunus's (ibid.) perspective the basis being that the rewards gained relate to a personal satisfaction of helping others improve their lives. This emphasis of a reliance on philanthropy illustrates the strong ethical issues and principles that underlie the condition of poverty, and an assumption that as most people care about the world and about each other, they would prefer to live in a world without poverty, disease, ignorance and needless suffering.

There are, however, key differences to a pure act of philanthropy and an investment in a business, which will need to become self-sustaining to survive. A social business has to subsequently recover its full costs whilst achieving its social objective, a characteristic that differentiates it from a charity or non-governmental organisation. Social businesses actively compete in the market with PMBs on traditional terms of market competition, including the quality and price of their service or product. They require unique selling points like any other business, part of which may be provided by the social benefits ethos that drives the mission of the business, which may provide a motivation for a consumer to purchase this product. In terms of differentiating social business from PMBs, there are three main criteria that can be used: (i) they achieve social objectives – for example, reduce poverty and clean up the environment; (ii) they work to alleviate ills – for example, drug and alcohol abuse, crime; and (iii) it covers its costs through the sales of goods and services, but pays no financial dividend to its investors.

Yunnis (2007) further distinguishes between two types of social business: (i) companies that focus on providing a social benefit rather than profit maximisation, which are owned by investors who seek social benefits – for example, poverty reduction, health care for the poor, global sustainability – typically through the services and products they offer; and (ii) profit-maximisation businesses that are owned by the poor, that is, the social benefit is derived from the dividends and equity growth produced by the PMB going to benefit the poor, helping them to reduce poverty or even escape it altogether. This latter category would characterise many CBT schemes for example.

To encourage the development of tourism entrepreneurship and provide people with the skills of work in the mainstream tourism industry, it is also necessary to enhance the capacity of the poor. This involves ensuring both the prioritising of opportunities for children to receive basic schooling and the provision of specialist tourism training, such as through hotel schools. There is also a requirement for the creation of market opportunities so that the poor may sell their goods and services; e.g., guiding, handicrafts and fruits, directly to the tourists within the informal economy. It is essential to ensure that the provision by local authorities of any designated physical space for this interaction to take place is in a locale that encourages tourists to visit it through characteristics such as ease of access and the provision of a welcoming environment. The use of primary locations is also critical as tourists are unlikely to visit places that are difficult to reach or are seen as being threatening. The provision of information to tourists about local products and training to raise the capacity to provide products of a quality that meets tourists' requirements is a further important part of this equation.

Action to strengthen the links to local enterprises in the tourism supply chain with the aim of maximising the retention of tourist expenditure through reducing economic leakages and involving the poor in the supply processes is essential for poverty reduction. Typical inputs could include food, fuel, or building materials to tourism operations. Support can vary from marketing and technical support (e.g., by nearby mainstream operators), to shifts in procurement strategy, or direct financial and training inputs. The PPT Partnership (2012) stresses that livelihood benefits for the poor is an important consideration for tourism poverty reduction strategies. The tourism industry needs to be able to demonstrate that it can provide wider social and environmental benefits to a cross-section of the poor and not just those either directly or indirectly engaged with tourism. To gain the support of the wider community, the industry has to have a demonstrable impact on the improvement of services that are essential to the poor. This would include a contribution to education, health care, sanitation and other infrastructure improvement programmes. The development of collective community capital is important, and funding for this could be raised as the UNWTO (2012) suggest through a tax or levy on tourism income or profits, with the benefits going to the poor. Such a mechanism will ensure that all the poor benefit from tourism, not just those with direct or indirect engagement with the sector.

Whilst these measures represent sound practical measures of how to reduce poverty using tourism, whether they will work effectively or not is uncertain. To what extent they can overcome the structural inequalities and injustice of the wider political economy is uncertain. As Scheyvens (2007: 135) puts it: 'it is relatively straightforward (and good for public relations) to pump money into community tourism initiatives, but it is far more difficult and controversial to endorse labour rights for all tourism sector workers worldwide, or to challenge the control that foreign companies and local elites often have over the tourism sector.' We shall see.

SUMMARY

- The future use of tourism for poverty reduction will be influenced by the changing political economy in which it is grounded. The questioning of the purposes of development, what it means and is hoping to achieve, combined with shifts in the global political economy, and the environmental constraints on development that will become more evident in the course of the next decades, presents challenges and opportunities to maximising tourism's poverty reduction potential. The post-development paradigm condemns the development project itself as creating mass poverty under an illusion of social improvement based upon Westerncentric economic paradigms of advancement, and after six United Nations development decades, global economic development is still failing to have relevance and make positive links to hundreds of millions of the world's population.

- The growing political and economic importance of the 'South', being led by the BRIC countries, may eventually lead to shifts in the political make-up of the World Bank, IMF and World Trade Organisation, leading to loaning, trade and regulatory frameworks more favourable to the developing countries and LDCs. Tourism may increase in its economic importance in developing countries and has the potential to offer significant potential for the creation of livelihood opportunities and improvements in well-being for the poor. To realise this potential will rely upon political will, good governance and productive partnerships between the private sector, government, NGOs and critically the poor. Within the move towards a global 'green economy', progress towards the greening of the tourism sector should reinforce the employment potential of the sector and supply chain with increased local hiring and sourcing. A key feature of a green economy is that it seeks to provide diverse opportunities for economic development and poverty alleviation without liquidating or eroding a country's natural assets.

- The global financial crisis of 2008 has led to a questioning of unbridled capitalism and calls for greater state intervention and regulation, particularly of financial markets that act as the key driving force of economic globalisation. This recognition for an increased role at least at a national level to direct economic development is partially reflected in the shift of the World Bank and IMF from SAPs to PRS, within which tourism has a significant role in many LDCs. An increased role for the state in directing economic development provides opportunities for it to be pro-active in developing policy for the use of tourism for sustainable economic growth and poverty reduction. This is important, as for tourism to play a serious role in poverty reduction strategies it needs recognition and careful planning to produce a holistic approach in place of ad hoc schemes that have only a local economic impact on the poor and can only help limited numbers.

- The emergent trends towards a green economy and the shifting geographical dynamism of the global political economy presents opportunities for the comparative advantages of the natural and cultural resources of many LDCs to be used in a sustainable approach to tourism that can reduce poverty. A major consideration in tourism's use for poverty reduction is its geographical scale and the political economy within which it operates. To play an effective role in poverty reduction, tourism needs to be able to work within different development paradigms and at various spatial scales. Fundamental to ensuring the effective and equitable use of tourism for poverty reduction is good 'governance', which establishes the framework for economic, social and environmental progress through participation, transparency and accountable processes.

Bibliography

Agnew, J. (2005) 'Space: Place', in Cloke, P. and Johnston, R. (eds) *Spaces of Geographical Thought*, Sage, London, pp. 81–96.

Ashley, C., Boyd, C. and Goodwin, H. (2000) 'Pro-Poor Tourism: putting poverty at the heart of the tourism agenda', *Natural Resources Perspectives*, 51, Overseas Development Institute, London.

Ashley, C., Roe, D. and Goodwin, H. (2001) *Pro-poor Tourism Strategies: Making Tourism Work for the Poor: A Review of Experience*, Overseas Development Institute, London.

Asthama, A. (2012) 'Family of four "needs" £37000 to maintain basic life standards', *The Times*, London, 10 July, p. 8.

Badger, A., Barnett, P., Corbyn, L. and Keefe, J. (1996) *Trading Places: Tourism as Trade*, Tourism Concern, London.

Baker, V. (2012) 'Easter Rising', *The Guardian*, Travel Section, London, 11 February, pp. 2–3.

Beaudoin, S.M. (2007) *Poverty in World History*, Routledge, London.

Becken, S. and Hay, E.J. (2007) *Tourism and Climate Change: Risks and Opportunities*, Channel View Publications, Clevedon.

Belle, N. and Bramwell, B. (2005) 'Climate change and small island tourism: policy maker and industry perspectives in Barbados', *Journal of Travel Research*, 44, pp. 32–41.

—— (2007) *In Defense of Globalisation*, Oxford University Press, Oxford.

Bianchi, R. (1999) 'A critical ethnography of tourism entrepreneurship and social change in a fishing community in Gran Canaria', unpublished PhD thesis, University of North London.

Bird, B. (1989) *Langkawi: From Mahusri to Mahathir: Tourism for Whom?* INSAN, Kuala Lumpur.

Blair, T. (2009) 'Sierra Leone rises again', *The Guardian*, London, 30 April.

Boluk, K. (2011) 'Fair Trade tourism South Africa: a pragmatic poverty reduction mechanism?' *Tourism Planning and Development*, 8, 3, pp. 237–51.

Brandt, W. (1980) *North-South: A Programme for Survival*, Pan Books Ltd, London.

Britton, S.G. (1982) 'The political economy of tourism in the Third World', *Annals of Tourism Research*, 9, pp. 331–58.

Brohman, J. (1996) 'New directions in tourism for Third World development', *Annals of Tourism Research*, 23, 1, pp. 48–70.

Burns, P. (2004) 'Tourism planning: a third way?' *Annals of Tourism Research*, 31, 1, pp. 24–45.

Castells, M. (1996) *The Rise of the Network Society*, Blackwells, Oxford.

Castree, N. (2003) 'Place: connections and boundaries in an interdependent world', in Holloway, S.L., Rice, S.P. and Valentine, G. (eds) *Key Concepts in Geography*, Sage, London, pp. 165–86.

Chamberlain, M.E. (1974) *The Scramble for Africa*, Longman, Harlow.

Chok, S., Macbeth, J. and Warren, C. (2007) 'Tourism as a tool for poverty alleviation: a critical analysis of 'Pro-Poor Tourism' and implications for sustainability', in Hall, M. (ed.) *Pro-Poor Tourism: Who Benefits? Perspectives on Tourism and Poverty Reduction*, Chanel View Publications, Clevedon, pp. 34–55.

Clayton, J. (2012) 'Africa shrugs off global slowdown as investors seek new horizons', *The Times*, CEO Summit Africa Supplement, 19 March, p. 3.

Cleverdon, R. and Kalish, A. (2000) 'Fair Trade in tourism', *International Journal of Tourism Research*, 2, 3, pp. 171–87.

Collier, P. (2008) *The Bottom Billion: Why the Poorest Countries are Failing and What Can Be Done About It*, Oxford University Press, Oxford.

Commission for Africa (2005) Our Common Interest: Report of The Commission for Africa, London. Available at: www.commissionforafrica.org.

Cowen, M.P. and Sheraton, R.W. (1996) *Doctrines of Development*, Routledge, London.

CPRC (2009) *The Chronic Poverty Report 2008–9: Escaping Poverty Traps*, Chronic Poverty Research Centre, The University of Manchester.

Crowards, T. (2000) *Comparative Vulnerability to Natural Disasters in the Caribbean*, Caribbean Development Bank, Staff Working Paper No. 1/00.

De Blij, H. (2009) *The Power of Place: Geography, Destiny and Globalisation's Rough Landscape*, Oxford University Press, New York.

de Rivero, O. (2001) *The Myth of Development: The Non-Viable Economies of the 21st Century*, Zed Books, London.

DFID (1999) *Tourism and Poverty Elimination: Untapped Potential*, Department for International Development (UK) Briefing Paper, London.

—— (2000) *Eliminating World Poverty: Making Globalisation Work for the Poor*, White Paper on International Development, Department for International Development, London.

—— (2004) *What is pro-poor growth and why do we need to know?* Pro-Poor Growth Briefing Note 1, Department for International Development, London.

Dieke, P. (1994) 'Tourism in Sub-Saharan Africa: development issues and possibilities', in Jenkins, C. and Seaton, A. (eds) *Tourism: the State of the Art*, Wiley, Chichester, pp. 52–64.

—— (2000) *The Political Economy of Tourism Development in Africa*, Cognizant, New York.

Duralappah, A. (2004) *Exploring the Links: Human Well-Being, Poverty and Ecosystem Services*, United Nations Environment Programme and International Institute for Sustainable Development, Winnipeg, Manitoba.

Easterling, D. (2005) 'Residents and tourism: what is really at stake?' *Journal of Travel and Tourism Marketing*, 18, 4, pp. 49–64.

Edington, J. and Edington, A. (1986) *Ecology, Recreation and Tourism*, Cambridge University Press, Cambridge.

Eilers, R. (2012) 'Floating asset', *The Guardian*, Travel Section, 18 February, pp 10–11.

Elliott, A.J. (1994) *An Introduction to Sustainable Development: The Developing World*, Routledge, London.

Ellwood, W. (2001) *The No-Nonsense Guide to Globalisation*, New Internationalist Publications, Oxford.

Engels, F. (1845) *The Condition of the English Working Class in England*, republished (1987) by Penguin, London.

Entriken, J.N. (1994) 'Place and region', *Progress in Human Geography*, 18, 2, pp. 227–33.

Forna, A. (2009) 'Tourism will not be a quick fix for Sierra Leone', *The Guardian*, 13 May, p. 33.

Frank, A.G. (1967) *Capitalism and Underdevelopment in Latin America: Historical Studies of Chile and Brazil*, Monthly Review Press, New York.

Friedman, T.L. (2005) *The World is Flat: A Brief History of the Twenty-First Century*, Farrar, Strauss and Giroux, New York.

Garman, J. (2006) 'If I were . . . Aviation Minister', *The Ecologist*, pp. 23–4.

Gentleman, A. (2009) 'I want an education. I want to change my life', *The Observer*, 29 November, pp. 16–17.

George, S. and Sabelli, F. (1994) *Faith and Credit: The World Bank's Secular Empire*, Penguin, London.

Gilpin, R. (2001) *Global Political Economy: Understanding the International Economic Order*, Princeton University Press, Princeton.

Goodwin, H. (2006) *Measuring and Reporting the Impact of Tourism on Poverty*, School of Management, University of Surrey and International Centre for Responsible Tourism, London.

—— (2009) 'Contemporary policy debates: reflections on 10 years of Pro-Poor Tourism', *Journal of Policy Research in Tourism and Leisure*, 1, 1, pp. 90–94.

Gordon, D. (2002) 'The international measurement of poverty and anti-poverty policies', in Townsend, P. and Gordon, D. (eds) *World Poverty: New Policies to Defeat an Old Enemy*, The Policy Press, Bristol, pp. 53–80.

Gossling, S. and Hall, M. (eds) (2006) *Tourism and Global Environmental Change: Ecological, Social, Economic and Political Interrelationships*, Routledge, London.

Gossling, S., Schumacher, K., Morelle, M., Berger, R. and Heck, N. (2004) Tourism and street children in Antananarivo, Madagascar, *Tourism and Hospitality Research*, 5, 2, pp. 131–49.

Goudie, A. and Viles, H. (1997) *The Earth Transformed: An Introduction to Human Impacts on the Environment*, Blackwell, Oxford.

Green, D. and Allen, I. (2008) *The Urgency of Now*, Oxfam, Oxford.

Hall, C.M. (1994) *Tourism and Politics: Policy, Power and Place*, John Wiley and Sons, Chichester.

Harrison, D. (ed.) (1992) *Tourism and the Less Developed Countries*, John Wiley and Sons, Chichester.

Harvey, D. (1989) *The Condition of Postmodernism*, Basil Blackwell, Oxford.

Hawkins, D.E. and Mann, S. (2007) 'The World Bank's role in tourism development', *Annals of Tourism Research*, 24, 2, pp. 348–63.

Hayter, T. (1981) *The Creation of World Poverty: An Alternative View to the Brandt Report*, Pluto Press, London.

Heffernan, M. (2003) Histories of Geography, in Holloway, S.L., Rice, S.P. and Valentine, G. (eds) *Key Concepts in Geography*, Sage, London, pp. 3–22.

Hobsbawm, E. (1962) *The Age of Revolution*, Abacus, London.

Holden, A. (2005) *Tourism Studies and the Social Sciences*, Routledge, London.

—— (2008) *Environment and Tourism*, Routledge, London.

—— (2009) 'The environment-tourism nexus: influence of market ethics', *Annals of Tourism Research*, 36, 3, pp. 375–89.

—— (2010) 'Exploring stakeholders' perceptions of sustainable tourism development in the Annapurna conservation area: issues and challenge', *Tourism and Hospitality Planning & Development*, 7, 4, pp. 337–51.

Holden, A., Novelli, M. and Sonne, J. (2011) 'Tourism and poverty reduction: an interpretation by the poor of Elmina, Ghana', *Tourism Planning and Development*, 8, 3, pp. 281–96.

House, J. (1997) 'Redefining sustainability: a structural approach to sustainable tourism', in Stabler, M. (ed.) *Tourism and Sustainability: Principles to Practice*, CAB International, Wallingford, pp. 89–104.

Houston, R.A. (2001) 'Colonies, enterprises, and wealth: the economies of Europe and the wider world', in Cameron, E. (ed.) (2001) *Early Modern Europe: An Oxford History*, Oxford University Press, Oxford, pp. 137–70.

Ibrahim, M. (2009) 'Measuring the unmeasurable', *This is Africa: A Global Perspective*, Financial Times Ltd., London, September.

IBRD (2009) *Atlas of Global Development*, 2nd edn, HarperCollins, Glasgow.

IMF (2000) *Annual Report of the Executive Board*, International Monetary Fund, Washington, ch. 1, p. 2.

—— (2012) 'International Monetary Fund Factsheet'. Available at: www.imf.org/external/np/exr/facts/prsp.htm (accessed 21 June 2012).

IPCC (Intergovernmental Panel on Climate Change) (2001) *Climate Change: Synthesis Report: Summary for Policy Makers*. Available at: www.ipcc.ch/pdf/climate-changes-2001/synthesis-spm/synthesis-spm-en.pdf (accessed 2 November 2012).

—— (2007a) *Climate Change 2007: The Physical Science (Basic Summary for Policymakers)*, IPCC, Geneva.

—— (2007b) *Climate Change 2007: Impacts, Adaptation and Vulnerability*, IPCC, Geneva.

Kakwani, N. and Pernia, E.M. (2000) What is pro-poor growth? *Asian Development Review*, 18, 1 (page numbers are not defined).

Kane, S. and Kirby, M. (2003) *Wealth, Poverty and Welfare*, Macmillan, London.

Kennedy, P. (2002) in Kennedy, P., Messner, D. and Nuscheler, F. (eds.) *Global Trends and Global Governance*, Pluto Press, London, Ch1, pp. 2–19.

Kennedy, P., Messner, D. and Nuscheler, F. (eds.) (2002) *Global Trends and Global Governance*, Pluto Press, London.

Koroma, E.B. (2012) 'Natural wealth will be a blessing and not a curse', *The Times*, 19 March, p. 9.

Landes, D. (1998) *The Wealth and Poverty of Nations*, Little, Brown and Company, London.

La Trobe, S. (2002) *Climate Change and Poverty: A Discussion Paper*, Tear Fund, Teddington.

La Viña, G.M., Hoff, G. and DeRose (2003) 'The outcomes of Johannesburg', copy of text accepted for publication in *SAIS Review: A Journal of International Affairs*, Winter-Spring issue, vol. XXIII, no. 1.

Lea, R. (2012) 'Nobody said that getting Africa into the air was going to be easy', *The Times*, 7 August, pp. 30–31.

Lines, T. (2008) *Making Poverty: A History*, Zed Books, London.

Lister, R. (2004) *Poverty*, London, Routledge.

Maathai, Wangari (2009) *The Challenge for Africa*, William Heinemann, London.

Macbeth, J. (2005) 'Towards an ethics platform for tourism', *Annals of Tourism Research*, 32, 4, pp. 962–84.

MacGillivray, A. (2006) *A Brief History of Globalisation: The Untold History of Our Incredible Shrinking Planet*, Robinson, London.

Mackinnon, D. and Cumbers, A. (2007) *An Introduction to Economic Geography: Globalisation, Uneven Development and Place*, Pearson Education Limited, Harlow.

MacPherson, S. and Silburn, R. (1998) 'The meaning and measurement of poverty', in Dixon, J. and Macarov, D. (eds) *Poverty: A Persistent Global Reality*, Routledge, London, pp. 1–19.

Mankils, N.G. (2001) *Principles of Economics*, 2nd edn, Harcourt College Publishers, Fort Worth.

Massey, D. (1994) 'A global sense of place', in Massey, D. (ed.) *Place, Space and Gender*, Polity, Cambridge, pp. 146–56.

McClenaghan, M. and McVeigh, T (2012) 'Fears of health disaster for thousands of refugees hiding in the Nuba Mountains', *The Observer*, 20 May, p. 23.

McGrew, A. and Held, D. (eds) (2007) *Globalization Theory: Approaches and Controversies*, Polity Press, Cambridge.

McMichael, P. (2004) *Development and Social Change: A Global Perspective*, 3rd edn, Pine Forge Press, London.

Mieczkowski, Z. (1995) *Environmental Issues of Tourism and Recreation*, University Press of America, Lanham.

Mitchell, J. and Ashley, C. (2010) *Tourism and Poverty Reduction: Pathways to Prosperity*, Earthscan, London.

Mowforth, M. and Munt, I. (1998) *Tourism and Sustainability: Development, Globalisation and New Tourism in the Third World*, Routledge, London.

—— (2003) *Tourism and Sustainability: Development and New Tourism in the Third World*, 2nd edn, Routledge, London.

—— (2009) *Tourism and Sustainability: Development, Globalisation and New Tourism in the Third World*, 3rd edn, Routledge, London.

Nash, D. (1989) 'Tourism as a form of imperialism', in Smith, V.L. (ed.) *Hosts and Guests: The Anthropology of Tourism*, 2nd edn, University of Pennsylvania, Philadelphia, pp. 36–52.

Neate, R. (2011) 'Soaring food prices will be devastating for the world's poor', *The Guardian*, 18 June, p. 35.

Nielsen, L. (2011) *Classifications of Countries Based on Their Level of Development: How it is Done and How it Could be Done*, IMF Working Paper. Available at: www.imf.org (accessed 3 November 2012).

Novelli, M. and Hellwig, A. (2011) 'The UN MDGs, tourism and development: a tour operator's perspective', *Current Issues in Tourism*, 14, 3, pp. 1–17.

NSAC (1999) *Nepal Human Development Report*, Nepal South Asia Centre, Kathmandu, Nepal.

OECD (2012) *Framework for an OECD Strategy on Development*. Available at: www.oecd.org (accessed 2 November 2012).

Pass, C., Lowes, B. and Davies, L. (2000) *Dictionary of Economics*, 3rd edn, HarperCollins, Glasgow.

Pieterse, J.N. (2010) *Development Theory*, 2nd edn, Sage, New Delhi

Ponting, C. (1991) *A Green History of the World*, Sinclair Stevenson Limited, London.

Power, M. (2004) *Rethinking Development Geographies*, Routledge, London.

Pro-Poor Tourism Partnership (2012) *What is Pro-Poor Tourism?* Available at: www.propoortourism.org.uk/what_is_ppt.html (accessed 13 February 2012).

Radcliffe, S. (1999) 'Rethinking development', in Cloke, P., Crang, P. and Goodwin, M. (eds) *Introducing Human Geographies*, Arnold, London, pp. 84–91.

Ramesh, R. (2010) 'London's wealth gap: £930,000 from top to bottom', *The Guardian*, 21 April, p. 12.

Ransom, D. (2001) *The No-Nonsense Guide to Fair Trade*, New Internationalist, Oxford.

Reid, D. (1995) *Sustainable Development: An Introductory Guide*, Earthscan, London.

Reinert, E.S. (2007) *How Rich Countries Got Rich . . . and Why Poor Countries Stay Poor*, Constable and Robinson, London.

Rice, X. (2009) 'Slumming it: poverty tours come to Kenya', *The Guardian*, 26 September, p. 26.

Roberts, J.M. (1995) *The Penguin History of the World*, Penguin, London.

Roe, D., Ashley, C., Page, S. and Meyer, D. (2004) 'Tourism and the poor: analysing and interpreting tourism statistics from a poverty perspective', PPT Working Paper, Overseas Development Institute, London.

Rowlands, A. (2001) 'The conditions of life for the masses', in Cameron, E. (ed.) *Early Modern Europe: An Oxford History*, Oxford University Press, Oxford, pp. 31–62.

RGS (Royal Geographical Society) (2011) p. 17, London. *Geographical*, 83, 1.

Rose, E.M (1972) *The Relief of Poverty*, The Macmillan, London.

Rossetto, A., Li, S. and Sofield, T. (2007) 'Harnessing tourism as a means of poverty alleviation: using the right language or achieving outcomes?', *Tourism Recreation Research*, 32, 1, pp. 49–58.

Saarinen, J. (2006) 'Traditions of sustainability in tourism studies', *Annals of Tourism Research*, 33, 4, pp. 1121–40.

Sachs, J. (2005) *The End of Poverty: How Can We Make it Happen in Our Lifetime?* Penguin, London.

—— (2008) *Common Wealth: Economics for a Crowded Planet*, Allen Lane, London.

—— (2010) 'An age of fear and loathing', *The Guardian*, 24 September. Available at: www.guardian.co.uk (accessed 3 November 2012).

Sachs, W. (1999) *Planet Dialectics: Explorations in Environment and Development*, Zed Books, London.

Saville, N.M. (2001) 'Practical strategies for Pro-Poor Tourism: case study of Pro-Poor Tourism and SNV in Humla District, West Nepal', PPT Working Paper No. 3, DFID, London.

Scheyvens, R. (2002) *Tourism for Development: Empowering Communities*, Pearson Education Ltd., Harlow.

—— (2003) 'Local involvement in managing tourism', in Singh, S. Timothy D.J. and Dowling R.K. (eds) *Tourism in Destination Communities*, CABI, Wallingford, pp. 229–51.

—— (2007) 'Exploring the tourism-poverty nexus', in Hall, M.C. (ed.) *Pro-Poor Tourism: Who Benefits? Perspectives on Tourism and Poverty Reduction*, Channel View Publications, Clevedon, pp. 121–44.

Scott, L. (2005) 'International history, 1945–90', in Baylis, J. and Smith, S. (eds) *The Globalisation of World Politics*, 3rd edn, Oxford University Press, Oxford, pp. 93–110.

Seabrook, J. (2007) *The No-Nonsense Guide to Poverty*, 2nd edn, New Internationalist, Oxford.

Sen, A. (1992) *Inequality Re-examined*, Russell Sage Foundations and Clarendon Press, Oxford.

—— (1999) *Development as Freedom*, Oxford University Press, Oxford.

Shah, H. and McIver, M. (2006) *A New Political Economy*, Compass, London.

Sharpley, R. (2009) *Tourism Development and the Environment: Beyond Sustainability?* Routledge, London.

Slattery, M. (1992) *Key Ideas in Sociology*, Nelson, London.

Smith, D. (2011) 'Tutu's dreams for Cape Town fade as an informal apartheid grips the city', *The Observer*, 9 October, p. 2.

Sofield, T. (2003) *Empowerment for Sustainable Tourism Development*, Pergamon, Oxford.

Spero, J.E. (1985) *The Politics of International Economic Relations*, 3rd edn, St. Martin's Press, New York.

Srisang, K. (1991) 'The problematique of tourism: a view from below', Paper presented to the ASEAUK Conference on Tourist Development in South-East Asia, 25–28 March, University of Hull.

Stephan, H., Power, M., Hervey, A.F. and Fonesca, R.S. (2006) *The Scramble for Africa in the 21st Century: A View from the South*, Renaissance Press, Cape Town.

Stern Report (2006) *Stern Review on the Economics of Climate Change*, HM Treasury Office, London.

Stiglitz, J.E. and Charlton, A. (2007) *Fair Trade for All: How Trace Can Promote Development*, Oxford University Press, Oxford.

Storey, D., Bulloch, H. and Overton, J. (2005) 'The poverty consensus: some limitations of the "popular agenda"', *Progress in Development Studies*, 5, 1, pp. 30–44.

Telfer, D. (2002) 'Tourism development', in Sharpley, R. and Telfer, D. (eds) *Tourism and Development: Concepts and Issues*, Channel View Publications, Clevedon, pp. 1–34.

The Government of Maldives (2009) *National Adaptation to Climate Change*, Ministry of Housing, Transport and Environment. Available at: www.maldivespartnershipforum. gov.mv/pdf/Adaptation%20to%20Climate%20Change.pdf.

The Travel Foundation (2012) 'Practical steps in sustainable tourism: developing and marketing a sustainable Maasai Village Tourism Experience in Kenya'. Available at: www.thetravelfoundation.org.uk (accessed 1 July 2012).

Torres, R. and Momsen, J.H. (2004) 'Challenges and potential for linking tourism and agriculture to achieve Pro-poor Tourism objectives', *Progress in Development Studies*, 4, 4, pp. 294–318.

Tourism Concern (2012) *Tears and Blood of the Kalpitiya Fishermen*. Available at: www. tourismconcern.org.uk/index.php/news/269/154/The-tears-and-blood-of-the-Kalpitiya-fishermen.html (accessed 2 November 2012).

Townsend, P. (1979) *Poverty in the United Kingdom*, Penguin, Harmondsworth.

Townsend, P. and Gordon, D. (eds) (2002) *World Poverty: New Policies to Defeat an Old Enemy*, Polity Press, Bristol.

Turner, L. and Ash, J. (1975) *The Golden Hordes: International Tourism and the Pleasure Periphery*, Constable, London.

United Nations (2011) *Human Development Report: Sustainability and Equity: A Better Future for All*. Available at: http://hdr.undp.org/en/ (accessed 2 November 2012).

—— (2012) 'World population prospects, the 2010 revision'. Available at: http://esa.un. org/undp/wpp/Analytical-Figures/htm/fig1.htm (accessed 23 May 2012).

UNDP (1995) 'The Copenhagen declaration and programme of action: World Summit for Social Development 6–12 March 1995', UN Department of Publications, sales no E.96. IV.8, New York. Available at: www.visionoffice.com/socdev/wssd.htm.

—— (2003) *Human Development Report: Millennium Development Goals: A Compact Amongst Nations to end Human Poverty*, United Nations Development Programme, Oxford University Press.

—— (2006) *Human Development Report*, United Nations Development Programme, New York.

—— (2008) *Creating Value for All: Strategies for Doing Business with the Poor*, United Nations Development Programme, New York.

—— (2011) *Human Development Index*. Available at: http://hdr.undp.org/en/statistics/hdi (accessed 25 May 2011).

UNEP/UNWTO (2005) *Making Tourism More Sustainable – A Guide for Policy Makers*, World Tourism Organization, Madrid.

UNEP (1999) *Overview GEO 2000: Global Environmental Outlook*. Available at: www. unep.org/geo2000/ov-e/ov-e.pdf (accessed 2 November 2012).

—— (2011) *Green Economy: Pathways to Sustainable Development and Poverty Eradication: A Synthesis for Policy Makers*, United Nations Environment Programme, Nairobi, Kenya.

UNWTO (2003) *Climate Change and Tourism: Proceedings of the 1st International Conference on Climate Change*, Djerba, Tunisia, 9–11 April, United Nations World Tourism Organisation, Madrid.

—— (2006a) *Poverty Alleviation Through Tourism: A Compilation of Good Practices*, United Nations World Tourism Organisation, Madrid.

—— (2006b) *Tourism and Least Developed Countries: A Sustainable Opportunity to Reduce Poverty*, United Nations World Tourism Organisation, Madrid.

—— (2007) *Davos Declaration: Climate Change and Tourism, Responding to Global Challenges*, Davos, Switzerland, 3 October, United Nations World Tourism Organisation, Madrid.

—— (2007b) *Sustainable Tourism-Eliminating Poverty*, United Nations World Tourism Organisation Madrid.

—— (2009) *Tourism Highlights 2008*, United Nations World Tourism Organization, Madrid.

—— (2012) *The Seven ST-EP Mechanisms*, United Nations World Tourism Organisation. Available at: http://step.unwto.org/en/content/seven-st-ep-mechanisms (accessed 18 January 2012).

UNWTO and SNV (2010) *Manual on Tourism and Poverty Alleviation: Practical Steps for Destinations*, United Nations World Tourism Organisation, Madrid.

Valley, P. (2012) 'A life free from hunger: tackling child malnutrition', *The Independent*, 15 February, p. 35.

Wall, G. (1997) 'Sustainable tourism – unsustainable development', in Pigram, J. and Wahab, S. (eds) *Tourism, Development and Growth*, Routledge, London, pp. 31–47.

Wheeller, B. (1994) 'Sustaining the ego', *Journal of Sustainable Tourism*, 1, 2, pp. 23–29.

Whyte, I. (2008) *World Without End: Environmental Disasters and the Collapse of Empires*, I.B. Tauris, London.

Willis, K. (2005) *Theories and Practices of Development*, Routledge, London.

World Bank (2000) *Attacking Poverty: World Development Report 2000/1*, Oxford University Press, New York.

—— (2008) *Poverty Data: A Supplement to World Development Indicators 2008*, The World Bank, New York.

—— (2010) http://web.worldbank.org/wbsite/external/countries/southasiaext/0,contentM DK:22531481~menuPK:2246552~pagePK:2865106~piPK:2865128~theSi tePK:223547,00.html

—— (2012) What is Pro-Poor Growth? http://web.worldbank.org/wbsite/external/topics/ extpoverty (accessed 9 February 2012).

WCED (World Commission on Environment and Development) (1987) *Our Common Future*, Oxford University Press, Oxford.

WTO (1998) *Tourism Economic Report*, 1st edn, World Tourism Organisation, Madrid.

—— (2002) *Tourism and Poverty Alleviation*, World Tourism Organisation, Madrid.

—— (2003) *Climate Change and Tourism*, World Tourism Organisation, Madrid.

WTTC (2004) *World Travel and Tourism Forging Ahead*, World Travel and Tourism Council, London.

—— (2012) Country reports www.wttc.org/site_media/uploads/downloads/world2012.pdf (accessed 11 May 2012).

Yunus, M. (2007) *Creating a World Without Poverty*, Public Affairs, New York.

Zhao, W. and Ritchie, B.J.R. (2007) 'Tourism and poverty alleviation: an integrative research framework', in Hall, M.C. (ed.) *Pro-poor Tourism: Who Benefits? Perspectives on Tourism and Poverty Reduction*, Channel View Publications, Clevedon, pp. 9–33.

Index

Numbers in **bold** represent terms within a figure
Numbers in *italics* represent terms within a table